NANCY
PELOSI

NANCY PELOSI

Political Powerhouse

ANNA LEIGH

LERNER PUBLICATIONS ◆ MINNEAPOLIS

Lerner Publications Company
An imprint of Lerner Publishing Group, Inc.
241 First Avenue North
Minneapolis, MN 55401 USA

For reading levels and more information, look up this title at www.lernerbooks.com.

Image credits: Alex Wong/Getty Images, pp. 2, 30; JOSH EDELSON/AFP/Getty Images, p. 6; Matt McClain/The Washington/Getty Images, p. 8; Bettmann/Getty Images, p. 11; John F. Kennedy Library, p. 12; Earthscapeimagegraphy/istock/Getty Images, p. 13; James K.w. Atherton/The Washington Post/Getty Images, p. 14; Matthew Naythons/The LIFE Images Collection/Getty Images, p. 17; LEE SNIDER/PHOTO IMAGES/Corbis/Getty Images, p. 18; Manny Ceneta/Getty Images, p. 19; Scott J. Ferrell/Congressional Quarterly/Getty Images, p. 21; Chip Somodevilla/ Getty Images, pp. 22, 33, 34, 35; Win McNamee/Getty Images, p. 24; MANDEL NGAN/AFP/ Getty Images, p. 26; Selcuk Acar/Anadolu Agency/Getty Images, p. 27; SAUL LOEB/AFP/Getty Images, p. 29; Mark Wilson/Getty Images, p. 31; BRENDAN SMIALOWSKI/AFP/Getty Images, p. 32; Drew Angerer/Getty Images, p. 36; Paul Marotta/Getty Images, p. 38; Tom Williams/CQ Roll Call/Getty Images, p. 39; Cover image: Tom Williams/CQ Roll Call/Getty Images.

Main body text set in Rotis Serif Std 55 Regular. Typeface provided by Adobe Systems.

Library of Congress Cataloging-in-Publication Data

Names: Leigh, Anna, author.
Title: Nancy Pelosi : political powerhouse / Anna Leigh.
Description: Minneapolis : Lerner Publications, 2020. | Series: Gateway biographies | Includes
   bibliographical references and index. | Audience: Ages 9–14 | Audience: Grades 4–6 |
   Summary: "Nancy Pelosi is the first woman to serve as Speaker of the House—and she's done
   it twice. Learn how the most powerful woman in US politics is redefining leadership for
   future generations"—Provided by publisher.
Identifiers: LCCN 2019028782 (print) | LCCN 2019028783 (ebook) | ISBN 9781541577466
   (library binding) | ISBN 9781541588899 (paperback) | ISBN 9781541583078 (ebook)
Subjects: LCSH: Pelosi, Nancy, 1940–Juvenile literature. | Women legislators–United States–
   Biography–Juvenile literature. | United States. Congress. House–Speakers–Biography–
   Juvenile literature. | Legislators–United States–Biography–Juvenile literature.
Classification: LCC E840.8.P37 L45 2020 (print) | LCC E840.8.P37 (ebook) | DDC 328.73/092
   [B]–dc23

LC record available at https://lccn.loc.gov/2019028782
LC ebook record available at https://lccn.loc.gov/2019028783

Manufactured in the United States of America
1-46769-47760-9/16/2019

CONTENTS

Nancy Pelosi, US Speaker of the House, speaks at the California Democratic Party State Convention in 2019.

One by one, the members of the House of Representatives in the 116th US Congress stood up, spoke a single name, and sat down. It was January 3, 2019, and the newly elected Congress was meeting for the first time. The group of US lawmakers had already made history. Of the 535 people elected to Congress, 127 of them were women—a record number. This Congress was also the most racially diverse in US history. At their first meeting, the lawmakers were about to make history again.

The representatives were voting for the person who would become Speaker of the House—one of the most important positions in US politics. The Speaker is the leader of the House and decides what the representatives will discuss and what issues they will bring to a vote each time they meet. For the first time in almost ten years, the majority of representatives in the House were part of the Democratic Party. This meant they would also select a Democratic Speaker.

Pelosi calls the House to order after becoming Speaker a second time.

In 2010 the Speaker of the House had been Democratic representative Nancy Pelosi. In the 2010 congressional elections, the House Democrats had lost their majority position to the Republican Party. Pelosi was the minority leader of the House while Republicans were in control. When the tables turned again in 2019, Pelosi was hoping to become Speaker once more. However, she wasn't sure she would win this election.

In the months before choosing a Speaker, many Democrats had said that they didn't plan to vote for Pelosi. Many thought that after thirty-one years, she had been in Congress too long, and it was time for a change in leadership. These Democrats planned to vote for other representatives instead.

After about an hour, the representatives finished casting their votes. The officers in charge began to count. Pelosi needed 218 votes to win. Finally, the Clerk of the House, who was leading the proceedings, said that 430 votes had been cast. Pelosi had 220 of them.

Those who voted for Pelosi broke into applause as she made her way to the front of the room and sat in a high-backed brown leather chair. She smiled and stated that she was ready to take her oath. First, however, she wanted to invite her grandchildren and any other children in the room to join her at the front. As the children crowded around her, she smiled and laughed. After several minutes, she raised her right hand. She promised to support the US Constitution and to take on the duties and responsibilities of her new position. She then picked up a wooden gavel and said, "I now call the House to order on behalf of all of America's children."

Twelve years earlier, Pelosi had stood in the same place, surrounded by children, as she became the first woman in US history to serve as Speaker of the House. This time, she was the first woman and the first person in more than sixty years elected as Speaker for a second time. At seventy-eight years old, she was one of the oldest people to hold the position, and she had no plans to quit anytime soon.

Born into Politics

Pelosi was involved in politics from a very young age. She was born Nancy Patricia D'Alesandro in Baltimore, Maryland, on March 26, 1940. She was the youngest of six children and the only girl. Her parents, Thomas D'Alesandro Jr. and Annunciata D'Alesandro, were both Italian Americans, and the family lived in the Little Italy neighborhood of Baltimore. When she was born, Nancy's father was a Democratic congressional representative (1939–1947). The family were devout Catholics. By the time Nancy turned seven, her father had become the first Catholic mayor of Baltimore.

Nancy often attended events with her father. She visited the White House for the first time when she was four years old, and she participated in his swearing-in ceremony when he became mayor. At the age of twelve, Nancy attended her first Democratic National Convention. The Democratic Party holds this event every four years to help select the party's nominee for president. In 1957 she met John F. Kennedy and attended his inauguration when he became president in 1961. She had always been a Democrat, but Kennedy's liberal views had a big impact on her future political ideas.

While Nancy's father was mayor, the D'Alesandro home became a gathering place for politicians and businesspeople who worked with him. Nancy learned to answer the phone and give answers to people who needed help from her father. She wrote notes for him about questions people had and kept track of political deals he made. She tracked favors he did for others and favors others owed him. These political favors were D'Alesandro's way of ensuring people voted for him and supported his policies. Nancy caught on to this way of political strategizing, including negotiating deals and keeping track of how people would vote.

Nancy's father, Thomas D'Alesandro Jr. (*second from left*), meets with other mayors in 1948.

Nancy and her brothers went to Catholic school, and they were encouraged to become leaders. Nancy's older brother Thomas III went on to become the mayor of Baltimore in 1967. However, nobody expected Nancy to become involved in politics as an adult. At the time, many people did not expect women to have careers. Instead, most women married and became mothers. Nancy later said that she always wanted to follow a different path, but she felt that she had no choice but to stick to conventions.

Pelosi (*far left*) watches President Kennedy swear her father into a government position in 1961.

She attended Trinity College, an all-women's Catholic school in Washington, DC, where she studied political science. While there, she took a class at nearby Georgetown University and met Paul Pelosi, whom she married in 1963. He became a businessman, and the couple moved to Manhattan, New York, and later to San Francisco, California, where he was from. Within six years, they had four daughters and one son, and Nancy settled into her life as a mother.

Stay-at-Home Mom

The Pelosi children—Nancy Corinne, Christine, Jacqueline, Paul, and Alexandra—say that their mother ran an efficient household. She expected her children to do their homework and prepare for the things they did. The children formed an

San Francisco's diverse community shaped Pelosi's priorities when she became involved in politics.

assembly line to make their lunches each morning. They took turns doing different chores. To make sure mornings ran smoothly, the children set the table for the next day's breakfast immediately after finishing dinner. Sometimes they even wore matching outfits.

Along with raising her family, Pelosi soon became involved in political events in San Francisco. The family lived in a large home, and the San Francisco mayor, Joseph Alioto, was one of their neighbors. One day, Alioto called Pelosi and offered her a position on a San Francisco library committee and she accepted. Pelosi began hosting fund-raisers and other Democratic Party events in her home. Her children helped serve food at these events. Pelosi had a talent for fund-raising and making political connections. In 1976 she worked with Governor Jerry Brown of California on his presidential campaign. Brown did not win the nomination, but Pelosi soon became the chair of the California Democratic Party and helped plan the 1984 Democratic National

Congresswoman
Sala Burton

Convention. She did her work well, but she never planned to take on greater responsibilities. She was content to stay behind the scenes.

Then, in 1987, Congresswoman Sala Burton called Pelosi. Burton was dying of cancer. She encouraged Pelosi to run for her seat in Congress after she died. By then Pelosi was forty-seven years old. Her youngest daughter, Alexandra, was in high school. Pelosi asked Alexandra what she thought about Pelosi having to travel frequently. Did Alexandra want her mother to be available during her final year of school? If she did, Pelosi wouldn't run. But Alexandra told her mom to go for it. With her daughter's blessing, Pelosi entered the race.

Pelosi's campaign did well. Though she was not an experienced public speaker and sometimes struggled when speaking to crowds, her other strengths made up for this weakness. Pelosi held one hundred parties to gain support, and she enlisted thousands of volunteers to work for her campaign. In seven weeks, she was able to raise $1 million for her campaign—more than any of her competitors had raised. Pelosi went on to win the election by about four thousand votes.

When Pelosi arrived in Washington, DC, in June 1987, only twenty-three other women were in Congress. Pelosi said it didn't seem as though the men in Congress saw the women as equals or colleagues. Pelosi had never planned to be in Congress, but she took her role seriously and fought for her voice to be heard.

HER GREATEST ACCOMPLISHMENT

People often ask Pelosi about her accomplishments, commenting that it must feel exciting and important to serve in Congress. While Pelosi acknowledges that her work is important, she says that it's nothing compared to her role as a mother and grandmother.

When Pelosi talks about herself, she always introduces herself first as a mother and grandmother before talking about her career or political achievements. She says that her family is her greatest accomplishment and that her main goal in life was to become a grandmother. If she had to, she said, she wouldn't hesitate to give up her role in Congress for her family.

In fact, children got her into politics. "What took me from the kitchen to Congress," she said, "was knowing that 1 in 5 children in America lives in poverty. I just can't stand that." Her own children taught her how to be efficient with time, make compromises, and navigate competition among others. Pelosi says that more than anything else, being a mother shaped her and helped her to become an effective political leader.

Pelosi worked very hard. She woke up at five thirty in the morning, stayed up late, and worked on weekends and holidays. She would often call members of Congress during the night or on days off, expecting them to be working too. Pelosi gained a reputation for being excellent at raising money. Drawing on the lessons of her father, she knew how to negotiate with both Democrats and Republicans to get them to vote the way she wanted them to. She was organized, efficient, and persistent.

Pelosi in 1987, campaigning for Congress for the first time

Moving Up

In Congress, Pelosi served on committees working with finance, banking, and government operations. She worked to promote policies that would benefit the people of San Francisco. She fought for better health care and lower taxes. She spent five years convincing the government to turn an abandoned military base near the Golden Gate Bridge into a large park. Pelosi's district within San Francisco had a large gay community, and Pelosi made sure to promote policies that benefited this community. She supported gay marriage and wanted to spend more money on research into AIDS, a disease that affected many in San Francisco in the 1980s and 1990s. She was persistent in going after what she wanted, and she was able to convince other lawmakers to agree with her.

The AIDS Memorial Quilt celebrates the lives of those lost to AIDS.

In 1994 the Republican Party won a majority of the seats in the House of Representatives for the first time in almost forty years. By then the Democratic Party knew that Pelosi was a great fund-raiser. Still, many were unwilling to listen to her ideas about how to get a Democratic majority back. In 2000 the Democrats were still the minority in the House. Pelosi began to consider pursuing a leadership role in Congress. In 2001 she campaigned to become the party whip, one of the most important roles in the House. The whip's job is to know how representatives are going to vote on each issue Congress debates. The whip counts votes and tries to convince representatives to vote so it will benefit the party. The position was the perfect opportunity for Pelosi to use the skills she had learned from her father.

Pelosi won the position. A year later, she moved up again to become the House's Democratic minority leader. She was the first woman to lead a party in Congress. She led with order and discipline, similar to

Pelosi is sworn in as House minority whip in 2002 with the help of two of her grandchildren.

BREAKING THE MARBLE CEILING

Historically, white men have held most positions of power in business and public life in the US. People began using the term *glass ceiling* to refer to the invisible boundary that seemed to be keeping women and people of color from being able to reach higher positions. When women and people of color do achieve top positions, they talk about breaking the glass ceiling. Pelosi, however, has said that her barrier was much stronger than glass. In Congress there was a marble ceiling.

When Pelosi was sworn in as Speaker of the House in 2007, she said it was a "historic moment for Congress . . . a historic moment for the women of this country. It is a moment for which we have waited over 200 years." Pelosi continued, "For our daughters and granddaughters, today we have broken the marble ceiling."

Pelosi said her new position was a responsibility. She believed that her becoming Speaker would help all women in the United States and encourage more women to participate in politics. To her, nothing could be more important or helpful for the country than having more women involved in politics.

Pelosi and other top-ranking Democrats celebrate the party's electoral victories in 2007.

how she ran her house when her family was young. She insisted that the Democratic Party needed a unified message on the issues they were fighting for. Soon Democrats were voting together on issues more often than they had in decades. But in 2004's congressional election, the Democrats again failed to win a majority in the House.

At the time, George W. Bush was president of the United States, and the country was involved in the Iraq War (2003–2011). Pelosi spoke harshly about Bush's leadership abilities and made it clear that she was against the controversial war. Other Democrats also criticized Bush and the ongoing war. Some wanted to impeach the president, or remove him from office. Despite her own feelings about Bush, Pelosi refused to consider impeachment. Instead, she said, Democrats must focus on winning a majority in the House of Representatives so they could give the country better leadership and policies. In 2006 Pelosi teamed up with other Democratic representatives to come up with a strategy for campaigning and winning more seats. The plan worked, and the Democrats finally won back their majority position in the House.

Following their win, the Democrats voted unanimously to make Pelosi the first woman Speaker of the House. By then Pelosi had been in Congress for almost twenty years. She was sixty-six years old and had six grandchildren, all of whom joined her on the House floor on January 4, 2007, while representatives cast their votes. When she took the oath of office, she invited her grandchildren to stand with her. "Today, I thank my colleagues," she said. "By electing me as speaker, you have brought us closer to the ideal of equality that is America's heritage and America's hope."

When she was elected Speaker in 2007, Pelosi became the highest-ranking woman in government in US history.

Three days later, Pelosi visited Baltimore, Maryland. The city was honoring her by holding a rally and renaming the street where she grew up. The street's new name was Via Nancy D'Alesandro Pelosi. When Pelosi spoke to the crowd that had gathered to celebrate her, she said, "I wanted to come back here and say thank you to all of you. Every step that I took to the speakership began in this neighborhood."

Crisis and Criticism

In 2008, just weeks before the election that made Barack Obama the country's first African American president, the US economy collapsed. Millions of Americans lost money, homes, and jobs. The US government planned to pass a bill that would provide $700 billion to large financial institutions. The bill aimed to help make the economy stable again, but it was very unpopular with many Americans. The government was planning to give money to the same people who had caused the economy to crash.

Many members of Congress planned to vote against the bill. But the government needed to do something. If it didn't, businesses around the world were likely to keep losing money, creating an even larger financial crisis. Pelosi went to several Democrats and asked them to support the bill. She managed to get the support she needed, and the bill passed.

Pelosi watches Obama sign the Affordable Care Act into law in 2010.

Soon after, with Barack Obama as president, Pelosi helped make several other important changes. The House passed bills that aimed to ensure better pay for women, help more students attend college, and assist those living in poverty. Pelosi became especially interested in climate change. She believed it was important to take care of Earth and to work on policies to help Americans live in more environmentally friendly ways. She passed a climate change bill in the House, but the Senate ultimately voted it down.

In 2010 Pelosi achieved one of the biggest successes of her career. The Democratic Party had been trying for years to pass laws that would change health care and health insurance in the United States. They hoped to make health care more accessible and affordable for more Americans.

Pelosi helped write the Affordable Care Act. This act granted access to health insurance to more than thirty million Americans who had not previously been able to get it. When Pelosi found out that sixty-seven people in the House weren't sure they would vote for the act, she got a list of their names, spent the night calling them, and persuaded them to vote for the act. The act passed.

Many consider the years under Pelosi's leadership some of the most productive years in Congress's history. But some Americans were unhappy with the new health-care laws. People were also frustrated that the government had spent so much money helping financial institutions after the economic crisis. An election was coming up, and many voters were critical of both Obama and Pelosi.

Republicans took advantage of this criticism. They spent $65 million to create more than 160,000 ads that ran during the election season and spread negative messages about Pelosi. Because so many people viewed Pelosi negatively, she couldn't help her fellow Democrats campaign for the 2010 congressional election. People might not want to vote for a candidate whom Pelosi supported. Instead, Pelosi stayed behind the scenes and ran fund-raisers. The Democrats lost their majority in the 2010 election, and some Democrats blamed Pelosi for the loss. Many expected her to step down from her position in Congress. Instead, she once again became the Democratic minority leader in the House. She knew she still had work to do in Washington.

Taking Back the House

Over the next few years, the Democrats remained in the minority in the House, and Pelosi was not involved in as many big policy changes as she had been in 2009 and 2010. Many people wondered if it was time for her to retire. But Pelosi did

Presidential nominees Donald Trump and Hillary Clinton on a debate stage in 2016

not intend to step down. By 2014 she was thinking ahead to the 2016 presidential election. She was making plans to have a Democratic president and a Democratic majority in the House once again.

Pelosi did not get her wish in 2016. Instead, Republican Donald Trump became president, and the Democrats remained the minority in the House. Pelosi continued to face criticism from both Republicans and Democrats. Representative Tim Ryan even ran against Pelosi for her position as the leader of the Democrats. It was one of her toughest campaigns, but Pelosi managed to keep her position. Once again, she began thinking ahead to the next opportunity to bring more Democrats into Congress.

Following Trump's election, many people in the United States were shocked. Trump did not have any political experience, and in the months leading up to the election, he had made many negative comments about women and people of color. He often posted controversial statements on social media. Many in the United States thought he was unfit to hold political office. They had been certain that Trump's opponent, the politically experienced Hillary Clinton, would become the first woman president.

When Clinton lost, women all around the country took action. They planned a huge march in Washington, and many decided to become more politically active. They thought it was time for change in Washington. Trump's win confused Pelosi too. She respected the office of the president and tried not to speak negatively about Trump in public. But she acknowledged that he often did not act or speak as a world leader should.

The Women's March took place the day after Trump became president. It was the largest single-day protest in US history.

The 2018 congressional elections reflected many Americans' belief that the government was not properly representing the interests of American citizens. The candidates campaigning for seats in Congress included more women and people of color than ever before. Democrats didn't just want a majority in the House. They also wanted new leadership for the Democratic Party. Pelosi once again came under fire. During their campaigns, many Democrats promised to vote against Pelosi for Speaker of the House. Republicans also attacked Pelosi, again spending millions of dollars on ads that spoke against her.

Pelosi wasn't concerned about the negative ads. She had learned to take criticism over her long career. She knew that she was a good leader and the best fund-raiser, and she believed that Republicans only targeted her because they knew how effective she was in her job. Pelosi did worry, however, that the attacks on her would discourage other women from running for office. She didn't want women to hesitate because they were concerned about the criticism they might face. She appreciated those who were brave enough to run despite the criticism. The morning after twenty-eight-year-old Representative Alexandria Ocasio-Cortez won her election in New York, Pelosi called her. "Thank you for your courage to run," she said. "This is not for the faint of heart."

Pelosi greets new representative Alexandria Ocasio-Cortez at the start of the 116th Congress in 2019.

Facing the President

The Democrats won a majority of House seats in the 2018 elections. Immediately, Pelosi went to work. She spoke to those who planned to vote against her for Speaker and tried to convince them to change their minds. She offered representatives good positions on committees in exchange for their votes. She also promised to limit her time in the role. If she became Speaker again, she would serve only until 2022.

In December 2018, Pelosi attended a televised meeting with Trump where he made a comment about her lack of popularity within her own party. Pelosi fired back, saying, "Mr. President, please don't characterize the strength that I bring to this meeting as the leader of the House Democrats, who just won a big victory."

Pelosi walked out of the meeting wearing a bright red coat and dark sunglasses. A photo of her instantly became popular on the internet, and people all around the country began taking notice of Pelosi. They recognized that she was willing to stand up to Trump. Pelosi knew how to respond to him and how to get what she wanted from him. When she spoke of her strategy in dealing with the president, she said, "He has things that he says about women or whatever—immigrants and the rest—don't be offended. Ignore it."

Members of Congress noticed too, including Republicans. Meanwhile, Pelosi's party realized that her experience in Congress was helpful and that her ability to stand up to Trump was important. In January

Though some Democrats threatened to run against Pelosi for Speaker, most ended up endorsing her.

2019, the House chose Pelosi to be Speaker for the second time. Just fifteen Democrats voted against her. Republican minority leader Kevin McCarthy acknowledged that Pelosi's meeting with Trump had a big impact on her becoming Speaker. "She won it because she stood up to him," he said.

Pelosi quickly proved that she was the right person for the job. The government was in the midst of the longest shutdown in history. Each year Congress and the president must agree on a budget to determine how the government will spend money that year. If they do not approve a budget on time, the government shuts down. Many government agencies close and workers go unpaid until a new budget passes. In 2019 Trump wanted the budget to include funding to build a wall between the United States and Mexico—one of his main campaign promises. Trump claimed the wall would help stop illegal immigration

Pelosi meets with (*from right*) Senator Chuck Schumer, Trump, and Vice President Mike Pence about border security in 2018.

31

into the United States. But Pelosi refused. She and the House Democrats said the wall was unnecessary and too expensive. They would not agree to grant this funding.

Pelosi strengthened her position by recommending that Trump postpone his State of the Union address, a speech the president gives each year to Congress. He agreed to do so. She also got him to admit on TV that he was the one behind the shutdown. Neither Republicans nor Democrats in Congress wanted the shutdown. Rather, Trump was the one holding up the government. Trump's admission drove his approval ratings down. After thirty-five days, he finally agreed to reopen the government—without getting what he had demanded. Many saw the end of the shutdown as a victory for Pelosi, as she solidified her power within the government.

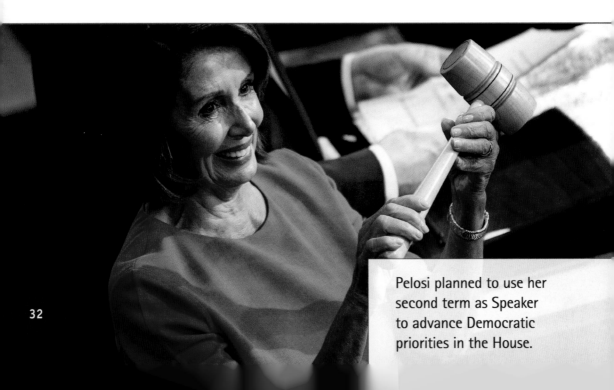

Pelosi planned to use her second term as Speaker to advance Democratic priorities in the House.

STATE OF THE UNION

When the State of the Union address finally happened on February 5, 2019, Pelosi once again became popular online. Politicians are often strategic about how they show support for the ideas presented in the president's speech. They clap only for statements that align with their political ideas and represent the interests of those who voted them into Congress. At one point in Trump's speech, Pelosi, who was sitting behind him, stood and clapped, pointing her hands in his direction.

Pelosi later said that she had clapped because she agreed with that part of the speech and was complimenting the president. However, many interpreted her action as sarcastic, and a photo of Pelosi clapping spread quickly. It became another example of people's faith in Pelosi to be able to stand up to the president.

A Cautious Approach

Within a few months, Pelosi was engaged in another political battle. In April the Department of Justice released the Mueller report detailing an investigation into the 2016 election. The investigation was to determine whether Russia had interfered in the election results and whether Trump had worked with the Russians and then attempted to interfere with investigations.

The report said that the investigators did not have enough evidence to say for sure that Trump had interfered and committed crimes. The report had been heavily redacted—parts of it had been covered up to protect sensitive information.

Special Counsel Robert Mueller was chosen to investigate and report crimes surrounding the 2016 presidential election.

Representative Jerrold Nadler reads from the redacted Mueller Report at a hearing in 2019.

The House demanded that the Department of Justice release a full version of the report without redactions. The House wanted to know all the facts about the investigation and about what had occurred in 2016. If Trump had interfered with the investigation, then he had not lived up to his duties as president and Congress could take action to remove him from office.

Over the next two months, many Democrats called for impeachment. They believed that Trump had not acted appropriately and was unfit to be president. At first, Pelosi refrained from calling for impeachment. She encouraged the House to move carefully. She said that they needed to be sure they had all the facts before

Trump began his 2020 campaign almost immediately after becoming president in 2017.

deciding whether impeachment was the best action.

Pelosi was, as always, thinking ahead to the next election. In 2020 Trump would have to run for the presidency again. If he lost, there would likely be a Democratic president, and Pelosi and her fellow Democrats would have an easier time passing legislation that they believed was right for all Americans. Pelosi was considering impeachment in this context. She believed the government should pursue impeachment only if it was for the good of the country, rather than because of political parties and ideas.

In September 2019, Pelosi's views on impeachment shifted. An official complained that Trump had improperly used his power by asking a foreign government to find damaging information on a Democratic presidential candidate. When the White House tried to keep the official's complaint a secret, Pelosi launched an impeachment inquiry. She and House Democrats would investigate whether Trump should be removed from office.

INSPIRATION AND EXAMPLE

Pelosi has been honored several times for her accomplishments and contributions to the United States. In 2013 she was inducted into the National Women's Hall of Fame, which recognizes the achievements of women in art, business, sports, and politics. Pelosi accepted the award on October 12, 2013, in Seneca Falls, New York, where the first women's rights convention took place in 1848. When Pelosi accepted the award, she spoke about the importance of getting more women involved in politics.

In 2019 Pelosi was honored two more times. *Time* magazine listed her as one of the year's top one hundred most influential people. She also won the Profile in Courage Award. The family of former president John F. Kennedy established this award to recognize those who have shown political courage. Kennedy's daughter, Caroline Kennedy, spoke about why they had chosen Pelosi. She said that Pelosi is "the most important woman in American political history" and that she is "an example and an inspiration for generations of Americans, men and women."

A Long Career

Pelosi (*left*) receiving the Profile in Courage Award from Caroline Kennedy in 2019

When she became Speaker of the House for the second time, Pelosi was seventy-eight years old. In the United States, many people retire in their sixties. For years, people have wondered when Pelosi will decide to retire from politics.

Many people, including her family members, have wondered about her reasons for staying in government. Some think she will retire after certain changes occur. She may be waiting for the right president to take office or for the right person to take over her position. She once said that she might have retired if Hillary Clinton had become president. However, as she sees it, there is still work to do in Congress.

Pelosi says that she sees her job as a mission. She wants the Affordable Care Act expanded. She wants better policies concerning climate change, taxes, and income equality. She would still like to see more women in politics. "When the mission is accomplished," she said, "then I can have satisfaction that when I was needed to get the job done, I was there to do it."

Despite the many challenges facing the United States and its government, Pelosi has hope. When she held the gavel for the first time in her second term as Speaker, she said, "We enter this new Congress with a sense of great hope and confidence for the future and deep humility. Our nation is at a historic moment. Two months ago, the American people spoke and demanded a new dawn."

Pelosi in 2019

IMPORTANT DATES

March 26, 1940	Nancy Patricia D'Alesandro is born in Baltimore, Maryland.
September 7, 1963	She marries Paul Pelosi.
June 2, 1987	She becomes a congresswoman for the first time.
January 15, 2002	She becomes the minority whip in Congress.
January 3, 2003	She becomes the first woman to lead a party in Congress.
January 4, 2007	She becomes the first woman Speaker of the House.
January 20, 2009	Barack Obama takes over as president of the United States.
March 23, 2010	The Affordable Care Act becomes law.
January 3, 2011	Pelosi becomes the minority leader for the second time.

January 20, 2017	Donald Trump takes over as president of the United States.
January 3, 2019	Pelosi becomes the Speaker of the House for the second time.
April 2019	*Time* magazine names her one of 2019's one hundred most influential people.
May 19, 2019	She receives the Profile in Courage Award.

SOURCE NOTES

9   "Nancy Pelosi Takes House Speaker Oath with Children at Her Side," YouTube video, 8:57, posted by *CNN*, January 3, 2019, https://www.youtube.com/watch?v=vt-dVB7sKUU.

16 Ellen McCarthy, "'Makes Going to Work Look Easy': Decades before She Was House Speaker, Nancy Pelosi Had an Even Harder Job," *Washington Post*, February 12, 2019, https://www .washingtonpost.com/lifestyle/style/makes-going-to-work -look-easy-how-being-a-full-time-mom-prepared-nancy -pelosi-for-this-moment/2019/02/12/416cd85e-28bc-11e9-984d -9b8fba003e81_story.html?utm_term=.c8d47b34d9bc.

20 "Nancy Pelosi Becomes First Female Speaker of the House," History, January 4, 2019, https://www.history.com/this-day-in -history/nancy-pelosi-named-speaker-of-the-house-2004.

22 Associated Press, "Speaker of the House Pelosi Makes History," *NBC News*, January 4, 2007, http://www.nbcnews.com/id /16449288/ns/politics/t/speaker-house-pelosi-makes-history/# .XOSzxchKg2w.

23 Ron Cassie, "The Gavel Goes Back to Nancy D'Alesandro Pelosi of Little Italy," *Baltimore*, January 4, 2019, https://www .baltimoremagazine.com/section/historypolitics/the-gavel-goes -back-to-nancy-dalesandro-pelosi-of-little-italy.

28 Molly Ball, "Nancy Pelosi Doesn't Care What You Think of Her. And She Isn't Going Anywhere," *Time*, September 6, 2018, http://time.com/5388347/nancy-pelosi-democrats-feminism/.

30 Anthony Zurcher, "Nancy Pelosi: The Remarkable Comeback of America's Most Powerful Woman," *BBC*, January 2, 2019, https://www.bbc.com/news/world-us-canada-46739947.

30 McCarthy, "Pelosi Had an Even Harder Job."

31 Todd S. Purdum, "The Second Coming of Nancy Pelosi," *Atlantic*, February 4, 2019, https://www.theatlantic.com/politics /archive/2019/02/nancy-pelosi-has-emerged-best-anti-trump -leader/581953/.

37 "Nancy Pelosi Named Recipient of Profile in Courage Award," *CBS News*, April 7, 2019, https://www.cbsnews.com/news/nancy -pelosi-profile-in-courage-award-john-f-kennedy-library -foundation/.

39 "Nancy Pelosi: Checks and Balances," YouTube video, 9:38, posted by *CBS Sunday Morning*, January 6, 2019, https://www .youtube.com/watch?v=EA_3jsnwoCk.

39 Clare Foran and Ashley Killough, "Nancy Pelosi Elected House Speaker, Reclaims Gavel to Lead Democrats' New Majority," CNN, January 3, 2019, https://www.cnn.com/2019/01/03/politics /nancy-pelosi-house-speaker-vote-new-congress/index.html.

SELECTED BIBLIOGRAPHY

Ball, Molly. "Nancy Pelosi Doesn't Care What You Think of Her. And She Isn't Going Anywhere." *Time*, September 6, 2018. http://time .com/5388347/nancy-pelosi-democrats-feminism/.

Editors of Encyclopaedia Britannica. "Nancy Pelosi." *Encyclopaedia Britannica*. Last modified April 29, 2019. https://www.britannica .com/biography/Nancy-Pelosi.

"From the *60 Minutes* Archives: Nancy Pelosi." *CBS* video, 13:16, April 14, 2019. https://www.cbs.com/shows/60_minutes/video /Kxd9m4zpq1gfco8T1iWMiVRr5CDzRYh8/from-the-60-minutes -archives-nancy-pelosi/.

Klein, Ezra. "The Vindication of Nancy Pelosi." Vox, January 25, 2019. https://www.vox.com/policy-and-politics/2019/1/25/18197685 /nancy-pelosi-trump-shutdown-over.

Kroll, Andy. "The Staying Power of Nancy Pelosi." *Atlantic*, September 11, 2015. https://www.theatlantic.com/politics/archive/2015/09/the -staying-power-of-nancy-pelosi/440022/.

McCarthy, Ellen. "'Makes Going to Work Look Easy': Decades before She Was House Speaker, Nancy Pelosi Had an Even Harder Job." *Washington Post*, February 12, 2019. https://www .washingtonpost.com/lifestyle/style/makes-going-to-work-look -easy-how-being-a-full-time-mom-prepared-nancy-pelosi-for-this -moment/2019/02/12/416cd85e-28bc-11e9-984d-9b8fba003e81_story .html?utm_term=.c8d47b34d9bc.

"Nancy Pelosi: Checks and Balances." YouTube video, 9:38. Posted by *CBS Sunday Morning*, January 6, 2019. https://www.youtube.com /watch?v=EA_3jsnwoCk.

"Nancy Pelosi Discusses Mueller Investigation, Impeachment and More." YouTube video, 7:16. Posted by *Today*, January 3, 2019. https://www .youtube.com/watch?v=xx50k42aLqE.

"Nancy Pelosi: The 2019 *60 Minutes* Interview." *CBS*, April 14, 2019.
https://www.cbsnews.com/news/speaker-of-the-house-nancy-pelosi
-the-2019-60-minutes-interview-2019-04-14/.

"Pelosi: I Want Women to See That You Do Not Get Pushed Around."
CNN video, 8:03, September 11, 2018. https://www.cnn.com/videos
/politics/2018/11/09/badass-women-of-washington-nancy-pelosi
-dana-bash-orig.cnn.

Purdum, Todd S. "The Second Coming of Nancy Pelosi." *Atlantic*,
February 4, 2019. https://www.theatlantic.com/politics/archive
/2019/02/nancy-pelosi-has-emerged-best-anti-trump-leader/581953/.

Wagner, Alex. "Pelosi Won, Trump Lost." *Atlantic*, January 25, 2019.
https://www.theatlantic.com/ideas/archive/2019/01/pelosi-beats
-trump/581344/.

Zurcher, Anthony. "Nancy Pelosi: The Remarkable Comeback of
America's Most Powerful Woman." *BBC*, January 2, 2019. https://
www.bbc.com/news/world-us-canada-46739947.

FURTHER READING

BOOKS

Braun, Eric. *Taking Action for Civil and Political Rights*. Minneapolis: Lerner Publications, 2017.

Read about ordinary people who stood up to make a difference in their communities.

Howell, Janet. *Leading the Way: Women in Power*. Somerville, MA: Candlewick, 2019.

Read about more inspiring women in politics, including the first woman elected to Congress and the first woman to sit on the US Supreme Court.

Leigh, Anna. *Alexandria Ocasio-Cortez: Political Headliner*. Minneapolis: Lerner Publications, 2020.

Learn about Alexandria Ocasio-Cortez, another member of the 116th Congress, who is raising her voice to fight for issues that affect her community.

WEBSITES

Nancy Pelosi
https://www.speaker.gov/
Visit Nancy Pelosi's website to read more about her life, career, and positions on important issues.

Our Government
https://www.whitehouse.gov/about-the-white-house/our-government/
Read about the three branches of the US government and about electing representatives and changing laws.

United States House of Representatives
https://www.house.gov/
Learn more about the House of Representatives, current members of Congress, and their work to bring about change in the United States.

INDEX

"Martin, pray me out of this," I said, and so joked as best I could, trying to avoid the trap the boy was setting for me.

"It's a matter of love, Owen," Woofer said.

"Worse and worse," I said.

"You've never been in love?" Woofer asked me, incredulous.

"Yes," I said, "but not lately."

"You have a woman in Richmond, sir, I understand," Betsy said to me.

"I did have one, from New Orleans. I saw her courting a major, so I won her heart away. Then a general saw her and won her heart away."

"You might become a general any day now yourself, the rumor has it," Betsy said.

"I don't think so," I said cautiously.

"General Manger is sick, I've heard."

"He's an able general and a tough man," I said.

"It's rumored he'll be replaced and you'll be advanced again, which the men believe, knowing how lucky you are with rank, sir."

I watched him thoughtfully, respectful of the cutting edge of his remark. "I'm not anxious to be a general," I said, still trying to hide the ambition I suffered from.

That night when Betsy and Martin prepared to leave, I asked Woofer to remain, and I asked him what was the matter with him and his woman.

"I don't want to worry you, Owen," he said.

"Well, you do."

"I worry about you too," he said simply.

"What is it?"

"She's pregnant, Owen."

"Ah, come on, boy. You got your woman in trouble?" I said, astonished.

"I did. I sure did. And I'm scared."

"Well, that's rough, Woofer. My lord, boy."

"I worry day and night about it."

27

"Is this her first one?"

"Well, no, Owen. It's her second one, though it's my first one."

"Her first one was by some other fellow?"

"Yes."

"Who is she, anyway?" I said. "She seems to get attention."

"A planter's daughter," he said.

"My good lord, worse and worse. How old is she?"

"About twenty."

"Well, you can't marry, not at your age, not under these circumstances."

"I must, Owen, but it would help if you'd talk with her people and with papa."

"I last saw papa lying on the ground where I'd thrown him."

"Owen, he loves you."

"Oh, hell—"

"Owen, he'll do anything you ask, you being the one in command of—"

"No, no."

"Owen, maybe twice a year he would get to drinking brandy at night, and he would talk about you more'n anybody, even more'n Jesse, how you could hunt and ride crazy and race faster than anybody and swim, and how you went out into the world and won. He said one night you and he were the same, except he had never had the nerve."

"Shut up, Woofer." I sat totally still, and tried to force from my mind what he had said, for it wasn't an honest portrayal of papa, I realized. It troubled me deeply, even to consider papa loving me. "I want you to know I have no—regard for papa, and as for your woman, you'll not be marrying while you're in my regiment."

"I'm your brother, Owen."

"You're just another boy who got a woman in trouble and ran off to the army. You'll stay here."

He sat for a while longer, watching the fire. "It'll break mama's heart if my baby is born a stranger, mama loves me so

28

much. I don't love her quite as much, Owen, for she clings to me, won't let me alone. Papa I love, but he has had so many rules, and I obeyed as many as I could, then finally broke them all with this woman, for she's all that papa dislikes. She can't even cook, Owen. She can't garden. She won't clean the house. About all she can do is ride a horse and swim. She used to come down at night and swim in the river with me."

"She has bewitched you with the moon, sounds like to me."

"I don't know. I feel like she might have. I'm under her spell, all right. I love her so much."

"Yes, well, you forget her."

"It would require two letters, Owen, one to papa, one to her brother-in-law. You have such power in our part of the country, decorated four times, the highest-ranking officer from that region—"

"You don't stop, do you, Woofer?"

"It matters so much to me. You don't seem to realize I love—"

"No no," I said.

He considered that silently, sat there brooding over it. "Damn it, Owen. If you knew."

"Woofer, I don't want to be reminded of it again. No opening of family wounds or talking about love or your woman. You are not to trouble me again, for I do have worries of my own."

"Yes, Owen."

"I have work to do. I'm in a war. I suspect papa disfavors it. Well, I disfavor papa. I escaped him, but not without force, as you remember."

"I remember."

"Now you've escaped. Welcome home, Woofer. Make a home of it. It's not a damn thing but the army, and I'm the father here if there is one. Or Bob Lee is—not the General, but that mongrel dog there. Salute Bob Lee. He's in love too."

He had no idea, of course, as he left, despondent and woeful, what emotions I had tried to dismiss long since of the woman

29

of my own. Let them be, leave them. God knows, a soldier must keep his mind on the hard work at hand.

But I have seen a seed of grass grow to break a rock, to splinter it. I began to wonder how I might help him, how at least I might inquire further into the involvement which troubled him. Also I began to dream of women I had known long ago when I was a young man, even before I married, when I had been like Woofer, a tall, slender blade of a boy walking proudly down the road, smiling at life.

CHAPTER TWO

General Manger came to my headquarters, accompanied by a new colonel whose name was Penny, a handsome, overbred planter-family type of man; they walked through the main room and into my bedroom, Manger waving for me to follow them. He propped my knapsack against the wall, there at the head of my bed, and plopped himself down. He raised his boots one at a time, groaning as he lifted each one, grunting contentedly as he set it down on my blankets, mud and all. "Owen, I need to talk to you, Penny and me do," he said. "Shut the damn door."

He was an old man. He had been a judge in Charlotte. He had once weighed over 200 pounds; now he weighed about 120. His eyes were always hungrily watching for a prey. He was a bull-dog type of fighter, in battle and in his personal life, tough of mind; even as I closed the door and turned to face him, I saw him close his eyes suddenly, tightly, as a spasm of pain—I cannot imagine what else it could have been—swept through him. When he opened his eyes again, his face was covered with moisture and his eyes were glassy, but there was no attitude of softness or regret about him. "Yes, God damn you, Owen, come here and sit down so I can talk to you." He had a habit of saying "damn you" to most everybody, even General Heth, but it was softly said, almost a sigh; it was more a term of endearment than criticism.

"I been wondering how you are, General," I said.

"Sit down, sit down." He began to cough, a phlegm-filled spasm. He put a clean handkerchief to his mouth and spit into

31

it. "How is my favorite colonel today?" he asked me. He twitched his lips and nose and blinked at the papers Colonel Penny had laid on the bed beside him. "Oh, for God sake, sit down, Penny, sit down, damn you."

Colonel Penny moved to a place near the window, where he stood looking out at the glassy, wintry scene and the men slodging up and down the road. He was dressed as a cavalry officer. Of late many new officers had entered the army, most of them but recently out of college. On the whole they were well-to-do, educated men, and they all wore cavalry uniforms, which were the nattiest, neatest, most colorful ones in the army.

The General snorted, a dry chuckle that he kept tightly controlled. "Ay, Lord, I have so much help I don't know how to do with it." He leaned toward me and grunted sharply. "I need it though, Owen. We're coming to a hell of a fight by spring. General Heth has the figures on it. Biggest army in the history of the world, that's what the Yanks are building, bigger than Napoleon's, bigger than the Russian army at Moscow, bigger than the Roman legions, bigger than the army of that Chinese what's-his-name."

"Genghis Khan?" I said.

"Bigger'n his. All of it amassed by the North to decide whether the United States will become one country again or remain two." He paused. He breathed in deeply in puffy gasps. "Which side will win, Owen?"

"The South."

"Why?"

"We're better fighters. We've won most all the ground battles."

"So." He nodded emphatically. "Why are we fighting?"

"To be free of them."

"Why be free of them?" he said, much in the manner of a trenchant schoolteacher.

"The South is agricultural and the North is industrial, and we want our own laws and ways," I answered. "And they keep robbing us every time we get a start—"

"Some say freeing the nigger slaves is the reason we've got in this war. Some seem to think the blacks started it." He began to chuckle; his body shook with his dry mirth. "What say to that?"

"I don't know any blacks," I said.

"Some people say the abolitionists started it, them and their monkey president—as if we could free the niggers and not go bankrupt as a people, ever one of us. Of course slavery is an evil, but so is child labor, so is bringing over shiploads of Irish immigrants and working them day and night in Yankee factories, so is dumping second-class products on us and refusing to let us buy from France and England, so is robbing us of our wealth. What money-seeking, cold-eyed bastards the Yanks are. Slavery is an evil just like sickness is an evil, but every culture, the Babylonian, the Chinese, the Eygptian, the Jews, the Greek, the Roman has used it. Which is what you believe, is it, Owen?"

"Yes, I suppose it's so," I said.

"But your family don't agree, do they?" Flatly, bluntly the words came out, sharply he asked me, a stunning comment, really, the smile vanishing in a moment. "Yes, you see your family has been mentioned to us, Owen. As you know, we have to be careful here in what the Yanks call a civil war. I get damned tired of loyalty checks. It was easier that first year, when we were all soldiers together and everybody who was a soldier went out to fight the enemy."

"What are you saying, General?" I said, watching him carefully.

Colonel Penny straightened his immaculate cavalry jacket. "Shall I go on with it, sir?" he asked.

General Manger nodded. "Yes," he said. "Tell him."

Colonel Penny calmly approached me, smiled down at me, ever so efficient in his crisp attitude. "We are trying to put the brigade in order for spring, Colonel Wright. As you can imagine, this is difficult. I have been assigned by General Heth to help

33

General Manger review his situation, and we have come upon a number of items concerning you and your regiment. Your regiment is understrength."

"Yes, it's down to about 350 men on duty," I said.

"It's down to 304 men precisely."

I was annoyed by that correction, by the sharpness of the rebuff. Officers were usually courteous, respectful of one another. Always before Manger had shown a paternalistic attitude toward me, had excused my exaggerations with a laugh. "We received forty, fifty volunteers a week or two ago," I said.

"Thirty. Yes, thirty, wasn't it? So we find your regiment is in weak condition and is sluggish in recruitment."

"My regiment never has been weak," I said.

"It is half-strength."

"The Yanks didn't think it was half-strength attacking before Richmond. I held the point for General Jackson's charge—"

"You lost twenty percent of your regiment, too, Colonel, in that first day."

"I held the point for that first day, all of it, and into the second day—"

"Fifty-two men the second day, Colonel, dead and wounded, and sixty men lost in the Shenandoah, and thirty more at Fredericksburg, one hundred four dead and wounded the previous year, and you have done nothing to attract replacements for them, even though you are highly regarded in your home region and we do have a conscription law, one much enlarged last autumn."

"I don't like that law."

"Don't you?" He shrugged. "Oh my," he said. Wearily he referred to the sheaf of notes in his hand. "We also find a number of references in your file to your family, which has a history of abolitionism."

"My father has, I admit."

"And your brothers."

"I—don't know about my two older brothers. Woofer is—"

34

"One brother for years has been active helping slaves to escape north, hasn't he?"

"No, not to my knowledge."

"He is now also engaged helping groups of white men get to the North in order to fight with the Yank army."

"I don't think either one of my older brothers—"

"These matters are documented, Colonel."

"Which brother is it?"

"I don't know which brother it is. I don't remember. I would have to go through these papers—"

"Well, go through them," I said.

"Yes. Perhaps later," he said.

I stared at him incredulously. He was as rude an officer as I had found, yet he was all spit and polish in his shiny uniform, speaking with his immaculate, soft, Southern accent, a gold chain, a diamond ring—all signs of attainment decorating him to a sheen.

"Was it Jesse or Phillip?" I asked.

"I—it was both, wasn't it, General Manger?" he said.

"I don't recall. I think it was the oldest one."

"Jesse? Well, I left home six years ago," I said. "I've not seen them. My brother Woofer is in my regiment."

"Which is pertinent, I suppose," Colonel Penny said casually, as if dismissing it from his mind. "It must all be weighed as we seek to identify weaknesses which hopefully we can correct by transferring a few officers to the Western theater of operation."

"You allowing them to do this, General?" I asked bluntly, turning on him.

"Oh, I don't know what to do," he said evasively. "You can't talk to the third floor any more since Lee has got the command. President Davis used to be commander in chief, and I knew him, but now it's Lee. I talked with him about something a while ago. It took a week to get in to see him, and his response was so moderate it didn't amount to anything. None of us Southerners cares about organization, that's the truth of it." He sat there

35

in the bed, looking at me, studying me. "I hate to hear you still won't use conscriptees, Owen. Your state can send recruiters up into those mountains most any time."

"I've never fought with conscriptees, General."

"You've never faced this new Northern army, either," Colonel Penny said.

"Neither of us has, Colonel," I said.

"That's true," he said, "and I realize that I am not a battlefield soldier and am, of course, despised by those who are. But I do have work to do, I have an assignment here."

"My command is stronger today than it would be if I took 300 recruits and tried to make soldiers out of them by spring," I said.

"Paper is what I have to deal with," Colonel Penny said, tapping the papers in his hand, "and on paper—"

"Well, I deal with Yankees," I said.

"Like your father and brothers," he said. He was crafty and keen of mind, all right. A hog killer for General Heth is what he was. A general's hog sticker. I was caught awkwardly unprepared for any such attack as this, was unable to meet it.

General Manger said, "We also heard a few remarks you're said to have made, Owen, references to Virginians and South Carolinians as having big asses, or was it big balls? I can't remember the facts of it. But General Lee and General Jackson and General Heth are all Virginians, to name but three. And you claim that South Carolina started the war impetuously."

"It doesn't hurt to joke with the men," I said. "If we don't entertain them, they might go home."

"We would expect you to detain them," Colonel Penny said.

"I would try, Captain Crawford and I," I said, entering his name into the conversation.

Penny looked up at me thoughtfully. "Why do you mention him?" The reference troubled him. No doubt he realized I had guessed he knew Crawford and that Crawford had collaborated with him.

I turned from him. "I have fought for two years with you,

General, and have never troubled you, have I, and for you to turn on me—"

"Your loyalty is not in question by me personally, Owen," he said without inflection or much concern.

"But you have heard rumors that I am trying to take your place?"

He shook his head. "I wouldn't—I don't think so."

"I believe you have, and you have turned on me, but I wouldn't harm you, after your advancing me from one rank to another—"

"Now, your generousness toward me, Owen—"

"We've been comrades-in-arms—"

"There is no need for you to flop all over me. Don't plead with me—"

"I know you would hold on to your post in the army, just as you do your life, for losing your post would cost you your life, wouldn't it?"

He watched me steadily. "Cost me my life? Why?"

"Because of your illness," I said, staring back at him.

"Illness?" he said. "I'm old, I admit . . ." His voice trailed away and faltered. He shook his head erratically, not looking directly at me now, nor at Penny. Both of us were staring at him, measuring the extent of the wound I had found it necessary to deliver to him. Manger murmured, "What you trying to do, damn you? Did you start the rumor that I'm ill?"

"I think as much of you as I do my father, General. You and General Jackson are the two who have befriended me consistently—"

"Owen, I want you to know this, if you go to General Jackson about this or any other matter, if you go over me and over Heth, then you will certainly answer to us in the strictest manner."

"I couldn't answer to either of you from out west, could I?"

The fire was in his eyes now, the old fire; he was the warrior now, all right. "You defy me, Owen? Are you threatening me?"

"You've seen me in the war and know I never threaten anybody without cause. I hope what I've said convinces you I'm loyal as needs be, and that there's no need in the world of me going all the way to the West, while my regiment falls to Captain Crawford, or some such man." Neither he nor Penny had expected my defense to be as open and blatant as this, I suspect. Lord knows, I had never talked to Manger like this before. But when a man is losing a battle which is dear to his own life, sometimes the only defense he has available to him is to attack, even awkwardly. "People have been saying to me, 'Owen, is General Manger ill?' and I say, 'No, no, why he's out there on the line with us, like he always has been.' I never do mention that spitting in the handkerchief."

"God damn you, Owen."

"Yes, sir. I know. But losing my command in this army is about the same as losing my life too, and I don't plan to lose it without kicking the walls down. I'll kick every wall down I see."

General Manger cleared his throat. "Yes, yes," he said, painfully annoyed. "Well, I ought to have known."

"I suppose you don't mind my admitting all this to you," I said.

"You wouldn't bother Jackson about such lies as my sickness, would you?" he demanded.

I said nothing.

He sat there frowning at me, sucking on a tooth, sniffing and clearing his throat. He dabbed at his handkerchief, spit into it. "I never know how to deal with you, Owen, for you do lie from time to time."

"The years I've—with you like a father to me—"

"God have mercy, listen to him," he said. "You've made mighty rapid advance in this army, Owen, to be so tender, and no need for me to ignore it—"

"Never over a friend—"

"—or to believe you're through advancing."

"Why would I want to be a general? My regiment is what I've cared about."

38

He considered that fretfully. He nodded finally and motioned to Penny to come closer. "Penny, I'm going to trust him," he said. He sat there waiting, but there was no comment from this young colonel at all; he was staring at us both, unhappily frowning at us. Manger waved his hand suddenly, dismissing him from his thoughts. "I trust you, Owen. I do, damn you," he said, "but I can't fully trust anybody in this army now, there being so many new ranks to fill and changes having to be made all the time, and I did hear reports of my retirement that your friends were starting, and they got to be so generally believed that Mrs. Davis mentioned my leaving as a matter of fact to my wife one afternoon."

"Never in this world," I said gently.

"No? Well, these rumors start among the men—I don't know just where. My God, I worry. I do. My health isn't impaired one bit—"

"Isn't it?" I said innocently.

Colonel Penny snorted and turned to the window, his back to us.

"Don't mind him, Owen. He's a young jackass."

"If there's anything I can do to squelch these rumors—" I said.

"Yes, yes," he said, his mind wandering. "I believe General Heth has called a meeting for four to announce certain changes," he said, "so we'd best settle for a few agreements now and worry about details later." Suddenly a spate of irritation seemed to sweep through him. "Owen, we do need to worry about how we are going to defeat the biggest army in history, don't you realize that? We have taken on more men, more money, more machines, more organization, more government than we can defeat, I'm afraid. We are a poor region by comparison with the North, about a fourth as rich, we have a tenth their industry, and we are sparsely populated by comparison. We are deep in the road ruts on this thing, and soon now we must go out to meet them for a third year. They are thirsty for us and we will bleed, my God, we will bleed, my boys will bleed again. Two bloody campaigns we have won, but the Yanks won't stop. They grow stronger after each defeat and we weaker after each victory. This spring we will have it to do again. We'll be bleeding on the fences again, we will bleed, damn them, for they will not let us be, and I worry, I do, I worry. It isn't my safety, not my own health, Owen, that rattles me. Do you believe it?"

"Oh, yes," I said.

"It's my boys. I have to help my boys. My death is nothing. It is soon upon me, for I'm seventy. It's true, Owen, I'm seventy. I could retire home and tend my place but my boys need me. My God, I think of it of a night. My wife says not to worry about it, for it's not my worry, she says. 'You only carry out somebody's commands, like everybody else,' she says. But I say to her, 'No, no, for they are my boys and their lives are in my hands and they must go out to fight come spring ...'" His voice trailed off into a little gasp and his mind seemed to hesitate on the threshold of a thought.

"Yes, sir," I said.

"But, Owen," he said slowly, "we have your papers drawn up to send you out west to the Mississippi, for you're more their type of blustery soldier, anyway, with your obstinacy and tricky tactics. I'm going to tear up the papers," he said, picking up two papers from the bed and scanning them, "provided we can agree on a few general matters."

"What are they?" I said guardedly.

"We need soldiers, or Heth is going to spew us all out. He's got too small a division to suit him. When all the generals sit down with Jackson, he's the smallest division in manpower. Now then, I want you to get three hundred more men out of that mountain region of yours."

"I won't conscript any men at all," I said.

"I don't care how you get them. Bribe them with promises of visits to the whorehouses of Washington, I couldn't care

40

how you get them. Talk them into it."

"There are not three hundred men who will agree."

"Send that swishy captain of yours up there to scout the ground out for you."

"Swishy captain?"

"Crawford. Send him."

"Why, he can't get ten, and I can't get more than thirty to volunteer."

"Three hundred men, damn you."

"I don't think we need more than fifty, General—"

"Three hundred men."

"Seventy would be too many. The people are scattered up there, live off to themselves in coves and hollows, each with his own homeplace. I don't—I don't see how I could force any of them to come to this war, or even convince myself a government has the right to force a citizen to fight."

"Owen, the question with Heth is your loyalty, ain't it, and for you to insist on seventy soldiers when you need and can legally get three hundred—well, I don't see that you prove your loyalty a damn bit. Do you?"

"Will eighty prove it?" I said.

"No," he said bluntly. "You are infuriating to a fault."

"Then I can't do it," I said, "so we come to the wall, that's all."

He sat there staring at me like a baffled bulldog. "All right with Heth—two hundred men?" he asked Penny.

"Not enough," Penny said.

"Tell General Heth 200 is all Owen can train," Manger said.

"Sir?" Penny said indignantly.

"You get 200, Owen, or you'll have your ass fighting in Mississippi come spring."

"I can't do it," I said.

"You want me to tear these orders up or give them to you?" he said bluntly, and he held them out to me. "You want them? You can go west now if you want to. I don't give a damn, but I want two hundred men if you stay, even if you have to con-

41

script them out of bed, and I want you to go home and tend to this yourself."

I hesitated, which he noted, I'm sure. I didn't know what to say to him, for I couldn't afford to abandon my regiment to Captain Crawford; also, I remembered Woofer, and that woman of his. I permitted myself in a single flash of a thought to wonder about helping them somehow, once I got home.

"I see you'll do it," Manger said, waving me aside. "Penny, you tell Heth we're keeping Owen with us."

"I don't know, I don't know," Penny said angrily, as he went through the doorway, slamming the door after him.

"He's swishy-assed and raw as hell, ain't he?" Manger said. "Owen, tell those mountain men we give every soldier beef for supper and a feather pillow to lie on. Yeh. Come spring they'll sleep maybe in the North. What say to that? Tell them this is their big chance to travel," he said, and a dry laugh came out of him and shook him, and abruptly he began to cough and a spasm gripped him cruelly and he doubled over, his handkerchief to his mouth, his body wracked with gasps for a long while, and when he drew the handkerchief away I thought I saw blood on it, but he was so careful to guard his movements that I could not be sure.

That day the men heard I would be going home, so I was pressed tight by requests for assignments to accompany me. I have never been more popular nor felt more miserable. The men also got word that I was going to conscript men, and a delegation came to petition me not to do anything like that, the men saying they would not fight with conscripted men, even if they were trained and able.

I was still being harassed by petitions that night when I retreated to my bedroom and tried to write out a letter to my state government, asking them to conscript 200 men for me. In the letter I expressed my dismay at having to make such a request; I suppose I hoped the Governor would turn me down. Crawford kept coming and going, asking what I was doing. I wouldn't tell him. He sat down on the bed finally and fretted as he watched me. I went on writing. He offered me a bit of brandy he had confiscated, and I drank that with him trying to conceal my anger, my fury at him.

"Sometimes, Colonel, I feel a strangeness, a coldness come over you, and it worries me," he said.

"We've been together a long time, Captain," I said, writing. "We know each other very well."

"We don't. We don't really know each other."

"No," I said, "I suppose not."

"Even as a boy I would have given you anything I owned to have you as my friend, you and the others."

"Uh-huh. Well, I didn't know that, Skip."

"My pony, my saddle, my slave—whatever I owned."

"You were such an exclusive fellow. Do you know this new colonel, this Penny?"

He closed his eyes tightly. "I don't know him."

"He mentioned knowing you," I said, watching him.

"I don't know him intimately."

"I wondered," I said, and went back to writing.

"I knew him in Raleigh when I worked there."

"I'll want you to visit home with me, Skip," I said, writing. Soon I heard him get up from the bed, sighing, moaning to himself, and go out, mentioning that he would see me again tomorrow.

About nine o'clock Woofer opened the door. "I got tired waiting," he said, and when I asked him why he was waiting, he said he wanted to thank me for deciding to go home to help him with his girl.

"Oh my. Well, I'm not going home to talk to her, Woofer," I said.

"Owen, you will take me with you?"

"No, I wouldn't want you around," I said.

"Owen, be serious. You will take me, won't you?"

43

"If you'll help me with papa. I'm afraid of him, Woofer."

"I will," he said.

"If my men find out, they'll kill me, for you're not even due a furlough. My Lord, boy, you get me in trouble on every hand." He was so pleased, though, that I couldn't help but be pleased for him, so we had a drink together and celebrated his good fortune. I kept telling him how much I worried about seeing papa again, and Jesse and the others, and I told him I was suspicious of Skip Crawford. "He always has been hanging around me, and I should have been more careful. He's jealous of me, Woofer—those Crawfords are all jealous of us Wrights, you know it?"

"I never have thought so," he said. "But I only know one of them, old man Eli's wife."

"How come you know that old woman?"

"I don't know any old woman. She's about twenty."

"Why, he must be eighty years of age."

"Yes, but you see, she got into trouble with a man down near Raleigh where her parents live, and they married her to her cousin Eli to give the baby a name. But you know, once they married they came to love each other, Owen. They held hands in church."

"That's proof of it, is it?" I said.

"Usually the women sit on one side in church and the men on the other, as you know. She sat with him, even with her belly poked out with her baby. He would lay his hand on her belly, as if to feel the baby kicking inside, and she would lay her hand on his hand, ever so tenderly."

"Woofer, you're drunk as a lord."

"I am. I know. I can't drink as much as you can."

"What did they name the baby?"

"Named it after him, Eli, and he was so happy he fell down his own porch steps. Papa told it on him. Then he went off to help save Tennessee from the Yanks over on the western front."

"Yes, where Manger was trying to send me today. Woofer,

44

I'm going to send Crawford home for 200 men, and I'm going to be helpful and kind to him, but when we get back into the war, I'm going to have to even my score with him in order to protect my regiment." I ordered some eggs from Sergeant Silver. I like a few eggs of a night, especially when I'm plotting and thinking. He brought us hot biscuits and molasses too, but Woofer wouldn't eat anything. "You're not hungry?" I asked him.

"Owen, my stomach has shrunk from not eating in camp."

"What do you do with your rations?"

"Men come around, say they're sick."

"Maybe they are, but you have to think of yourself in the army. Most of all in the army, where there are people after your food, after your rank, after your women, after your life before it's over, shooting at you with cannon and God knows what all. I learned, so can you."

"If they try to kill me, Owen, what do I do?"

I looked up at him surprised. "Don't worry about what they do, you worry about your aim."

"I don't know, Owen." He smiled wistfully with that twisty smile of papa's.

"If they are going to kill you, you don't know?" I said.

"I—don't know yet, Owen."

"My Lord have mercy, boy. I ought to take you home and leave you."

"If they were trying to kill you—" he said.

"I believe I will leave you."

"I could kill them then."

"What?"

"If they were trying to kill you, I could kill them."

It struck me odd, that silly comment. I knew he meant it too—there while I was trying to educate him to be selfish. "I'm full, Woofer," I said abruptly, to hide my embarrassment, "and ready for bed. It has been a bad day for me, you know it? I got caught by surprise. Didn't have my skirmishers out

45

far enough to give me warning."

"You look tired," he said. "Your face is drawn. Your eyes are so dark they look like caves, with maybe a squirrel peering out of each."

"Those two men put me on the rack, boy. They tied me hand and foot, Lord knows, and Crawford helped them. He's a traitor to me, and I will need to even the score, Woofer."

When he got up to go—I always had to prompt him a number of times to go—he stopped near the door. Just before opening it he said to me, "Owen, I hope you won't hurt Captain Crawford too much."

I thought about that. "What is it with you and Crawford?" I asked him.

"N-n-nothing, Owen."

"Give me some help with it," I said.

He considered the problem for a while. "Well, it's Eli Crawford's woman that I w-w-want to marry."

"Where is Eli?"

"He was shot at Shiloh."

"She's a widow? You've got involved with Eli Crawford's widow?"

"I—did, Owen, and it's about to k-k-kill me."

"You— What relation is she to Captain Crawford?"

"His aunt, I think."

"You knocked up Captain Crawford's aunt?"

"Yes."

"Ohhhhh, Loooooooord, Woofer."

"Papa's going to die, and Captain Crawford will die."

"Well, Woofer . . . well, Woofer," I said. I blurted out a laugh which quite well startled him. "Oh myyyyy Lord, Woofer, you've—you've got her pregnant, boy. Good for you. Oh myyyyy Lord, Woofer, you've crossed over to the far side of the river."

I hugged him. I never had been so surprised and pleased about anything. I pounded him on the back, congratulating him.

46

"Will you, Owen, will you, Owen?" he kept saying to me, and I was saying, "Yes, hell, yes," to whatever it was he wanted me to do—to arrange his marriage, I suppose, since I was a bloody colonel. "Yes," I said, laughing, for it was funny to me, my family marrying into that family, especially in the middle of this war, my kid brother becoming a slaveowner, this kid becoming Crawford's brother or his uncle or something. This kid would be Captain Crawford's uncle!

"Oh my!" I shouted, choking. "Yes, hell, yes, I'll talk to them," I was telling him, "I'll make her marry you," and he was consumed with joy, for he seemed to think whatever I attempted would be the law of the land.

"I love her, Owen," he told me.

Which struck me as the funniest thought of all.

CHAPTER THREE

Isn't it remarkable that a government will assume the power to conscript a man to fight for it? I never think of the government fighting for itself; I never think of President Davis fighting, and Lord knows the legislature of these Confederate States of America leaves Richmond whenever the Yanks begin moving that way. Last spring the government officials even took their families, their furniture, they moved the files of government, the money, the gold, when the Yanks were approaching. That same covey of officials had made it legal for the government to draft men to protect them and the common cause. Never before in the history of this continent had there been such a thing as conscription.

Yet in December, in my log room, with Captain Crawford standing nearby watching, tight-lipped, attentive, I signed a letter officially requesting of my state's conscriptors the sum of 200 human beings, and I offered the services of Captain Crawford and myself to help bring them into the fold. Then without a word I went out into the road and walked, walked, walked up and down, talking to the soldiers about incidental matters, trying to find little ways to make their lives happier, easier, as if in such courtesies I could salve my guilty soul.

I began to read their mail, too, secretively, of course, for I had no authority to violate the personal lives of my men this way, as Captain Crawford reminded me, giving me the number of the official order. Stiff of manner Crawford was now, and frightened. Penny must have told him I suspected the truth. I never mentioned the matter to him myself. I would not mention it and let him ever after be able to claim I was seeking revenge. Within his own little world he could scheme against me, and within that world he could fear what I might do, and when. Just now he could ask himself why it was I was sending him ahead to the home region.

Honey,
If men com to conscript Rog or Harris, writ me and I wil com home to hep. I fer the South has lost its hed honey and is despert, for we are a much smaler army than the North has. The North has Germans, other foreners, bring them in by ships, give them guns, send them agin us. Irish to. Niggers to, I spect. I wish they wuld com therselfs one time.

My dear wife,
I wil be shoting Southerners next, if ary one com nigh you and Ben. Tel yor brother to hid himself so he can continu to work my farm. If he dont work it, who in hel wil. How ar yu Annie. Let Willis or Lary carry a gun for that is the best pasport anywhere I ever did see.

My son Steven,
I fear for the South, our dear new land, it is desperate, they turn on their own people. But if a bear is wounded, won't it slash out at one and all? All I ever saw did so. I try to excuse our dear country. But I cannot understand why they want to send untrained men here to starve with us? If there is more food, feed us for we are hungry. If there are more uniforms, give them to us for we are cold.

Dear Charlie,
If I ever get home, there'll be heads knocked over this thing. I com to fight a short time for my country and have been here 18 months and have missed most of two years work and have not got much pay and I have had running bowels most of the time. My God have mercy, what do they have in mind, them that stays in Richmond? If a cunnel or general ever runs for any office, I'll vote agin him as many

times as I can buy votes. Nobody here cares about us a damn bit. Our own cunnel has sold his sol ...

And directly, coming to these men from home were reports of strangers moving along the roads, asking: How many sons in your family? How old is your father? Where is your father? What does he think about the Union?

... And un man com to me and sad hows yr helth budy and I sad except for being cripled in both knes its fin and he sad whats the mater with yr knes and I sad they giv way under me when I her gunshots ...

Dear Marshall,
I have only a tiny bit of ink left here at the house and no way to get more, it's so dear. Now your brother Charlie wants to go off to war. And the conscriptors come yesterday and talked for an hour with Sims and him with a wife and youngin, so he might have to go. I would have nobody left to home but your mama and a pack of hounds. Lord God, what have we got into? I hope the South wins it, for I love the South, I do. But I can't do all that's here to do by myself. Tell the army it ought to have its fill by now. Never has anybody ever been conscripted, never before, Harmon says. Why now? Your mama and Sims say hello. Charlie is out hunting foxes or rabbits, either one that flushes first.

Dear Husband,
The night is col
The day is hot
Our partin hours
Is not for got.
In pleasant dreams or Sorrows' hours
In crowded hills or lonely bowers
The pleasure of my mind shall be
Forever to remember thee.

As I got ready to break away from camp for two, maybe three, weeks I realized that I had created a number of special arrangements which could not be put off on Lieutenant McGregor

50

without explaining. I was keeping eight alcoholics in liquor, for example, this being the easiest way to keep them in condition. I also had arrangements with eleven men who had their wives in Virginia, living in farmhouses near the camp or in Richmond; they could spend the night with their wives two nights a week.

Lieutenant McGregor, a planter's son, an educated, refined man, was astonished by my conspiracy with common soldiers.

"And about once a month, Lieutenant," I explained to him, "some father or other will come in here to say his daughter has been wronged and he is looking for the culprit. I have found it best to discourage all such fathers, lest one gets involved in legal complications. I tell the father to marry her off to a relative and leave me be. If he won't, I offer him Fetcher or Private Balcum. Either of them will marry most anybody."

"Colonel, are you serious?" McGregor said, his handsome, clean face contorting suddenly.

"Now rape is more serious. Again, try to discourage official complaints. If you have to go through with an investigation, it means all sorts of entanglements, beginning on a Sunday morning when the offended girl walks with you when you make your rounds of the regiment. You've seen this done. Every poor man in my regiment has to have his few moments to quake before her. I suggest you say to the girl before starting out, 'You will see hundreds of men and you might become confused, so don't try to decide the first time round.' I try to give the men a break that way. Even worse are the children. You recall the morning there came that fat girl in the yellow dress. I made a speech of discouragement, told her that she shouldn't identify anybody unless she was absolutely certain. I think she wasn't listening to me. She was anxious to be out there looking, and as we made the rounds, her father kept saying, 'Don't you see him yet?' and I kept saying, 'See how the flag flies from that pole over there,' I introducing most any distractions I could think of, but she had only one thought in her head. Oh, she was a strange little girl.

51

She stared at every face. All my men got put on trial. So I kept telling her, 'We have one more street yet to go on,' and when we reached the end of the first one, I asked, 'Nothing yet, nothing yet, Elizabeth?' And she said, 'No, not yet.' Three times I asked her. 'Not yet,' she said, 'but I will see the next street now.' The Adjutant had heard her clearly and her father had too. 'That's all the men there are,' I told her, and she looked up at me stunned. 'You promised me,' she screamed. She kicked me in the shins and began beating on me; she was beside herself, and she began to shout at me, 'Him, him, him,' and point at me, 'him, him, him!'"

Poor Lieutenant McGregor was white as a ghost. I suppose he had thought being acting regimental commander would be a lark, that he would sit by my fire and scatter his power about beneficently, along with his handsome smiles. "My God, Colonel," he said. "Anything else?"

"Yes. I wouldn't punish the homosexuals publicly. It gives the regiment a bad name. One of the best punishments for them is to make them strike ten or twelve lashes each on the other's back. Not the other's butt. The back, Lieutenant, so as not to excite them. No branding of anybody. No notching of ears. No marking of face or hands. I would ignore thefts unless a serious one occurs. In that case I would call in Sawyer, Ball, or Wimple and accuse him of it. He will find out who did the theft, likely as not, and report the culprit to you."

"And if he does not?"

"Then punish him for the crime, as you said you would. All three of these men are thieves, anyway."

"But—why not discharge them, Colonel?"

"I need them to catch thieves for me," I said. "Don't you understand?"

Woofer was ready to go home too. He had packed his one extra set of "smalls," as our mother called underwear. He pestered me daily, it was pathetic how anxious he was to be underway, to see his little widow. He showed me letters in her pretty handwriting, on blue paper, perfumed with a sweet piny scent. I was even required to read one of them.

>Dearest Woofer,
>I miss you. I miss you. Where are you dear? I wonder. I look for you on the road across the bridge, expectin to see a tall, handsom young man with his head high, smiling, coming to see me. I want to meet you again and in my arms hold you and have you tell me life is laughin and music. I have never known anybody who was hapier than you. Where are you dear? What will you tell my people? Do you know yet. I got your letter of last Christmas day but it said much about the camp singin and nothing about when you might talk with my father or uncle or your father. Will your brother hep you? Oh I hope so, Woofer. A cunnel would only have to whisper in my fathers ear for him to say yes, for he thinks God started this war hisself. Oh, if he would.
>I sit by the river, our river as I write this, in the stand of birchs, our private woods, in our silver kingdum by the see, my hand, our hand, tremblin for wanting to touch you, my body, our body fretful within itself. Oh Woofer come to me soon as you can . . .

My own hand trembled when I handed the letter back to him. "Women go on and on like that, don't they?" I said, trying to hide my embarrassment. "Women are more romantic than men," I told him gruffly. "Listen here, don't show your love letters around like that, Woofer, you hear?"

On Friday night—we were to leave at 4 A.M. for home—I began to drink. I had a delicious apple brandy I had confiscated from Company D, from hut Jezebel. I drank more than I meant to, wondering what my parents would say to me and what my older brother Jesse would say and whether they would kill the fatted calf or not. Woofer got me on the train to Richmond, which we reached at 10 A.M.

He said I must buy gifts for the family. It was his idea, and he picked them out for me, a lace blouse for my mother and a pretty blue hat with a veil for Nell. For each man, papa, Jesse and Phillip, he selected a leather belt beautifully tooled with birds on one, animals on another, and snakes on a third. I would as soon not get papa and Jesse anything, I told him. "God knows what they're going to think of me." But he assured me everything would work out well, so I bought the gifts, and then he and I strolled down Broad Street, which was lined on both sides with two- and three-story buildings, stores on the street level and apartments upstairs. Several of the older Richmond stores had gone out of business because of the scarcity of commodities to sell, and their quarters were now occupied by a busier, more hustling management, many of them newly arrived Jews who stocked all sorts of expensive goods. I don't know how they got them unless it was overland from the North or from Europe on blockade runners. They had linen, furs, silver and gold jewelry, diamonds, pearls, rubies, perfumes—goods which would not lose value should our money suffer further inflation, all sold in a single shop, called stores in Richmond. Woofer, who had never seen a Jew, and who had been reared and educated on the Old Testament as well as the New, was captivated just watching them walk about talking with one another.

Nearer the center of the city the jeweler's window under the street clock was another marvel to Woofer. He had never seen such a large pane of glass before, and, of course, displayed behind it was a ransom in wealth—half a million dollars would not buy that window's merchandise. Yet there were men in Richmond who could easily buy it with money earned recently from speculations made possible by the army and the war, trading coffee, salt, sugar, medicines . . . Negro men, some free and others slave, were everywhere, driving carriages, holding doors open, sweeping sidewalks, stepping out of the way to allow white men to pass freely, bowing to us from the waist, averting their eyes whenever a white woman appeared. Most all the civilian white men knew each other, and all the officers of the War Department knew each other, so there were many polite exchanges of greetings along the way—not with Woofer and me, of course, for we were strangers, and a sorry-looking pair of strangers we were, too: a colonel dressed in a battle-worn uniform, with a gangling private dressed in the dirtiest, most tattered of clothes, the private gawking at everyone and everything he saw, constantly on the lookout for Jews.

"See here, Woofer," I told him, "look down Broad Street as far as you can." It was a long street, reaching to the horizon line. "I've seen it full of Yank prisoners, shoulder to shoulder, being marched to Libby Prison and Belle Isle." I told him all about that certain night when Lieutenant Hal King and I, both wounded, had walked into town, all the ambulances being filled, and arrived to find the sixty hospitals filled. We were herded into a store building. I recalled lying on a counter, nobody to tend to me.

Down one street Woofer and I could see two auctioneers' flags, which meant slave auctions were taking place. Even from a distance I could identify many groups of soldiers. The Georgia soldiers wore brown uniforms with full-skirted pants and green trim. The Alabama uniform was blue. Many of the soldiers from Tennessee wore coonskin caps. Texans, including the Texas Rangers, wore cowboy hats. Arkansas men did too. The Washington Artillery, which was from New Orleans, wore white gloves. We saw a cluster of New Orleans Zouaves, dressed in baggy scarlet trousers, white gaiters, low-cut blue shirts, their jackets heavily embroidered and braided, each man armed with a bowie knife held in a blue sash. The Floridians, the Mississippians, and most of the rest of us wore gray. And at the Richmond South Station we saw hundreds of deplorable-looking conscriptees, some of them young, most of them old and sickly, forced into service by the militia or lured into service by the $300 payment offered for substitutes, paid by the rich so that they could avoid conscription entirely. All of them were sad and cold and discontented.

Our train car, which was the officers' car, had a hole in the side of it big enough for a piano to go through. The cold wind came in there, as did the engine smoke whenever we rounded a curve. There was a coal stove huffing away at the center of the car, and an old coffee pot was perched on top of it, but there was no water on hand and I had no coffee with me. Only two other officers were aboard, and they huddled near the front of the car, wrapped in blankets. The odor of anthracite coal was strong in the car.

Woofer and I took a seat together, I with my legs stretched out into the aisle. I like to ride the train. I always have. It massages my body and mind, it sets me to rest as it rocks and rants its way along, even then, after the army had all but worn out the railways. Iron was one of the many commodities the South was short of, and since the North had managed to blockade most every harbor, we couldn't replace worn-thin track. Our wheels rolled on faith and hope. Our bridges were about to fall too, and our boxcars and passenger cars were weirdly battered. To me they rasped as I rode along, "We'll make it through spring, *maybe*, we'll make it through spring, *maybe*, we'll make it through spring, *maybe* . . ."

"That mist is pretty, Owen, you know it?" Woofer said. "You take a mind as big as God has and figure out how he ever came to think up mist. Not a man I know could think up mist, given half a dozen chances at it, nor trees either. I'd never think to put a leafy ball like that on one leg, would you? Look at that woman like mama out hobbling her cow."

"Mama still wear those same long frocks?" I asked.

"I never have seen mama's ankles but once, and that was by accident. You see the way the paths have got worn into that hill by the cows crossing at that place. Looks like the lines in the palm of papa's hand."

We saw a hilltop where a farmer was working, foddering cornstalks, and he raised his long knife, saluting us. We crossed a river, clear water with no mud in it, in spite of the recent rains. "In rolling woods like these, come spring, Woofer, the battles

will take place," I said. "The birds will fly off, the r
hop in confusion, dogs will howl and roosters will cro
will warn everybody to beware, and then will come th
sound of all, the Ahhheeeee of the Rebels or the Ha
Haw of the Yank army, the battle cries."

Woofer stared out at the woods and fields disconso

"Out there I can take most any part of that land an
battle for it. Those woods near that hickory, I can d
regiment along that stretch of woods, hide men there. I c
a pastoral place and make history on it, make any field r
bered, any woods. That big rocky vale, you see it?"

"It's pretty in this misty sunlight. I wonder abou
more'n—"

"Night battle or day battle, you can infiltrate under
The stone wall over there would be cover for a company o
men, or even a three-company section. They would be a
as in their mothers' arms. The hedgerow over there would
good cover too, though not as safe, and up that draw—ass
the enemy is on the hilltop, has artillery by those oaks—up
draw men could advance without exposing themselves to a
lery at all—"

He listened politely, but I got the impression that I was ast
ishing him. I seemed always to be taking Woofer unawares

"What do you plan to do, come next fall?" Woofer asked
suddenly.

"Woofer, I haven't had time to figure out any life plans,"
said. "I've been risking my life every month or two, with n
many prospects even to survive."

He frowned at me quite critically, his face poked up close t
mine. "Now's the time to plan, Owen. Papa said the planters
were once the most powerful group in the South, even though
they have never been more than a fourth or a fifth of the white
population. Papa says as a rule the oldest son takes over the
plantation, and the others are turned into a lawyer, a doctor, a
teacher, a preacher, and finally an officer in the army. So these

57

younger sons have got the power for themselves, they have by now taken over the railroads, the governments, they put editors in prison if it suits them, and they've passed a law saying they can conscript men and make them fight for them, whether the men wanted to fight or not. Not even priests, back when they were the most powerful profession, had so much power, papa says."

I was idly listening, mildly interested in spite of myself.

"... Papa says when the war ends the officers will be as powerless as a once-was king. They won't have special cars on the trains to ride in, or special rooms at hotels, won't have special women, and unless the colonels think to find themselves a place to go to once the war ends, before next summer—"

"Oh, shut up, Woofer."

"I know two or three widows about your age, Owen, whose husbands have got killed in the war, and when we get home I'll take you to see them."

Once out of Richmond we rode by a few great estates, but quite soon we came to poor plantations and poorer slaves. In Richmond slaves are clean and often are educated, but here, on these typical plantations, the slaves lived in hovels, their clothes were changed only twice each year, most of them had no bed, no chair, no table, no fork, no knife. I have worked in this region, and even though I have never worked with the slaves, I know how they have to live. As our train rolled south we saw many groups of them working in the fields, men and women and children, Negro drivers moving among them.

The farms looked much better than the plantations, incidentally. That was one of the most interesting facts of life in the South just now, at least in this part of the South—the plantations were not prosperous. Up until sixty years ago, the planters were well-to-do, but as each generation divided the plantation among the heirs, the holdings became too small for slavery to be productive. As long as forty years ago the slaves were being herded south to the new slave states, Alabama, for instance, and to the

delta along the Mississippi River, where cotton could be harvested from the flat, rich land, and there the slaves were worked in massive gangs. Some of those plantations worked a man for only seven or ten years and then were done with him. I have been there, I have visited that section, and I liked the white farmers very well, but the planters had brutalized themselves; their profits were immense and the whip was their law.

One often hears, especially of late, of "Southern culture," and I admit there is a world of achievement in Richmond, in Charleston, in New Orleans, and maybe in a few other places, but on the whole, and particularly in the new cotton states, such as Alabama and Mississippi, the richer, more lordly whites are a lazy, greedy lot, without many traits of a civilizing influence that I can detect. And even here in Virginia, the best educated of the planters often spend their time away from the South; some of them live in the North, or even in Europe. The planter's family fortune might have come in part from the plantation, and maybe some of his income still comes from it, but all that the owners want now is a foreman's report on the annual profits. If it is a Virginia or Carolina plantation, the profits will be small, or there will be a loss, and I noticed now, even as we rode along, that ever so many of the plantation houses—two- and three- and four-room plank buildings, not the columned, spacious places in Northern press reports—that their porches were sagging, the paint was flaking off the boards. "You see out there, Woofer? They tell me in Pennsylvania, where we might invade come spring, there are no slaves at all, yet the farms are prettier than in any section of Virginia or North Carolina. They say the same for Ohio. They grow more crops too."

"You sound like papa," Woofer said.

"Look at that little baby nigger. Look a there, eight, nine little niggers in the coal dirt without shoes or a coat among them, next to this train track."

"Who takes care of them, Owen?"

"Why, they have to look after themselves until they are put in the fields."

When we reached North Carolina, the state by contrast to Virginia seemed to be even more unkempt. The little towns were straggly, board buildings staggered along muddy main streets, where chickens pecked for seeds in the horse dung and at the fence crannies. There were a few wagons and carts on the move, and now and then I saw a family walking, their goods tied to their backs, but the little show of traffic was wintry and impoverished. The train station in Raleigh had only a few piles of goods, marked "War Department." Not many people were about, and the station door had come off one of its two hinges. The stationmaster, a wheezy, distressed man, told me he was "tuppense tired of not being able to get help for love nor money."

Just after sundown we started moving west, rolling by fits and starts. We got to Burlington and lay there by the platform for a while, then moved on, and I began thinking about Jesse and how jealous I had been of him as a young man. I thought about my mother; I never knew her to be unworking. I never knew her —like I suspect some other women to be—simply to sit in a chair waiting. Waiting for maybe a child to come to her and put his head on her lap. I tell you, if you put your head on mama's lap it would land in a pot of beans she was breaking, or a basket of clothes she was darning, or a suit she was sewing, and since she was always busy, she never was embarrassed by some child wanting her, saying, "Yes, I need you" to her. My father was impersonal too. He was a man of books, as well as a farmer, vintner, carpenter, mason, banker. On Sunday he would plan a week's work for the family, and he would also bring his journal up to date, recording what had been done the past week as well as what births and deaths and sicknesses had been reported from close by. He had a record of the community, of farmers and planters both, and on Sundays he might divulge information from it if asked to. I recall listening from a rocker on the porch when a boy of fourteen named Henry Sims came by. Papa let him into his study and this boy Henry said, "Mr. Wright, I been wondering when my birthday is and how old I am."

After a while I heard papa say, "You sure you were born, Sims?"

"Why, yes," Sims said in a determined voice.

"How do you know?"

"I'm here, so I must have arrived."

"You aren't the boy that was born with his head one day and his ass end another, are you?"

"Sir?"

"And they had to sew them together?"

"No, sir."

"Come over here to the window and let me see."

The window opened onto the porch. I could see Sims was quaking with fear. Papa examined his neck, tut-tut-tutting with his tongue, frowning as if worried about what he saw, then a big smile came over his face. "You were born all of a piece, Sims. You wait and I'll look up the date."

Papa could do like that. He did have a sense of humor, of a wry sort. He was a man of hardness as a rule though. My horse got sick, stuck a nail in her foot, and papa didn't say anything to me about it. I was fourteen, fifteen. After a while I saw that she was sick and I found the nail and pulled it out, but the horse stayed sick. Papa said nothing to me about it, even then. The horse got in pain, and I would stand out there in the yard near the stable and hear her breathe, a deep, husky, irregular, threatening sound in her chest. I loved that horse very much and that sound grated on me awfully, and finally papa came to where I was waiting, this was after supper one night, and I said, "Papa, she's sick," and he said, "Yes, she is," and I said, "What are you going to do?" and he said, "She's yours, Owen, not mine." And I cried out to him, "What am I going to do?" We were in the barnyard in the moonlight, and I was straining to see his expression.

"Shoot her," he said. It was so God damn easy and simple the way he said it. Oh, Jesus, it was cruel.

"No medicine that—will cure her?" I asked.

"No," he said.

He started on off toward the lambing pens, and I said, "You shoot her for me, papa."

"You can use my gun, if you want to," he said, and he was gone. I heard from Nell that he didn't go far, that he watched me from back of the stable, but I don't know if she made that up or not. She was always trying to make him seem to be more human.

Phillip came outdoors, and I told him I couldn't shoot my horse, and he said, "I wouldn't shoot her then, if I was you."

"Will you do it?" I said.

"No," he said. "Papa wouldn't like that; he's been waiting for you to do it yourself."

"Well, I love that horse," I said, "and won't shoot her."

"She had probably rather be left painin' than be shot, anyway," he said, and went away.

I waited there an hour, her breathing pressing through my nerves every few seconds, before I went into the house and got the gun. I took the lantern from the porch and turned it up bright. I hung the lantern on a nail near the stall, so I could see my horse, and I got to crying and trying to hug her neck. I talked to her, said I hoped she was feeling better, said I could remember when we had ridden to Hobbs and back in two hours once and how I wished we could ride up on the mountain and see if there were antelope tracks in the snow and that I would always remember how she took to jumping and that I had hoped we could go riding together down to Morganton someday. Oh, my God, I cried. I got to crying so bad I couldn't aim the gun, but I pressed myself into one corner of the stall and pointed it at her head.

It was a big noise, louder than I had expected, an explosion, the shot itself and the indoor reverberations of it, and my horse lunged and tried to stand up, but she crumpled against the stall, fell, and tried to run, her legs began to move as in running, the hoofs were striking the wooden wall of the stall, so that there was the sound of a horse running on a wooden road. The lantern was swinging, trembling, its light shuddering, the noise a thundering sound of hoofs on the wall, and shadows were moving in great sheets and blobs of blackness.

Until it was quiet. Not a sound. Not a breath. In the place where the breathing had been so loud, not a breath. I touched her and broke in two in my heart, tears gushed from me, and I ran out of there. I went out fast, but at the big door somebody strong caught my arm, stopped me, held me firm, and I looked up to see papa's face, stern as it could be, and he said, "Don't forget to put your tools away."

We were somewhere west of Burlington. "How is Phillip?" I asked. "Is he any smarter than he was?"

"He's not one for thinking fast, but he's big, Owen. He and Jesse are both strong as oxen."

"How is Nell? Is she a loving woman or not?"

"Why, you know she is, her being your sister."

"Men court her much?"

"She's plain, Owen, with those old dresses and aprons she wears all the time."

"She dresses up to go to church, surely."

"Yes, but if somebody asks to walk her home, where's there to walk to, for she lives across the road, and mama watches her even that little distance. Once Joshua King was courting her in the kitchen, and I caught mama upstairs lying flat on the floor watching them through a hole she had made in the floor. And, of course, papa says no man is born good enough for Nell."

"I remember her fondly," I said, "a little girl about eighteen when I left. About Morla's age. Morla was a loving woman, Woofer. It was life she coveted, and when she looked at me, it was not only her eyes which saw me, but her life which saw me, and saw not my face only, but my life inside me, which was the life she coveted to be inside her, to give birth to if I would let her have it, to hold."

Woofer was staring at me strangely, as if he had never seen me before.

"Men touch with their hands and see with their eyes, don't they, and they can only learn about life from a woman," I said. "Morla was a good teacher, and I believe Nell was about to become one, unless she got pushed into the shadows by mama. We need to get Nell married, Woofer. She'll drive herself crazy if she doesn't get somebody to love."

"She loves papa and mama," he said.

"Not the same, not the same," I said.

"If she leaves them, Owen, the house will be lonely entirely."

"Even so."

"But isn't it unkind to them?"

"Don't go blaming life on me," I said.

He thought about that and sighed finally. "Well, Owen, I hope you won't try to change everything all in a few weeks, when you get home."

We became more and more weary as we approached Salisbury. When I get tired I begin to fidget inside my nerves, inside the nerves in my thighs particularly, and I can't seem to sit still for wanting to break the stress of it, to get up and walk about. If I can do knee bends until my leg muscles tire completely, then they won't stress me for a while afterward, but I didn't feel like doing knee bends in this train car.

"Do you believe in God at all, Owen?" Woofer said to me abruptly, in that utterly serious manner he often had.

"Woofer, you seem to get religious when you get weary," I told him.

"Are you saved? Yes or no, Owen?"

"I was saved years ago," I said. "I was thirteen and that evangelist Bill Toll came through swinging his arms. He was mostly an outdoors evangelist, but we had completed our new church and he was to dedicate it. Old Bill got loud and tested the roof timbers, and we had dust and sawdust falling all over us on the benches, and one rock fell from the chimney top. We got saved, all of us children, that night. I never was so close to God as with that dust falling on me in an untried building."

"You—you won't be serious about anything, Owen, will you?"

"I'm serious. When that fellow got through describing Hell and said what we had to do to avoid it was to come forward and accept Jesus, I hit the trail, and so did most everybody else. He was a mighty man, Bill Toll was."

"Owen, right now I mean, are you ready to die?"

"I suppose so, are you?"

"I'm not afraid of death, for I trust in Jesus and know I'll go to Heaven. But you don't seem to believe that."

"Oh, yes," I said. "I know about the golden streets. And they sing songs all the time. And there's no war. But it's—it's not as interesting as Richmond, Woofer."

"Law a' mercy, Owen."

"That's more my type of place. I prefer cities that have run-down sections and rainwater and puddles and people staring at one another, and I don't much want to go to any place that doesn't have dogs."

Woofer began laughing. He bent double laughing, and he kept trying to tell me to hush, hush.

"Golden dogs, think of that, Woof," I said.

In Salisbury we went to an inn near the station house, a plank building put up only a few years ago but tottering already. The innkeeper heated up what food had been left over from supper. We had rancid mutton with turnips and dried-out corn bread. I asked him to scramble me two or three eggs, but he complained about being tired and having had a long day. He said he employed a free Negro man to cook in the kitchen but the Negro had gone home for the night and couldn't use the streets again until dawn, since he was black.

When we asked for water to wash in, the innkeeper directed

us to a washbasin on a stump out in the back yard. The only towel was a rag that had been in use for days, and neither Woofer nor I would touch it. "Some people are so shiftless they ought to be beat," I told him. "There's no need to run a shoddy inn, now that we have a railroad and travelers coming through all the time. A Yankee will come down here and open a decent place and get all the business, and this man will complain about Yankees till his dying day." Nothing made me more angry, for here we were fighting a war to make ourselves free of the North, and we had no quality in most of what we were doing for ourselves.

I asked the innkeeper to come see his towel. "And look at that bowl of soap," I told him. He got to sputtering and saying some men were too clean to breathe, but later he sent me a clean towel by a little black girl who was trembling like a leaf—and who looked like him in the face, incidentally.

What did he learn from me? I suppose nothing. I am not much of a teacher anyway. I'm too impatient.

The bedroom. You should have seen our bedroom. There were two nails in the wall to hang clothes on, no chest or cabinet or chair. The bed—I know in the army we do no better, but it's my dirt I sleep in when I'm in my bed in the army. "I'll figure it out someday," I told Woofer, as I lay there sniffing the wood-smoke. "Something's wrong in us, you know it? Too many of our people are too content with sorry living. Papa never was."

"No, sir," Woofer said.

"Can you imagine mama putting up with such food as that supper or such a bed as this?" There were cracks around the window big enough for the winter gale to come through. "I want to be proud of what we're trying to do, you know? I see shiftlessness and want to wipe it out, for it's a fierce thing we are doing, this war. It's terrible to consider the cost to us, and I get embarrassed about my country."

"We're n-n-not worth a damn, Owen," he said. "Papa always said the South was too content with its own shiftlessness."

"Papa says, papa says. Don't you ever have a thought of your own?"

"No," he said. He got to laughing about that.

"What's the matter with you?" I asked him.

"You're like Papa when you argue, you know it?" he said.

Next morning we rode a train through the little town of Morganton, and an hour later the train came to a stop at the railhead, and from the car we could look out the windows at the range of blue mountains. On top of these hills, on the plateaus, and in the valley surrounded by still higher mountains, was our own country.

I rented two riding horses from the stable, and we rode out toward the northwest, toward the mountains rising raggedy and rocky in winter dress, their hides gray and black, bleeding cold clear water as we mounted onto the flank of them, the water running glistening silver rushing gushing over cascades, enlivening every nerve of my body, the mere sight of it.

We climbed through mist for two hours, then were out of it, were above the sea of it. The sun was clear and dazzling. We reached the gap, flung ourselves down by a spring to drink. To the west and northwest rose the peaks of many blue mountains, and to the southwest was a range of black mountains, a wall against the sky, their peaks rising almost a mile above the valley floor. I lay on the ground and gazed about, caught up in the vastness, stunned dumb by it.

There was no sign of the war here. There was no sign of government either. Everything up here was wild. Nobody controlled it, for it was not conquered yet. The first settler had arrived about eighty-five years ago. The first two in the Harristown area were my grandfather and his first wife, Evey. She died in the cold winter dampness that first year. She is buried up back of papa's house. They were from North Ireland, but were Scots. He later married a planter's daughter, a widow, one of the Harrison family, but he wouldn't keep slaves himself. She

67

had had two sons already, and together they had two sons of their own, and a daughter, who died of smallpox. Their oldest full son was my father, and he inherited the farm, most of the land, and all the stock. His two half brothers, Vernon and Fate, took money for their part and migrated to Alabama. His younger brother, Weatherby, who was called Bee, took up preaching for a time, and he tried to farm some land downriver from the homeplace. He died at 48, hating my father and the hardness of his life, and on his deathbed told his family to migrate to the North. His widow, his oldest son Weatherby, and his other children moved to Ohio soon after that. At the age of thirty-seven my father married, picking a hard-working, younger woman. That was in the 1830's. But even then there were but eleven of the two thousand acres cleared, most of it worn thin from planting, and of a night bears might bash in a pen and go off with a calf. A bear one night when my mother was suckling Jesse climbed to the roof of the room upstairs, where she lay, and she looked up to see his paw tearing off the shakes.

A wild place. I had forgotten in the outlands, which had been settled for several generations, how wild it was up here. And lonely. Only once did Woofer and I encounter a family along the road. The man had a pack on his back; so did his wife. They had tied two bundles to their calf. An oxcart loaded with furniture rolled along noisily behind them. Each of their five children, dirty little ragamuffins, carried a chicken, and behind them three pigs followed along. The man smiled and waved grandly at me. People up here are friendly even on first meeting.

That afternoon, near the end of our journey, the mist cleared and we could see off into the outlands to the east. Flung as far as the horizon line were ridges and hills, and clay roads like red wounds in the bare forest of this time of year. The several small houses each owned a gray field and one or two smoke plumes. I felt relieved, free of the war up here, and I wanted to shout out, to tell those cranky officers in Richmond to come see this, look out there, now turn around and look through those naked limbs past those two hemlocks at the high peaks rising where nobody lives, where only the loneliest go, and tell me why in hell I who am from here should return to fight your public war way off or should take men off to fight for you. "It's a new country, Woofer, you know it? It's not ruined yet. It makes me want to shout."

"My lungs ache from breathing of it already," he said.

"It goes on and on forever." I did shout out, I became so taken with it, so overcome with the grandness, greatness, wildness, wonder of it.

At dusk we could see Harristown to the west below us, its farms and plantations marked by the rows of stone walls and wooden fences, fifty or sixty houses in sight. The houses were built along the flanks of the valley, with the fields rising above them on all sides, with the river making its way along the center through river bottoms which now were cold-brown, though checkered with tan and gray. We saw the church with its unfinished steeple—nobody up here had known how to finish the top tier, once its builder died. The mill was on the river, its wheel idle just now. The forge was nearby. I saw our house, a gray-weathered, two-story, spider-structure sprawled out amid a multitude of sheds and buildings, which appeared to be its flock of children.

I saw two men walking away from the forge, going home to supper, most likely having spent the latter part of the day talking about the weather, and any births or deaths hereabouts, and any illnesses, any hunting going on, any accidents. Woofer and I saw a carriage leave the Crawford house, where Captain Crawford was now, and move down their drive, which was flanked on both sides by apple trees, black-limbed and twisty. The carriage turned to the left onto the south river road, which was little more than a trail, and went along that road past the other Crawford plantation, where Woofer's widow lived, which was the next house downriver. Her place had narrow fields along the river but huge pastures on the mountain up back; its house was lantern-lighted in most all its upstairs windows. "She must be having a party there tonight," I said, "with all that light."

"She does that way normally," Woofer said. "She gets scared, Owen, her and her boy, with nobody about but the blacks."

In that instant I saw papa coming down through the yard from the stable. It was this time most nights he put the horses up, just this time of night, and went in to eat. There he came staunchly, bent slightly, not as spry as in the old days at all. "There my old man goes, Woofer," I said.

CHAPTER FOUR

We were near the kitchen porch in the yard when we met. He took my hand, which I offered him, and gripped it briefly. There was this nervousness in his face, a dread, there was an effort at a smile, tentative and embarrassed. My mother came running noisily toward me, and I hugged her, she laughing. Nell came running, and I swept her into my arms. I gave her and mama the presents I had for them. Then I gave papa his, and he held it awkwardly, I think resenting it somewhat, even as he appreciated it. Abruptly he nodded to me. "Thank you," he said. "I been needing one."

We went indoors, papa asking how our journey had gone, but mama and Nell were so noisy with excitement, talking about how Woofer and I looked, that we couldn't reply. He asked what the army was like, but mama began fondling Woofer, cuddling him affectionately, talking to Nell about how long his hair had got and how brown his face was for wintertime. Papa finally told her, "You don't have to impress your own children, do you?"

"Why, Nell, look how he's got even thinner," mama said, poking Woofer's ribs experimentally, hoping to find some show of fat on him. "He's too thin, Owen. Either take better care of him or send him home." She was quite serious about it.

Jesse was over at his woman's place, Woofer whispered to me. Phillip was in the stable tending to a sick horse just now, Nell said. So the five of us ate, roast chicken and baked sweet potatoes, pickled beans, hot bread, sourwood honey, and cider cold out of the cellar.

71

"I've not done the rough cider as well this year," papa said. "My heart got to fluttering like butterfly wings, so I had to let Phillip do the pressings. Not been making any cheeses either. Seems like if the world is going to lose its mind, I might as well stop trying to do anything."

"We're not going to discuss the war, are we?" mama said.

"You and I can make cheese tomorrow morning," I said to him.

He sat there staring at the tabletop. He looked up finally, let his nervous gaze sweep over me briefly. "Woofer, how long you home for?" he asked.

"Whatever Owen decides," he said, glancing at me to see if I had been hurt by papa's slight.

Mama asked me how my army was. She asked who did our laundry. She probed for any hunger or healing or mending needs, and Nell went to get a salve to doctor the small tree-branch cuts on our faces. It was an exciting time for them. But even they gradually settled back into the warm, firelighted atmosphere of the room. It was a log room, of course, and the spaces between the hewn logs had been filled with red clay; over those places paper had been pasted, sometimes pages from magazines, or wooden slats had been nailed, some one year and some another. A few of them had fallen off by now. There was a big fireplace, and it was burning hickory logs, the kind of wood mama preferred to cook with, for it gave a hot fire with clear, slight flames, and the smoke made meat taste better than any other she had found, even oak or apple. Near the fireplace were four copper pots. The table at which we sat and talked about our family type of needs—food, comfort, healing—was big enough to seat ten or even twelve people. The top of it was two planks from a chestnut tree, each of them two feet wide and two inches thick, oiled and time-darkened. The benches had been made by my grandfather. The corner cupboard had been made by my father when he was a boy, and often he had told us about cutting the wild cherry tree that had made the lumber for it and pulling the trunk by oxen from up near the gap. He sat now in a cane-bottomed chair at one end of the table, his somber gaze resting on me whenever I wasn't noticing, his mind no doubt piecing together his old memories of me, his worries about me. I suppose I was a world he had never quite mastered, had never understood as well as the world of the pastures and fields, stock and pens, cribs and crops, loaning and trading, which he knew about and which he had patiently broken down into rules and order and had written down facts about, by day and month and season, by measurements on scales, as well as in pint, quart, peck, bushel, barrel, wagonloads. "I see you never got her any white dishes, papa," I said, looking at the yellow and brown earthenware plates and cups that were stacked on shelves near the washroom.

"Why would we want them?" he said, watching me carefully.

"For company," I said.

"I like colors, myself," he said.

Mama said, "If we had four white servings, to use when company comes, to serve the visitors in."

"No, no," papa said. "The potter up here can't make white."

"What about the preacher, papa?" I said. "What about when he comes to eat with us?" I said, prompting him, reminding him of an old tale, one so familiar it might relax him into the body of the family.

"Oh, yes," he said, but fell silent, a spate of nervousness twitching his face so that he put his hand up to his eyelids and pressed on them. "That preacher always wiped his dish with his shirt afore he ate," he said. "And wiped out his cup with his necktie."

We all laughed about it, as we had in times past.

"You're getting younger every year, mama," I said. "You're younger than you were when I left a few years ago."

She smiled in spite of her embarrassment. "Listen to him, Nell."

"You look like a bride waiting for her groom," I said. "You're

73

a bloomin' thing, mama, don't you think so, papa?"

"Oh, yes," he said, glancing uneasily at mama, who was gripped by embarrassment.

"You always was the worst flatterer in the family, Owen," she said.

"Pretty as springtime. And Nell's blossoming. Some man's going to come through here directly and snatch her off to himself."

"Ohhhhh," Nell said, swallowing, staring in a fascinated bewilderment at me.

"What kind you want, Nell—tall or short, blond or black-headed?"

"I—Owen, don't—"

"She's got a man; tell him, Nell," mama said.

"Hush, mama. I don't want Owen to know yet," she said, looking at me, her eyes soft, her mouth open as she breathed. "When you getting married, Owen?"

"Most any day," I said. "Soon as I find a rich widow."

Woofer laughed and choked on a bite of food.

"I'm looking for a rich one who's not too old. Any rich widows around, papa?"

He stared at the ceiling, searching his mind. "Oh, there's Mattie Davis."

Mama let out a sharp laugh and covered her mouth with her hand.

"She's closer to your age than mine, papa," I said. "She must be sixty by now."

"She's got good land," papa said. "Well, she has," he said, for Woofer was laughing at him. "She has twenty acres of bottom land."

Woofer let out a roar. "Oh, my, she's got bottom land, Owen."

"Twenty acres of it," I said.

"Now you can both laugh," papa said, "but she's got a barn big enough for eight horses and two wagons, got a lambing pen her second husband made that took him the best part

74

of two winters, and he hired a hand to help him make it."

"Well, would she marry me, papa?" I said. "Now that I'm persuaded."

"Oh—" He thought about it, suddenly waved the matter aside. "You don't want to settle around here, do you, Owen?" he said.

There was a startled silence.

"I hope he will," mama said quietly.

"I hope he will," Nell said.

"I think he will," Woofer said.

Papa said nothing more, until finally he shifted his weight in his chair. "Then there's the Howard widow."

"She's not rich, papa," Nell said. "And her teeth are bad."

"She has a right smart of land. I'd guess at half a section."

"Why, it's straight up and down," Nell said.

"No, not all of it," he said.

"Is she pretty?" I said.

He sat there studying about it, a little perplexed grin on his face. Nell was snickering, and so was Woofer. "You could put a poke over her head," he said.

Woofer got to laughing and choking on his food. "That's funny," he said, "that's funny, papa."

"What you laughing at, Woofer?" I said. "I have a problem to solve, mister. Papa's helping me."

"He's helping you all right," Woofer said.

Nell was laughing. "The idea of you and those old women, Owen," she said.

"What about Eli Crawford's widow?" I said.

That sobered everybody up. Woofer's laughter stopped in a startled cough and gasp. Nell was astonished and confused. My parents were perturbed even to hear that name spoken in their house.

"I hear old Eli got killed in the war," I said. "I suppose she's rich."

75

Papa cleared his throat. "Be better to leave her alone," he said solemnly.

"Is she pretty?" I saw that I was making Woofer a most unhappy, nervous boy.

"I've never noticed how she looks," papa said.

"Why, she looks at every man she sees," mama said.

"She don't," Woofer said suddenly.

"Well, I say she does and always has. She's got a pretty body and she knows it and talks to everybody she sees as if she's known them for years."

"She's not like that, is she, Nell?" Woofer said defensively.

"She'll strike up a conversation with a stranger," mama said.

Woofer stared at her. "What if she does?"

Nell said, "What you so excited about it for, Woofer?"

He went back to eating. "Never mind."

"How much land she got, papa?" I said.

"Lord knows," he said grumpily. "I would leave her alone." He was distressed about the matter, I could tell.

"Living over there without a white man on the place, them slaves about," mama said. "So far two different men have—"

"The land is all right, is it, papa?" I said.

"Not as good as mine is. Not as wide along the river," he said.

By now Woofer was giving me heavy, threatening frowns.

"How much stock she got?" I said.

"She has good stock, I'll allow," papa said.

"Barn is all right, is it?" I said, grinning at poor Woofer.

"It's the best on that side of the river, though not as good as the one my father and me made out there in the yard," papa said.

"Stables—has a fair stable, as I recall," I said. "Grape arbor, I suppose? Apple orchard?"

"Oh, yes."

"Woofer, what do you think? Should I marry her?" I said.

Woofer stared at me furiously—I think he would have choked me if he could. He grumbled something incomprehensible.

"Tell me, papa," I said, "the most important thing: does she have her wood cut for winter?"

Papa blinked in surprise, then he laughed. Even Woofer had to laugh.

"I'll marry her now if she does," I said, and winked at Woofer. "Otherwise, I'll wait till spring."

So we ate dinner that way, talking about foolishness, and even with all the hints we had made nobody seemed to realize that Woofer loved the Crawford widow.

Later when I went out to the stable to see Phillip, Woofer offered to come with me, but as soon as we were in the yard he went running down the hill toward the bridge, beyond which she lived. From the farmyard I could see her house, with its glass windows golden in the lamplight, a flare of its reflection shimmering in the river. I watched him until he was lost in the darkness of the road beyond the bridge, then I saw his silhouette as he ran across her lawn and onto her front porch. I suppose he stood there knocking on the door, and I thought to myself how excited and happy he was, how healthy and likable a boy he was, what a man he was going to make, for he was decent and alert and strong—yes, and persistent as a mountain stream.

Her door opened, a yellow glow fell out onto her porch, and I saw a shadow move as Woofer leaped forward. I saw them sway and hold one another, they moving slowly in the glow of light, and as they went indoors I saw a little boy rush up to Woofer to be carried high in his arms.

I went on to the barn, walking on the oak planks Phillip had split and laid. There was a network of narrow walkways going from sheds to barns to chicken house to dogtrot, the walkways forming a complex pattern. Not many men would spend the energy to split oak merely to make their work more comfortable, but Phillip would. He was powerful as an ox, anyway.

When I pushed open the stable door I got a stomach-sick sensation for a moment; I saw a lantern hanging from a nail at one of the end stalls and I could hear a sick horse breathing. I stood still, allowing my body to quiver with the sound, before I moved quietly along the aisle to the stall, where I saw my brother crouching, his back against the wood wall, and over in the far corner was a Plover girl, Katie, whom I recognized even though she was fading now. The Plovers reach a peak of bloom at seventeen and fade by thirty; they're a beautiful and fragile human flower. She was blond and lean, and she wore an old thin dress. Her breasts were small and their nipples were visible through the dress.

She said, "Why, I told Phil I thought maybe it was Owen coming to visit us here, and he said he expected it would be Woofer first."

Phillip stood. He was a huge man, about six feet, almost as tall as I, but heavier set, forty pounds heavier, I judged, and he had a round face which was trembling with emotions just now. He held out his big hand to me.

"You're the damn biggest man I ever saw," I told him. I poked at him on the chest and shoulder. "Lord a' mercy."

"Jesse's filled out too," he said. "So have you."

Katie said, "Jesse never done it like Phil, though, never growed up like he done it." She was proud of this one, conspicuous victory Phillip held over our oldest brother.

"And how you doing, Katie?" I asked her, kneeling by the sick horse, patting his damp neck.

"Why, I'm fighting off children all the time, down there in what mama calls a home, with papa off trapping fish. If it wasn't for the fish and the rabbits, we'd have our stomachs touching our backbones at our place."

"How is your papa?"

"He's fiddling for first one party and then another, but nobody pays him. You'd think they'd give him more'n his food and drink, but that's all he gets."

"Look how much he drinks, though," Phillip said, laughing gently.

78

"I'll pay him," I said.

"In the war, though," she said.

"Yes. I miss his playing."

"He might go to war if you tell him he'll have a bigger audience," she said, laughing.

I tried to remember Katie as she had been when she had worked for mama years ago. I wondered if she had fallen in love with our house first, and now with Phillip. And why were they courting in the stable—was it papa who would not allow her to enjoy the warmth of the house she coveted?

"He's not bad sick, Phillip," I said.

"I believe we'll save him," he said. "I've bled him twice today."

About eight o'clock I heard music. I was in the kitchen by then, talking with papa, was joking with him, and I heard a fiddle, a guitar, and a drum. Soon the musicians arrived, Elvir Plover, a slight wisp of a man, in the lead, and as usual he was woefully dressed, with patches protecting the pieces of patches remaining on his clothes. With him was a drunk friend of his who owned a guitar. Tagging along behind was his son Victor, who was beating a drum. I decided then I must have all three for my regiment. The miller's family must have heard them, and the smith's, and the German's, for all three families soon arrived. I had been talking quietly with papa about Raleigh, which he had visited twenty years ago and had not seen since, when this noisy commotion arrived at our door—arrived not to herald him, or even Jesse or Phillip, but me, the wayward son.

Music attracts visitors in this part of the world. Even though the weather was chilly, a dozen people soon arrived. We built two fires in the back yard, one for the women to talk around and one for the men. At our fire we had a whopping time of recalling old hunts and devilment. A dance started, women and men stomping and twirling between the fires, their shadows thrown on the sides of the barn and out over the pasture and the mountainside, humorous shapes sometimes, adding to the party spirit.

79

Maybe thirty people were there by nine o'clock when Phillip broke out the first pitcher of rough cider, papa having turned his back to the cellar door for a minute. Phillip got two or three more pitchers full and mulled it at the fires. Even the women took their part, mama and Nell among them, and directly Phillip and the smith were going into the cellar with two pitchers each. I suppose they were bringing out the planting party supply. I don't know.

Mr. Abel Crawford, himself, walked over from his house to witness the event, the welcome of the local Rebel colonel, his own son's superior officer. Mr. Crawford was one of the leaders among the planters in this valley, as papa was the leader of the farmers, and the two men distrusted each other but were never impolite to one another. Papa now had this courtly visitor to cope with.

Phillip, urged on by Katie Plover, went behind the barn and roped a calf. He and the smith slaughtered it and hung the two halves on a sapling rack at the women's fire, where papa at first didn't even see it. His lower jaw began to work rather frantically when he did, but Phillip was glorious in his kindly, big smile, for he had bested him and papa knew it. Phillip was patient and warm of spirit, and nobody could help liking him.

Papa was in a nervous state; he couldn't seem to decide what to do with his hands or where to stand, and he kept trying to avoid Abel Crawford, who dryly was congratulating him on his contribution to the Southern cause, and he kept glancing unhappily at that skewered calf, hung on green saplings which were sizzling now about as much as the meat was.

Plover called the dance as he fiddled, for he had the fiddle not under his chin, but against his chest.

> Hold your partner by the hand,
>   twirl her 'round,
> Hold your partner by the arm,
>   twirl her 'round,

> Hold your partner by the waist,
>   twirl her 'round,
> Oh my, let go of that, boy, let
>   go of that ...

Billy Furr, a hunter and trapper from Hobbs, arrived with a friend named Sole McKinney, who smelled about as sour as he did. They wanted to report to me on which men in the region were in sympathy with the enemy, believing, I suppose, that I would drop everything and come help them convert these traitors to a more acceptable frame of mind—my father and brothers among them, no doubt. We plied them with mulled cider, and before long I suggested they might want to butcher a pig out of papa's pen and rack its carcass to cook at the men's bonfire, which they did.

By ten o'clock the prettier women had danced six dances. Mama had danced three, not because she wasn't pretty either, and Nell had danced a time or two. Old man Abel Crawford had clogged for a few minutes, to everybody's pleasure and my surprise. His son, the Captain, had arrived. People from both sides of the river were mingling again, the first time in a year or so, for here I was, a Wright who was a Southern officer. Both the planters and the farmers could assemble to agree that Owen was all right, he was a great man, the leader of our regiment, of our boys off fighting.

Two other musicians were getting their instruments tuned now. More people came walking up from the road. Our little orchestra struck up for the next dance. A big party had broken out, and there was no way to stop it, not once it had got to spewing and sparkling like this, and I lent myself to it, went spinning off into pleasure dancing with one or two women, watchful for a prettier one. Maybe fifty or sixty adults were twisting and twirling before the fires, their children all over the place yelling, and we had meat roasting with delicious crackling noises and some spluttering, our cider and music were both intoxicating, and I got to laughing, dizzy with the shadows on

81

the hill and the sounds and color of the welcome, for it was all as fine as any welcome could be—

> One girl is not too few,
> two girls is not too many,
> three girls is what
> I'm hoping for ...

Papa wandering about with a pint of mulled cider in his hand, taking mighty draughts from it, at least halfway won over to my side.

> I love somebody, yes, I do,
> I love somebody, how 'bout you?
> I love somebody, yes, I do,
> Wish somebody loved me too!

Plover was up there on a barrel, calling those words while he stomped time with his foot and while the dancers twirled. A few went scampering, those young ones, through the fence rails and up into the pasture to see the stars better.

> Darling, you can love five,
> Darling, you can love six.
> Darling, you can love seven,
> And still go to heaven.

Mama was laughing with Abel Crawford, Nell was dancing with the older brother of my Lieutenant Hal King, the one who was wounded, the music was swelling to fill the valley like flour fills the hand.

> It's all around the mountain, charming Betsy,
> It's all around the mountain, Cora Lee,
> And if nevermore I see you,
> Sally Anne and Linda Joy, remember me ...

I got drunk on music. I love music better than anything, and I am romantic by type anyway, and admit it. Sometime during the festivities I got a notion to follow the shadows where they led, and I stumbled up after them onto the hillside above the house, walked through a pasture, a jug in my arms held like a baby, the music of the party faintly in my ears even yet. It was strange, really mystic, and above me was the whole, open, spangled Southern sky, glorious beyond churches and paintings, and I could see forever, I could see God's toes twitching at me, I could see his eyes looking down at me, and I raised my hand to him and shouted out, "Hey, see me, see me, see me, papa."

His two eyes twinkled back.

On a plot of grass I flopped down, flattened myself on my back and stared directly up into that jowled and heavenly face. "Hello, old man," I said. "I might be dying in the war soon, and when I come to see you, I hope you won't start off our first meeting talking about sins, like your preachers do." What a disappointment, I thought, after a spectacular journey through space, to come to the wide, golden streets, to the scarlet room with forty thousand singers dressed in white, to approach the throne of God at last, to see him lean toward me, all angels quiet now that the Wisdom of Ages was to speak to his child, Owen Wright:

"Colonel Wright, do I have it correct that on the night of the 24th of September, 1863, you slept illicitly with a New Orleans woman in Richmond?"

"Yes, your lordship."

"And is it true that you slept with her on other nights in October as well?"

"Yes, your lordship."

"And is it true that at the age of 28 or 29 you struck your father, not once but repeatedly, and cast him from your life and threw a sizable sum of his money to the hogs?"

"Yes, your lordship, but could I first ask about the creation of man, that most marvelous instrument which I myself, your lordship, have come to appreciate through war—"

"And is it true, Colonel Wright, that before you left home you buried a woman there, one pregnant at the time—"

"No, your lordship—"

"You did not?"

"She was not pregnant, your lordship?"

"Did she not tell you she was?"

"No."

"And the work and that cold winter and the pregnancy conspired to—"

"No, God, she never told me."

"She lost the baby just before she died. She lost it in a field up past that straggly yellow-apple tree."

"Your lordship, I suspected, but I didn't know. I feel unhappy and wicked, now that I am with you, God—"

"Yes, well, so you are wicked. You were born corrupt, Owen. All my children are sons of the devil."

"My father always thought I was corrupt."

"Your father never was sure you were his son."

"I—wondered about that too, sir."

"His brother's name was Weatherby, was it not? And he envied your father and often stayed in your father's house, which had been his own father's house."

"But you—you must know the truth of it—"

"Where two brothers are involved it is devilishly hard even for me to tell, for the seeds are similar, and I can't see everything firsthand, though I spend my time on the lookout for just such sins."

"Did my father ever mention this to me?"

"I think he would not."

"I seem to recall the sound of his voice—"

"You might have heard your parents arguing. No sparrow falls to the earth except I know and no man sleeps with another's wife except I know, but I lose track sometimes. I see such practices as would amaze you."

"I would—be pleased to watch with you."

"You don't have my purity of mission, Owen. I know you very well. I know you killed your colonel in a battle last summer."

"Sir, I beg to differ with you. I did not."

"You carry the guilt of it. Why do you carry the guilt on your soul?"

"Sir, purge it from me, for I did not. I was in a field at Port Republic, and he said to me, 'Should we go up that draw where all that laurel is, Captain Wright?' And I said, 'Yes, but I am lame, sir, I am lame in my right leg,' and he said, 'I will leave you here, then,' and he gave the command, and he and Major Dockery—believe me, your lordship, look into my heart. I did not at that moment know those two—"

"You were not wounded in that leg at all, as I recall."

"I did not kill them."

"Then forgive yourself, Owen."

"If you in your wisdom and purity would forgive me, I would be forgiven."

"I forgive you. You didn't kill him is the cold fact of it, I agree. Not like a murder out on a heath. I have seen murderers on heaths, Owen, that would shock you. What wicked creatures men are!"

"You forgive me?"

"Yes, I forgave you a moment ago, for you did not do it. But, lord, I see the scar is with you even now, so my forgiveness is not the issue at all."

"What is the issue then?"

"You must be more guilty than you've confessed. I suggest you knew that your commander ought not to go up there, for you must have seen—"

"No, God damn you—"

"Oh my. Well, it doesn't matter whether I forgive you or not, for you can't forgive yourself, can you?"

"I am not one for speechmaking in such company as this, but I will say as emphatically as ever in this world I've spoken that I did not see any enemy soldiers up that ravine, and yet I was afraid to go up there. I—did want him out of the army, but I did not want him dead or for those men with him to die; there were eighteen men in all who went up that draw, and there were at least a hundred Yanks waiting in those laurel thickets."

85

"Oh, don't play coy with me, Owen Wright. I see you clean through. You know you suspected all of it, and you got what you wanted from it. I don't think you knew he and Dockery would get killed, but you thought very well they might, and I suppose you hoped the others would not, and when all got killed you naturally went into a state of shock that lingers even yet, eight months later, and your own deliberate participation has been muted in your memory."

"Does Captain Crawford know?"

"I would have to inquire. I suppose so. But God knows I've seen men do worse for less. It was evil, but it was not as evil by earthly morality as sleeping with that Louisiana Frenchwoman. Or earlier those other tarts and servant girls. Those marks stand against you here. War does not. To kill eighteen soldiers is paltry. It isn't worth recording. Even you—why, you have—what's your total men shot in battle?"

"By myself about twenty and an unknown number of hundreds, thousands by my regiment."

"That's ghastly, isn't it? And how many have died or been wounded in your own regiment since the war began?"

"Three hundred—"

"Quite a commendable record. A most able regiment. I must watch it more carefully when it goes into battle. Good show, Colonel."

"Thank you, sir."

"It's a difficult sort of war, isn't it? A family fight. Only when the Negro gets involved is there much animosity. There have been riots in the North because of their new conscription law, and do you know what the rioters do after they shout and burn and demonstrate?"

"No, sir."

"They kill hundreds of Negroes. It is as if they say, 'Take the black man away and it will end forthwith, kill the blacks and we need not fight'."

"Yes, sir. I understand."

"I think if the Negroes were not one of the issues, the Southerner wouldn't fight, for he cares nothing about any other issue involved. He cares nothing about government—he cares more about God than government."

"Yes, sir."

"No people on earth are more religious than the Southerners."

"Yes, sir."

"They are among the kindest people—yet are the meanest too. The Northerner is more likely to hurt a stranger; a Southerner hurts his father, his brother, his son, his wife, his closest friend, he takes his best friend's wife—"

"Yes, sir."

"I'm always being asked to forgive some damn thing or other. It breaks your heart to hear how sorry they are."

"Do they love niggers or hate them, your lordship?"

"Negroes, Owen!"

"Sir?"

"To the Southerner there is no consistent way to separate love and hate. He blends almost everything, even accepts both the Old and the New Testament as companionable, one testament being fierce with racial pride and war and the other mild with forgiveness and love. They see themselves as the new chosen people in the promised land. So your father could hate and love you, and when you went to him and said you wanted land, that you had married Anna Morla Britt—was that her name?"

"Yes, your lordship."

"He at first said no, for that girl is not worthy of one of us—"

"I told him we had had to marry, which was not true."

" 'Let her use a knitting needle,' he said. He said he would not give you any land, any money, though he did. And when Anna

Morla died, her life flowing out of her, and her child's life too
—your child's life, Owen—"

"How desperately she wanted a child—"

"Yes, I put a quantity of that desire in women, maybe too
much—I don't know."

"After she died I went to him and asked for money so I could
go away and start off in a new place, with a chance, some
opportunity, for I was being made into a stone, a trunk of a tree
on that rocky soil he had given me—"

"As he knew you would be. Yet he said no, no."

"With such callousness. Not even hate. Only callousness."

"And he said again there was something different about you,
which was only his admission of the worry he could not tolerate,
that you were not his but were his brother's, that you were not
even his to love or hate, or to love and hate."

"I plan to talk with him, your lordship. Can he and I bury the
old animosity?"

"Perhaps. He is sick and is more vulnerable to his emotions."

"Will he die soon?"

"Tut-tut-tut, man, don't ask me for the secrets of time. You go
see your father, and do leave the New Orleans woman alone,
you hear me? Find a proper woman for yourself."

"Where?"

"Up here, I imagine, at home. Pick one for yourself. Find a
young widow with land and money, so after the war you can
retire to the place you're best known. You need a woman you
can love, land you can work, children you can rear—"

"Will I find her up here? Can I find her?"

"Owen, I told you not to ask me for the secrets of time."

CHAPTER FIVE

Later, much later, I lay in bed, my head swimming dizzily. It was about 2 A.M. and twenty gallons of cider were gone, and the pig, and the calf, and the guests.

I could hear my father and mother fussing at each other in the front bedroom.

I lay in bed in the little bedroom off the kitchen, my old room. Out the one glazed window I could see traces of the moonlit clouds. I crept deep into the feather mattress, deeper under the cotton and feather eiderdown. The room smelled of pine wood, even yet. Papa and Jesse and Phillip and I should have used oak or hickory, as we knew, but a big white pine had split off a branch, and papa said the tree endangered the house. The tree was four feet in diameter. With oxen we dragged logs of it to the mill, and used the power of the mill wheel to rip off planks. The belts broke several times, I recall.

On the boards we had pasted paper, using a mixture of flour and water. This helped keep the wind from sweeping through. We even used one of papa's books that way in the storm of 1847, when mama said we needed warmth more than we needed to read. Papa selected a book on the benefits of infant baptism, in which he did not believe. We pasted the pages right side up and in order, mama and I, and for years one could walk about the walls and read about baptism, until the paper faded and splotched.

The chair in the corner was of oak and had been cut and carved by my grandfather. The dressing table he and papa had made of cherry; the wood had bleached out its redness by now. The bench was of hickory. The broom was of hickory splits, which mama or Nell had cut and bound. The curtains my mother had made of linen, which she had made from the flax she had broken, and which she and Nell, and maybe Woofer, had dyed blue from a dye they had boiled out of alder bark, which grew along the river. The quilts were made of cotton from our own fields. The blankets were of wool cut from our own sheep, then carded and spun by my mother, or by one of my grandmothers. The sheets were of linen from flax grown and broken, spun and woven here. I was lying deeply comforted with feather mattresses, the feathers having been pulled from many an angry goose, and was listening to the wind which blew strong from the mountain, our mountain, up back of our house, as it always had.

$$\diamondsuit$$

Jesse was sitting at papa's place at the table when I got up. I could see him from the bedroom. His broad, hunched back and shoulders were toward me, but I could tell he was glowering. As he chewed his food, slowly he moved the cream pitcher, the sugar bowl, the honey server, the butter dish, the jam pot, the bowl of applesauce, the plate of hot biscuits. He wore a brown leather jacket, black riding boots, and black homespun pants. He had a six-inch knife in a sheath on his right hip. He had a thick neck, broad shoulders, huge arms, as large in girth as mine. His palms were massive, but his fingers were slender and long, as are mine. He was all power; there was no fat on him. When he spoke to mama or Nell, who were nimbly waiting on him, his voice had a growl in it.

Phillip noisily entered the room, became quiet when he saw Jesse sitting there, went to the outside door without speaking, looked back only when Jesse said, "You had no authority to—"

Phillip shut the door quickly as he left.

"I couldn't even come home to my own bed till morning," Jesse said, "and I saw enough of the party to know you were

90

drunk, Nell, so don't deny it. My own sister. I'll write Hal and tell him you were out flouncing with his brother while he's laid up in the hospital."

"Jesse, don't—you wouldn't—"

"No, you won't, Jesse," mama said.

Nell said, "Even if you did, Hal wouldn't think anything, out in the light of two fires."

"Burned two cords of wood," Jesse said. He brought his hand down on the table, making some of the cream slop out of the pitcher. "What do you think you are, out there dancing with that planter High Shoreman?"

"She was only welcoming Owen and Woofer home—" mama said defensively.

"And you dancing with old man Crawford," Jesse said. "I hope you've washed since."

"Hush afore you wake up Owen and Woofer," mama said huskily.

"Damn slaveholders, damn their souls, damn them, I say."

I was getting dressed by now, anxious to join the commotion. I watched as Jesse suddenly looked off toward the hallway and shouted, "Woofer, get your lazy self out of bed." Then to mama he said, "Where did he go off to last night?"

"I don't know, I don't know," mama said worriedly. "Don't you go ordering my baby around, you hear?"

"Baby?"

"I'm warning you, Jesse Wright, to leave my youngest to me. I've told you afore—"

"Oh, I know he's mama's baby and mama has to have a baby," he said.

"Hush. Not another word about him."

"I thought he was going to be a preacher, like you wanted, but a whoremonger is more likely."

Mama stomped her foot. "I said to hush about him, you hear?" She was on the verge of tears. "I don't know where you was either."

"Mama's little baby," Jesse said teasingly. "Papa got him untied from the apron strings at last, but where does he go off to but the war, and when he comes home he goes courting till three damn A.M."

Mama turned back to the fireplace, troubled deeply. Jesse began chewing food again. Suddenly he brought his hand down with a slap on the table. "Who said Owen could kill my calf?"

Nell hurried away, went into the washroom with the breakfast plates. Mama went on cooking, murmuring to herself, seeking to comfort herself.

"Who said they could eat my pig?"

"Your papa has so many pigs he don't even know their number. We should have announced a party, posted a notice, but nothing was done—"

"Well, I didn't know he would steal. Oh, yes, oh, yes, I did know, too. Oh, yes. I should have known to lock up my stock and mount guards."

"He'll hear you, Jesse," she said huskily. "Now I want his visit to be a happy one—"

"It was my calf."

"I don't know who killed it, but once it was hanging up broiling there was no point crying over it."

"Our best pig hanging up, too."

"It was not our best—"

"I know our own stock. And you dancing with Abel Crawford—"

"I was not dancing much—"

"Ask papa."

"Why not ask me?" she said. "You're such a big man, Jesse, you've growed to be so big I can't tell you anything, for you're so right about everything, you're always on the one just side and above complaints."

They glared at each other. I rather enjoyed seeing it. Quickly I rolled up the belt I had bought for him and shoved it into a pants pocket. I pulled the door wide open and went on into the kitchen.

Mama turned to me. "Why, you did get up finally, Owen," she said, glancing warily at Jesse, who kept his seat there at the table, his black back to me, his shoulders rolled forward. "Your papa's in the field," mama said, "but Jesse waited for you out of brotherly regard."

"Oh, he's a fine brotherly fellow," I said, nodding to his back and big neck.

"You let us talk, mama," Jesse said, growling.

"Yes, I'll go see if Woofer's up," she said, and went hurrying out.

Jesse spit a cherry seed onto the table. "How you, Owen?" he said, not looking at me.

I moved past him to the long side of the table, sat down about four feet from him. As yet neither of us had looked at the other's face.

"I'm all right, Jesse," I said. I picked up a spare biscuit and chewed on it.

"I'm all right too," he said, pouring two spoonfuls of sugar into his coffee and stirring it with the sugar spoon.

I reached the pot of coffee and poured a cupful for myself.

"I want to ask you something," he said, chewing on a dry biscuit.

I reached toward him, not bothering to look at him, picked up a piece of bacon from the serving platter. "You worrying about your calf and pig?" I said.

"I worry about people eating half-raw meat," he said.

"Farm must be getting on well if it can spare a fine calf and a pig for not much of a reason," I said.

"And a barrel of cider," he said.

Mama came scurrying back, went to the fire to stoke it, which was always her first duty whenever she entered the room. "Woofer's out of bed and will be down directly," she said.

"I ain't talking about Woofer," Jesse said. He chewed on a dry bite of biscuit and swallowed it. He was looking at the kitchen windows, not at her or me. He coughed and biscuit crumbs

93

sputtered over his plate. "Tell you what I wonder, Owen. I mean six years. I thought you were dead."

"I never thought he was—"

"Mama, will you let me talk?"

"Who are you to tell me—"

"Mama, do Owen and me have to go to the barn to talk?"

She stood blankly pale, a big cooking fork in one hand and a spoon in the other, her eyes flashing fiercely, but she relented, turned back to the fireplace, began muttering one complaint or other about his rudeness.

"Six years," he said, taking the last remaining egg off the platter, pulling it onto his plate, tapping the platter with his spoon to be filled again. "I thought you were dead, but here you are, all flesh and blood again."

"You knew Owen was in the regiment," mama said suddenly.

"And I knew he might get killed there, too," Jesse said. "But here he is. Here you are, Owen, flesh and blood. And I suppose after six years you came back because somebody sent you. What say?" He leaned toward me, sucking on a tooth, staring at me. "Somebody send you, Owen?"

"Yes, I suppose you could say so."

"Who sent you?"

"Woofer," I said.

He blinked. He tried to regain his sense of argument. Finally he grunted and sat back in his chair, returned to his eating. Then once more, slowly, deliberately, he laid his fork down. "If you won't say who sent you, maybe you'll say why you're here. Something to do with slaves, is it?"

"Runaway slaves?" I asked. There was nothing left for me to eat, because he had eaten it all or had it all on his plate.

"That's it, is it? They send you for that?" he said.

"I'm not here for that," I said.

Slowly he picked up his fork and went back to eating, but he looked up again, as deliberately as before. "If it's not about the blacks, is it about the soldiers?"

94

"The white men who need to be guided through the mountains to the Yank army?" I said.

He blinked. His smile faded. He reached up one long finger and scratched a bite on his chin. "That's it, is it?"

"No, that's not it," I said.

He went back to eating again, but for a fourth time he laid down his fork and carefully ventured forth. "Is it the conscription? I'll tell you now, Owen, if you come for me, I'll buy a substitute. If you come for Phillip, papa will pay his fee too, for we need him. You won't get either one of us that way. And if you try to take anybody else of a Union disposition you'll have trouble with guns going off in your face. I'll warn you of that now."

Mama set the platter of eggs and ham down between us. I took the platter and set it in front of me and began to eat from it. Jesse looked helplessly at the platter, then up at me, a hungry scowl on his face.

"No, I'm not here about the conscription either," I said, my mouth crammed full of food.

Suddenly he shouted at me out of his exasperation, "What the hell is it then? You are here. You did arrive last night and killed my calf and pig and drank a twenty-gallon barrel of cider, didn't you? You did arrive and got Nell and mama to a dance and got Woofer lost and put papa into the bed with a fluttering in his heart. You are here this minute eating every damn mouthful of food mama cooked, ain't you?"

"Pass the cream, Jesse," I said.

"Go to hell," he said, torn by frustration and passion. "It does have to do with me, does it, not with the war, not with the slaves, not with the white soldiers, but with me. I thought Woofer wouldn't be party to it—"

Mama said, "You leave Woof—"

"Let me tell you now, Owen, I'll not be set upon by the two of you. All you have against me is that I was born first, and it's for that I have been plagued all my life, and even my own

95

mother is jealous of me for Woofer's sake, and my own sister is jealous of me for Phillip's sake—I think she loves Phillip more than she loves herself or Hal King, either one—"

"Don't you mention his name to Owen—" mama said.

"Oh, she'll tell Owen about Hal King writing her three letters, don't you worry about that, she'll tell Owen forty times before he goes away. Jesus, mama—three letters—"

"Don't curse—"

"I'm telling you, Owen, if you try to take one damn square foot of this farm from me, I'll end this family argument in my own way." He was leaning far toward me, glaring at me. "You got sixty acres already, and you'll get your fair share of what estate papa has left, but it won't be another foot of this farm, nor another beast on it to eat. This has been promised to me since I could hear words spoke, and I've had to fight for it ever year, with Phillip trying for it and then you trying for it, and now Woofer has gone to fetch you, has he, to bring you back on me with all your colonel's buttons and the power of the army, has he? Well, I've been here for these six years, I've been here in this house and out there on that land every day. I've worked twelve years more than you to make something out of this place, while most of that time you were whoring around in Virginia—"

I tossed the gift onto the table. I threw it out there to him, that was all, to hush him with the gift, and it uncoiled at him, its buckle even seemed to snap at him like a snake. I didn't mean it that way. He was on his feet instantly, knocking papa's chair over backward, and he let out a yell that filled the house, a shout which unnerved even me, a soldier.

Of course, when he saw it was only a belt he became even more dismayed.

Well, what could I say? He had made a fool error, of course. What would he believe about what I had intended? "I brought you a gift, Jesse," I said, "that's why I came." Then, God forgive me, he looked so peculiar and out of sorts that I had to laugh.

I wandered about the yard with Nell, she telling me about how Hal King started writing to her last spring when he and I were fighting together in the Shenandoah Valley. He wrote her the first time he got wounded, said he had always watched her with interest and wished he had mentioned himself to her before. "And he said he had come to respect you so much," she told me.

"I suppose Hal likes me well enough," I said. "He's a fine officer, for he doesn't worry anybody, doesn't fret and plot; he's calm by nature."

"He seems to be on the surface," she said, "but his letters tell me more about him, Owen. He's troubled in many ways. I suppose he knows he's been too lucky for his luck to continue much longer."

"Well, let's not talk about the war," I said.

She told me about Phillip's attitude toward the Plover girl. "She likes him," she said, "and he's so embarrassed about it he acts as if he's doing her a favor to allow her to watch him work. He talks mean to her sometimes, says 'What, you back again?' Such as that. But he loves her, he really does, Owen. And of course papa won't agree to her even coming into the house, unless mama has hired her to help cook or clean."

"Does Jesse have a woman?"

"I think so, but it's not talked about. She's a Walker and has a cabin of her own about a mile away, down the hill from her father's place. They're close, Owen, but when they go to church they don't speak to one another, lest papa object."

"I think I ought to encourage Phillip to marry that Plover girl, don't you?"

She thought about it. "If you dare," she said.

She showed me her flock of chickens. She had about forty, and she had guinea hens, too, and ducks and a few turkeys. We looked for duck eggs along the brook, then I left her finally and went up to see how papa was doing. He was pruning apple trees, and I sat down on a rock in the orchard, with the sun warm on me and the whole world at my feet, with the settlement in clear sight below me and a few carts on the road winding their patient ways toward the mill.

Apple trees should be pruned in spring or fall, but I have seen papa prune them in the winter, with snow in their limb crotches, and in summer, in every month of every year. Whenever he would have some worry to get through, a decision to make which troubled him, he would go get his fruit saw and walk up through the pasture to one of his apple trees and would work on it, to shape it properly.

After a little while I wandered on down along the rail fence, made of chestnut rails split by my grandfather. I toured the rows of sheds and little huts, coming at last to the dog pen. I pushed the gate back and there they went, the pack of two hounds and four bear dogs, across the pasture on a trail of some sort, and I ran after them, shouting them on. Phillip came out of the barn, fussing about the dogs being out, but when he saw me, he smiled. "Jesse don't want them to run," he explained. "I don't care myself."

I went into the dye shed, which had stone walls and had a hearth and a chimney made of stone, every stone in its place, evenly, securely laid, with clay used as mortar. There was also a building to wash clothes in, and outside it was a battling block. There was a stone springhouse which papa, Jesse, Phillip, and I had built one winter long ago, the spring water running through the trough inside it.

I was looking at the crib, remembering my argument years ago with papa at this place, when an elderly woman came up from the road. She was toothless, had a snuff stick in her mouth, had a bonnet on, was wearing a pretty yellow dress with a blue shawl pulled tight around her shoulders. She was the mother of Caleb, she said. I didn't know who Caleb was, but I told her I was glad to see her. She told me Caleb had had ear trouble as a boy and she had feared he couldn't do the army work, but apparently he had succeeded for we had kept him. She was wondering how he was.

Several other people came by that day, some to see papa about money needs, others to see me. Three men came by worrying about conscription. I talked with them about volunteering but got nowhere. Several boys came by and said they wanted to join my regiment. They were quite young but I took their names. A man named Clancy, a fur trader, stopped by on his way to Old Fort, and we recalled hunting bears together nine, ten years ago, and I asked him to send a telegram for me to my regiment, which I wrote out. It was an instruction for Lieutenant King to be furloughed home, to finish his recovery here, if medically acceptable. It was time in my life I did another favor for Nell, I thought.

A few other women came by to ask about men in my regiment. "Can my boy come home," one woman asked me, "or can you at the very least send somebody home to do the plowing in his place next spring?" Another woman said to me, "They won't do any more fighting till you get back, will they, Owen?"

Woofer wanted me to come meet his girl, and he told me in detail about his greeting from her, the telling couched in such wonderfully romantic notions that I was swept along with him in spite of myself. He told me about his little widow being in the kitchen, where he had been courting her. It seemed he had decided he needed a bath, and she had agreed to heat water for one, and it seemed she helped wash him, and she splashed so much water on herself she had to undress too. I became quite excited listening to him. Woofer asked me to come see his woman that night.

"I'll take a bath over there," I told him, joking with him.

About dusk a man named Simmons came by, wondering if he might hope to bring his son's body home from the Shenandoah. I remembered the son very well. He had died at McDowell. We had buried him in a hilltop cemetery near there, a Methodist one.

"How will I find it, Owen?" his father asked. He sat down nearby. "If I go up there, where do I go to?"

"At McDowell take the northeast road, toward Harrisonburg, follow it for a mile, and off to your right you'll see a steeple rising from beyond a stand of ten-year yellow poplars."

"Is his grave marked?"

"I buried his canteen at the head of it, about six inches under the grass. I scratched his name into the wood."

"But nobody in that neighborhood saw him put away?"

"Yes, I paid the man who lives by the church three dollars to dig the graves, and your boy is the nearest one to the gate of the three, I believe."

He sat there chewing tobacco and spitting at the dirt. "Would you mind if I paid for the man who dug?"

"No, I wouldn't mind," I said.

"I'd rather do it, do something," he said, giving me a dollar. He sat around for half an hour after that, told me about his wife's sickness. Told me about a hunt he had been on in December. Told me about a coat he was hoping to make from a bearskin.

The day I arrived Crawford and the conscription officer, a major, moved a small company of state militia into Madison County to begin conscripting men there, and they got shot at from so many different laurel bushes—warning, worrying shots, that they retreated into the French Broad River and set up defenses on a little island, much to everybody's amusement. The conscriptors next gathered their strength at Burnsville and tried by court action to force men to sign the enlistment papers there, but their court processing turned out long and lame, so then the little militia major came creeping around papa's house wanting to shake my hand.

I advised him and Captain Crawford to settle down for a little while until I could see what development I could promote. So that night, instead of visiting Woofer's widow, I rode alone down to Hobbs to talk with Billy Furr and ask him what patriotic men could do to set matters to rights up here. He was a scheming man, as I knew, and he had fierce friends who were patriotic even in their breathing. "Are we going to let them get away with this, Billy, shooting at our people?" I said, sitting in his home, in one of the two log rooms he had, my creaky chair set firmly on the clay floor, his four young sons and five or six of his friends squinting at us from their places along the walls, where they crouched like young animals, whiling the night away just as they usually did the days too. In Hobbs, on the south side of the river, while the women worked the men thought and talked and hunted.

I went home by way of Burnsville and talked with a few men there, so I was late getting to my bed. Even so, Jesse was still out somewhere, and Woofer was too.

Next morning, sooner even than I had expected, we got a report that fifteen men from Hobbs, farmers and hunters led by Billy Furr, had on the previous night ridden to Andrews, to the large house of a wealthy farmer, Mr. Poston, who was seventy-two, who was a close friend of my father and was reputed to be one of those in charge of the underground for slaves and for white recruits trying to reach the Northern army. The raiders called him outdoors and demanded that he take the oath of allegiance to the Confederacy, which he refused to do, so the raiders drove his horses out of the barn and requisitioned them "for the Rebel army," meaning, I'm sure, for their own use as raiders, and they shot two steers and cooked steaks on fires made with rails from Poston's fences, stole brandy from his cellar and hams from his smokehouse, and after shooting a few sheep, rode off with pieces of meat and whole chickens dangling from their saddles.

This was a definite, provable act of vengeance, as the elderly gentleman who reported to papa and Jesse said. He was a friend and debtor of papa's, was doubtless a Yank sympathizer himself, which made his recitation somewhat difficult once he saw me sitting at the kitchen table, dressed in at least half a Rebel

101

uniform—the shirt I had on was Phillip's.

Jesse was present too. Jesse said it was treacherous to make a farmer swear a traitorous oath—he was fierce about it—and to kill his steer or even to trespass on his property was a burning evil.

I asked Jesse if he was going to allow these Rebels to get away with it.

I suppose there were many meetings that day of the Yank sympathizers. At any rate, that night a band of about fifteen met near Hobbs and rode into that settlement. They ordered Billy Furr out of his house, but when a thorough search proved he wasn't home—he was out raiding in Madison—they settled for his son, Beech, who was fifteen. They demanded that he take the oath to the Union, which he refused to do, so they held his hands between two chestnut rails and pressed the rails together until he screamed out the words. Then they stole chickens and hams and had a feast on the riverbank at the Hobbs church before huge fires. They shot their guns at midnight and sang "The Star-Spangled Banner," and rode toward their homes. Many of them were from right around here, from Harristown, and one report maintained that the smith was the leader of it.

It is a pity to bring a war into a remote part of the country such as this, to divide further the families and villages, but if the military intends to function here the disease of the war must contaminate the people until they call for military cures.

I could stop the raids, even after these initial exchanges. It was not too late, and I wrestled with myself—my sense of duty to my men off in the regiment contesting my sense of duty to these people—and I admit it was myself which weighed the difference, for I could not see any fulfillment of my own needs and hungry ambitions just now except in the army, which in return must be fed 200 human beings.

It was my duty to supply them. So I told myself, lying awake in my cold room asking myself what in God's name I was doing. Duty. A short, fluid word; one dispenses with it easily on the

102

tongue. It has in itself none of the hardness, the discipline which duty demands of us.

I talked with Nell about my dilemma. Can you believe I talked with Nell about a matter as personal as this, and treacherous? But it's similar, my predicament was not unlike hers when as a young girl she was loving in her heart and in manner, but was not attractive. "You are trapped, Owen," she told me. "Oh, Owen," and she sympathized with me, as only a woman can, and as only a woman can who herself has suffered her own pains.

CHAPTER SIX

I meant for Woofer to be with me when I went to meet his little widow, but I sent him to Hobbs to try to find out who had ridden with Billy Furr's band of raiders, and almost as soon as he was gone I began to wonder about her. I ate my part of the duck Nell had cooked for our noon meal, and after we had eaten and she and mama and I were left at the table, I asked them again about the Crawford widow. Mama picked up a piece of duck wing and began chewing on it—she preferred wings to any other piece of chicken or duck and always had. She began to tell me about last year when old man Crawford was brought home from the wars. "The other soldiers of his volunteer troop brought him home," she said, speaking without much emphasis, almost droning as she talked, "carrying him acrosss his saddle like a load of furs, and they took his corpse to his house to deposit him. His wife come out to greet her conquering hero, don't you know, and there he was, his skinny butt poked up toward the sky, and she said, 'What is this?' and that Crutch boy of Mabel's, who's no gentleman and is none too bright, said, 'It's your'n, ma'am, though its soul has flown.' And they say she cried."

"What's so surprising about that?" Nell said.

"Why, I don't know," mama said. "Did I say it was surprising? Nobody thought she cared about him is all. Charlie Crutch says she wailed the whole time they was getting his corpse off the horse. Then they found they couldn't straighten him up, and there was a big commotion about what to do about it, for he was stinking up the garden. They decided they would have to bury him hooped, in half a keg, so several of them drug a big barrel out of the cellar and drank what was left in it, and they got the body and the barrel and the widow and the boy Eli all over to the churchyard. Your papa and me went down there to see why the fires was lighted, and papa helped them saw the barrel in two, and the drunkest of them put old Eli in one half of it."

"Had to dig a circular hole," Nell said.

"I'm telling it, Nell."

"I only was mentioning—"

"Soon there was maybe thirty of us there shivering, with our hands on our hips, trying to act like there was no odor to it. The had-been soldiers put the barrel in the hole and covered over the top with sticks and cross-sticks, then they carefully poured on the first layer of dirt, enough to keep the odor controlled until they could finish burying him next morning with a service. His widow was all aflutter, leaning on first one man and then another. And the mite, the boy, who was about two, was not being paid attention to, and first thing I knowed—" She sat there looking at the wall as if she could see through it to the graveyard, an awful frown on her face. "That mite fell in, Owen."

"Fell in?" I said, startled.

"Fell in, and that little widow screamed. I was blood-cold in an instant, for the mite was caught with one leg down inside the coffin, his feet in among the sticks, and I— That woman was screaming, and she came rushing forward and fell on her knees at the grave and that mite was crying and she was trying to undo his foot. He was stuck in the slats, seemed like. I couldn't move to help."

"Neither could I," Nell said.

"But she got the mite out herself, and that youngin was screaming, I mean loud as a painter, and the boy's foot and her hands were—they was—that stink, you know, and she carried him clothed into the river, herself, and washed him, with him screaming like a poor man at a baptism."

"I don't know why mama likes to tell stories like that," Nell said critically. She was embarrassed, I could tell. "The way you go on, mama," she said.

"Why, it happened right out there," mama said.

When I finished eating I went on down to the mill to talk with the men there, who cursed the Yanks for a while, then I went to the forge and listened to the men there curse Rebs, nobody caring about my being present to hear it all said, either. I was going on toward home, wondering why Woofer was so late getting back, when I happened to decide to go see this little widow on my own. I was simply walking along the road and saw her house and said to myself, I must go see what Woofer has got himself attached to.

I crossed the bridge and went on around the back way, my breathing nervous and erratic for some reason. As I approached the house I noticed the fields were untended, had been left with the fodder and stalks standing, and the garden was in a woeful state; nothing had been plowed under or clipped for winter or mulched, even the party rosebushes had not been covered. The fence around the pig drove was down and the pigs were most everywhere marauding. A cow with a full bag was lowing at the gate and no one seemed interested in her, not a one of the blacks, who sat about insolently, not bothering about me even when I opened the broken gate and came down the stone walk, which had cow and pig dung on it. "Is your mistress home?" I asked a black man who was sitting on the ground, leaning against a rock wall.

"She might be." He was a huge man, black as night. He didn't move to help me.

The house was two-story. The bottom story was of logs, and the second story, which was quite high above the ground, was of chestnut planks left to weather brown in the sun—or to weather gray on the north side. Much effort had been spent on the place, but it was, like most all the houses up here, a conglomeration of rooms added to a central room over the years by one generation or another, and I judged the upstairs had been added last and had proved to be a risky venture. On the far side of the house was a covered porch. There was no porch on this side.

Nearby was a separate building, a row of three little rooms to serve as slave quarters, opening into a grassless path about six feet wide onto which slop was thrown out of one of the rooms even as I watched. Pigs began to oink and move that way, called by the slosh of the water. All about the slave quarters was the attitude of letting do, getting by, slanted and slurred and wobbly now, lame and lazy and filthy.

I knocked on the kitchen door, and a little Negro woman began to scurry about in there. She had been sleeping, huddled on the floor in a corner. I knocked again, louder. I opened the door finally and said, "Your mistress home, is she?" The black woman backed off, scared of me. I said, "Call her for me," and the little Negro went away, murmuring about spirits, praying to them, and did not return.

So I knocked again, quite loud, and directly I heard a woman call out, "In a minute."

Directly she appeared, at least her head appeared around the kitchen door, a pretty, shiny face with a full mouth and two dark large eyes. In age, a child, not much more than a child. She came around the door, watching me all the while. She had round breasts and her hips rounded out from her small waist. She was short, not much more than five feet tall.

"Why, I thought you were a bear abarking on that door, you beat so hard. I was afraid my second floor rooms were going to fall down. I never heard such knocking. You practicing to destroy the world?"

"I'm—not accustomed to knocking that loud, but I couldn't rouse anybody."

"That's your problem seems to me, not mine or my house's."

"How's that?" I said, surprised. The comment had been insolent, but the girl was not. At least, she was smiling.

107

"Huh," she said, a little friendly sigh, her two white, white hands on her hips, staring at me from out of her white, white, quite alert face with her dark brown, even black eyes. "You roused all the ghosts in this house. I suppose you scared them nigh to death, too, and they'll all run off up north, ghosts and nigras both, which is what they've threatened to do."

"They won't run off, Mrs. Crawford." I found the name unwieldy for such a small, young person.

"I tell them, 'Well, don't take everything I got when you go, for I'd as soon have you gone as have to feed you, with you doing nothing except holding down the ground.' There's not much work going on around here."

"I can see that, Mrs. Crawford."

She was still standing there in the middle of the kitchen floor, talking away in a Southern, a planter's accent, her words soft and modest even when her meaning was critical. "It's all going back to nature ever which of a way, and I don't know what to do about it, for whenever my brother-in-law comes by he takes more horses and sheep away, even has my husband's goat herd. He wants to run the plantation for me, he says, but it's his place that flourishes while mine diminishes, and when I tell the men nigras what to do myself, they snicker and say it's not the right work for this season, you don't plant potatoes in January, and yet they won't do anything else either. So I have decided to let it all go back to the way it was and let them go north and become kings, which is what they predict for themselves, and leave my boy and me in the weeds."

The speech ended plaintively, the soft sounds moaning to a close, she all the time staring at me with those two intense black eyes, now and then touching her black hair as if to assure herself it was combed, touching her white, white face with her white hand, her manner intense even though there was humor in what she said, standing flat-footed, staring at me, a stranger, who was framed in her kitchen doorway listening.

"What's your name?" she said, and before I could answer she

said, "I can tell that you don't much like me."

"I'm—I live across the way," I began.

"You the brother of the smith's, are you?"

"No. I didn't know he had any brothers living here now."

"Don't you think he don't, and him going around trying to raise a cavalry for the North so they can ride off and help the Yankees. Well, I wish they'd take some of my nigras with them. I worry about this place more'n I do eating, for we do have a cellar full of foods yet. My husband was a miser when it come to preparing for a hungry day. You'd a' thought he had grown up with his stomach attached to his backbone most of the time. He would load in onions, apples, potatoes, and about forty different kinds of wines, including daffodil. Have you ever tasted daffodil wine?"

"No."

"Or rose-hip?"

"No."

"Well, it's enough to turn your cheeks outside in, or inside out, and yet he would sniff it and say how dainty its nose was and didn't I think it was delicious. He would stare through it with a candle behind, to see how clear it was, and I would taste it and about die, but I would always say it was just fine, for he was my husband after all. You're not one of the smith's then?"

"No."

"Who are you?"

"I'm Owen, Woofer's brother."

She fell silent at last, her chin poked out, her full lips slightly pouting, her black eyes focused squarely on me, her hands once more laid firmly on her hips. She moaned once or twice to herself, as if considering some calamity. "You want to come on inside, Colonel Wright?"

She led the way into the next room, which was a pleasant room with a fireplace, but it was dusty as could be and even had dirty plates stacked on the table. "Oh, that woman," she said disgustedly. "She won't even clean up after herself." She went on into the parlor, where she began to straighten up things, the cushions and all, and a lot of dust filled the air. She threw a dirty cup and saucer out the front window. Threw them into the yard. "You can sit wherever you want to. My husband always liked that chair there."

I sat down in his big leather chair near the fireplace. She sat down in a smaller chair across the fireplace, which was un-lighted, which was a soggy pile of ashes. She clasped her hands together on her lap. "I suppose you think I'm about as strange as a pup trying to keep house, but when I was born I had a servant even to hand me my rattles, much less my spoons. I never did for myself one bit, Mr. Wright—Colonel Wright, I believe it is, or general—"

"Yes, colonel," I said.

"I never floured and fried my own meat, for there was always people standing there with the flour mill in their hand, and the meat, and the skillet, and the firewood, and the onions to chop in with it, and the almonds. Do you like steak amandine, Colonel Wright?"

"I—I do, yes," I said. "I suppose."

"I never even washed my face without a person standing beside me with a towel. If I ever went to the toilet, somebody was standing close by with a wad of paper."

I cleared my throat, embarrassed. Women didn't usually talk this plain, except in Richmond, and then only soldiers' women.

"I had myself washed every day, and my hair plaited and my shoes brushed and my clothes—I had so many different dresses that one whole room was nothing but cupboards and racks, for my papa idolized me, thought I was an angel because I could sing. Every now and then I would even sing in church, and that would get me another dress and two hats and a pair of black boots, or whatever I wanted, a horse for my own, or a big dog, or whatever. So I ran off from all of it." She sat there twisting her hands lightly, staring down at them, her tongue exploring the inside of her mouth, poking out her cheek, then her lips. She

110

seemed to be entirely relaxed and confident. "What was your childhood like?"

"Why, it took place just over there."

"You think you had a children's childhood or an old-aged childhood?" she said.

"I—don't know. I never had anything, anybody with me all the time, though."

"I got so I had to have somebody with me," she said, turning to look at me directly with those honest black eyes. "I got afraid if a nigra maid or boy wasn't with me, even if I went into the woods to walk. I couldn't be left alone, for I would cry and go running about seeking someone, no matter what I had on or didn't have on. I didn't care. All my people have spoken out what's on their mind, Colonel Wright."

"I gather that they have," I said helplessly.

"My family never takes much care about what it says, for it has a reputation in Raleigh that everybody just naturally lets us have the road. My brothers have all done awful things that you wouldn't know how to believe. But they're patriotic, I'll say that. One was killed at Bull Run, Colonel Wright."

"Oh, was he?"

"And one was killed at Seven Pines. A major he was, and he died on his hoss. They shot him with a cannon."

"I'm sorry," I said.

"And one was wounded and captured at Shiloh and might be dead too."

"On the western front was he?"

"I don't know where the Tennessee River is, but they say it's more'n a hundred rods wide and once was owned by Frenchmen."

"Yes, well—"

"I like French cooking the best in the world, don't you?"

"Well—no, not if—I'd rather have meat cooked without wine—"

"And we have the best fish in the world in that little river out

111

there, and here we are without an almond on the place."

"I—without what?"

"An almond."

"We need those, do we?"

"I should say we do. And we need some sort of person to tell me which mushrooms I can eat and which ones I can't, for I'm tired of wondering and feeding them to my cat. She died, Colonel Wright."

"Who?"

"She curled up on my bed and died one night while my boy and I was asleep. I awoke in the morning and said, 'Silly, you get gone, get off my counterpin.' She wouldn't do it, so I picked her up to put her down on the floor, and she was as limp as that pillow, Colonel Wright, and I thought of my husband and wondered why he wasn't limp like that when he died."

"Uh huh," I said, quite well under her spell, I must say, for her voice was soft and her accent was warm and comforting, nothing hard or sharp, all the corners of every word smoothed off and rounded.

"I had fed her mushrooms."

"What—where did you get them?"

"Oh, in the woods and fields. I have finally proved four kinds are safe to eat, but I walk past mushrooms every day from spring to fall that I have to let lie."

"Yes, we see them in Virginia too—"

"Do you? What are they like?" She sat back now to listen to me tell her about mushrooms in Virginia, I suppose, a most contented look on her pretty face.

"Why it—in Virginia the ground rolls some and has been mostly cleared, up where we are, and the—" I stopped, rather helplessly grasping for a way to describe mushrooms to her.

"You don't mean that's all there is to it, Colonel Wright?"

"I never tried to describe anything in Virginia before," I said.

"My papa used to say Virginia was so proud that they made even the little babies wear shoes in the summertime." She

112

laughed softly and smiled at me, a quick swift smile, showing sound white teeth. "He said it's an embarrassment to tell a Virginian you're from North Carolina."

"Well, we don't rank high socially, that's so."

"My papa says whenever a Virginian wrestles he keeps his watch and chain on."

I laughed out loud.

She cast another quick little smile at me. "He said they never undress without pouring powder down their shirt front first."

"Your papa knows, does he?" I said.

"He is a fine man, but he and I don't speak now."

"You don't speak to him at all?"

"No."

"That's hard to believe, Mrs. Crawford," I said.

She shot a look at me to see if I was serious, and fortunately I was smiling, for a dark look of wrath was settling on those black brows of hers. Slowly she smiled. "I do talk like a mill wheel, don't I? My papa always said I reminded him of a fifty-gallon crock of wine fermenting, for I never got done sizzling and gurgling. He said I was like a lamb that had lost its mama at the fair. He often told me he would give me a penny an hour to hush up."

"Did you make much money?"

"Oh, yes, until as I got older he swore he'd have to pay me more if he was to stay honest with himself, so I got angry and wouldn't take even a cent. And I wouldn't hush up either. But what can a person do that a dog can't, Colonel Wright?"

"Why—I don't know offhand."

"Talk. A dog can bark, but it can't talk, and I say we ought to use our talents. What can run and can't walk, has a tongue and can't talk?"

"I don't think I know."

"A wagon. I know a hundred ninety-three riddles like that which I can tell at a sitting."

"I hope not," I said.

113

"I hate them more'n anything, but that was the way a woman was supposed to be smart. The boys got to go to school, but a woman never even got to learn to write well. We were supposed to sing and be playful around the house and be gracious and entertain the gentlemen with our wit, and I hated it so much I almost died, Colonel Wright, for I always thought I would like to do something with my hands, if not my mind, but neither one was permissible."

"How do you manage up here?"

"Poorly."

"Doesn't Woofer help you at all?"

"Why, yes, he helps me forget. You know how he is, how he arrives and makes it all seem not to matter. He has a wonderful personality." She smiled at me quite frankly.

"Yes, he does. I agree."

"He's a wonderful encourager." She frowned at the wall beyond me. "But he isn't much of a farmer, I fear. And I am hopeless."

"And Mr. Crawford is not one you can look to?"

"I can look to him to end me up in the poorhouse. He takes it all, let me tell you. There's just one ham on a pig when he butchers it. He can count one for me and one for you and two for me and one for you and three for me and one for you, as if that's the way arithmetic is supposed to be."

I laughed, for I knew it was true. Everybody knew the old man stole on occasion.

"He's not going to be allowed in heaven unless he changes his ways before he dies, and him being sixty-nine years old too. Even if my husband was his brother, they never got along, except to drink together. If they drank together they could learn to accept one another unless they drank more'n three drinks each. Then they could be counted on to get into a fight."

"Not a fist fight, surely."

"No, not either one of them would even get out of his chair, but they would bellow at each other and say which one had robbed the other of the most, and how they had not got their even part of the inheritance, and how their older brother had killed himself because of the other brother. You never would have thought that either one of them while they were sitting down and drinking had been at all responsible, but each said the other one had done it all."

"Did he kill himself?"

"Drank himself to death, I'm told, and fell down in front of a stagecoach and was trompt and then run over by the wheels."

"My God."

"It was God watching, for they say the wheels cut his New Testament into bits and somebody said, 'Well, God got even with him.' But I said it was his brothers made him drink so much, and he gambled, and he got into the slave trade for a while, taking slaves from Virginia to Mississippi to be auctioned off. Nobody ought to sell slaves, I say. Let them grow up on their own plantation and marry among themselves and have their children and not none of them be sold, and maybe when they're old let them be freed to go see Raleigh or Richmond, or Washington, D.C., but don't sell a person. I think it's awful the way they take a mama's child away from her, even though nigras don't feel as acutely as a white mother would."

"Don't they?"

"They say not, though how do I know, I not being colored one speck, though I am dark of hair and eyes and my papa used to say I was so black eyed I must be a gypsy, but I'm not. My blood is gypsy-like, he said, and my eyes keep roving, he told me. Can you imagine your own papa talking like that to me when I was no more than thirteen, and then when—well, I tell you, when —" She got so tied up with tension that she ceased to talk at all, and she was twisting her hands nervously, was blinking nervously too, and finally she looked up and said, "Would you like a cup of tea, Colonel Wright?"

I stayed for tea. She and the nigra boiled the water, while I reflected on my impressions of her. She was a woman of extraor-

115

dinary depth of feeling at times, as when she had been talking about her father toward the end of the conversation. And I liked the looks of her. Bright, yes, with a sense of humor, a playful woman stranded on this farm, at nineteen or twenty the widow of a seventy-year-old man, the mother of another man's son, soon to be the mother of a third man's child.

We drank our tea in the kitchen, which was my suggestion, sitting at the big table there. She shooed the nigra woman out of the place. "You go and get your lazy self to your room, for you have about let the fire go out," she said. And she yelled after her, "Can't you keep one fire going if that's all you have to do?" She came back to the table, flopped onto a stool, and poured the tea with an angry motion. "No matches in this house, and I won't borrow from my brother-in-law one thing more, for he keeps a record of it all. He wants to trade me for what I've got. He'll say I owe him so and so, and I tell him no, and he gets furious, for he says I'm merely a slip of a girl and not to defy my elders. Oh, he is a sight, that man."

"I have some matches." I opened the match case on my watch chain. I gave her six matches to keep.

She seemed to be not at all grateful. She laid them aside on the table. "He says my fields should have been plowed under and oats should have been planted and all such as that, which a woman never knows about. I sent my men out to plow a field one day and he come fuming, said, 'For God sake, Sory, they're using the riding hosses.' So I called them in, tears in my eyes, and him saying, 'They've ruined two riding hosses,' and he got mad with them, said by God if they was his they'd be double beat and made to spade that field. He told them to get the oxen to use. He did help me that day and even stayed to lunch, and then he tried to kiss me." She was about in tears, seemed to me. "I never was so mortified as to be caught by that old lecher, and I told him to put his hands in his pockets and tend to his needs that way."

It was embarrassing to listen to her, yet intriguing, of course.

116

I was taken with her rapid changes of mind—

"Men think a woman can be set upon if she's alone. It makes them moist in their palms."

I felt my palms. "Mine are damp now," I admitted.

She laughed. "Oh, some men don't bother me, even with damp palms," she said. "But he did that afternoon. Don't you tell on him."

"Who would I tell? I only know his son."

She threw up her hands. "Oh, law, don't tell his son, and him so proper. My, he came to see me, brought me a pie. It was the first fresh food I'd had in days, and he got to standing around and shifting from foot to foot, but he never fooled me, Colonel Wright, for I don't mind a caller looking at the barns and stock and taking note of what's here, but I do expect him to notice me a particle of the time. My nephew was more attracted to figuring out how my farm could go together with his papa's one day. He took me for granted, as if I was stupid. Do you get that impression from him?"

"Yes, I do," I said.

"Course, he never asked you to marry him, I guess."

I laughed. "No."

"Nor me either. Not yet, but he is assuming it, seems to me."

"I understand."

"And he's never once looked into my eyes, nor held my hand at all, nor held me, which is to be expected. I'm not a virgin, after all. I don't think I'll break if touched. His father did try, and that much is to his credit."

"I hear Woofer tried."

"Tried?" she said, and began laughing, her eyes dancing, pleasure all over her face. "Why, he's the most reckless man in this world. Tried? He's got so many hands a woman can't keep track of where they are or where they're going to fall next. He no more'n gets your name in his mind than he begins to fondle you wherever he can. I slapped him four times and hardly interrupted his conversation. He used to come over here of an eve-

117

ning after most everybody hereabouts was asleep and sit in the rocking chairs in the porch. First night I heard the chair rocking I got nervous as could be, for ghosts do use rocking chairs, you know, that's one way they make their presence known. I found Woofer down there rocking away, and when I said, 'What are you doing here?' he looked up so startled and said he was a young man come to call, and I said, 'Who are you?' and he said he was a Wright, and I said, 'What are you doing on my porch?' and he said he liked to rock and his family always put their rocking chairs up of a night."

"That's true, that's true," I said, laughing.

" 'Why, go get them unput,' I told him. 'My goodness, what are you trying to do, scaring me and my boy to death?' And he got to smiling that flinty smile of his and lifting his head high like a colt and sniffing the air, and he said, 'You got anything to eat?' And I—I said, yes, for he was so clean and nice a man and didn't seem rough by nature. And he wasn't rough. He was like an octopus. When he got into the kitchen he decided to show me how he had once danced a polka in Burnsville. Let me tell you, I tried to dance him out the back door and would have if I hadn't been afraid the nigras would see us and tell the whole world he had been here. So I put up with some of it, even that first visit."

"He came back, did he?"

"Oh, yes. I suppose he's told you about us."

"He said something about a baby might be born."

"Might be born? Why, it's as certain as—as a rocking chair."

"You didn't—not in a rocking chair surely?" I said, amazed. She didn't know what I meant at first, then she guessed what my confusion was. She blushed red in the face and tried not to laugh, but she laughed anyway. "No, we never tried that, though sometimes I would lie awake lonely at night and listen for those chairs to rock out there."

"Then, if there is to be a baby," I said with some difficulty, for I was becoming concerned about this matter, "you will want to get rid of it before it is born?"

She stared at me for a long while. "I will not."

"You want to bear the child?"

"Woofer has never in this world suggested such a thing as getting rid of it."

"I'm only asking, that being a fairly normal occurrence."

"Nothing normal to it. Did Woofer say that to you?"

"Now don't get Woofer into—"

"You tell me."

"No, no," I said.

"Why, he can peddle his wares elsewhere if he comes around here with that argument. I don't ask for quarters from him. I want this baby, for I always have found a baby is the sweetest thing, the way they smile and carry on. I want to show him or her, and I don't care which it is, the wonders of this world before I die, and let him see what beauty is, for they don't know miracles by nature, and you can't see beauty without believing in miracles." She leaned far over the table toward me, passionate in her emphasis. "People don't believe in miracles, that's one trouble with them."

"Well, I—" I said helplessly.

"One has to have faith in what's not so," she said emphatically. "That teacher came in here last winter, teaching our local children that the moon is over 238,000 miles away." She slapped the table with her hand. "It's not, it's not, even if it is."

I was astonished.

"It is not. Say it is not," she said.

"It is not," I said. Then I had to laugh at her, for she was utterly furious, yet beautiful with all that anger settled on those black eyes, her lips pouting, that fierce little tongue ready to uncoil at me. "How far is the moon?" I asked.

"It depends on your moods," she said.

She was a beautiful little body of a woman. Her body and her face and her speech were all rounded.

"Sometimes I think it's near and sometimes I think it's far

away," she said. "I've often seen the moon not more than twice as far as the fartherest tree."

"Well, whatever you say, Mrs. Crawford."

"You call me Sory, will you? Not Mrs. Crawford, for that sounds like somebody's cow."

I laughed.

"And your name is—Owen?"

"Owen."

"I don't want to call you Owen," she said. "I sometimes name people for myself."

"Well, what would you name me?"

"You look a little bit like a sheep dog, with all that hair."

"I meant to get it cut—" I began apologetically.

"I can cut it for you."

"Can you?"

"I will sometime soon, of a daylight. We'll go out in the yard so the hairs can blow away in the wind. What would you call a sheep dog?"

"I had one once called Sam."

"No."

"I had one called Fiddler."

"Why?"

"His tail end wobbled when he walked, like a fiddle sounds. His little butt end vibrated."

She laughed, delighted with that. "I wish I could have a dog like that more'n any other kind I ever heard of. Maybe I could call you Fiddler. You vibrate, do you? Turn around."

"I had a dog named Comfort," I said.

"Oh, that's closer to what I think of when I think of you, for I do get so tired of trying to tell everybody what to do and how to do, when I don't know. I begin to worry, worry all the time, and I do so like to have a man to take over such as this and give me my comfort back again, which is maybe what I ought to call you. But it's too soft for you."

"Yes, I guess so," I said, lost in looking at her. "You can't go

120

back to Raleigh, I suppose?" I suddenly asked her.

"And be put in a drawer, be given a room upstairs in the southeast corner where my mother would tell me the sun is so pretty of a morning, and my son would be assigned a maid and a boy playmate, and I would be assigned a maid, and we would be awakened by them and helped to dress—oh, it is absurd, you know, it is absurd, it is awful, and you want to scream finally and say, 'Let me have that brush' and 'Let me pour that water' and 'Let me cook that chicken.' Which would be so shocking that my mama would die and papa would get to clearing his throat and saying I was always such a dangerous girl, so revolutionary, and that he had predicted a dire end for me. Well, he is not so, for I can read the stars myself, and I have a fine future as long as I don't marry a Virgo."

I roared. I really roared with laughter. "Oh, my God!" I said.

She sat there proud as she could be to have pleased me. She accepted my laughter as high praise and quickly leaned over the table a little ways and touched my arm. "Thank you," she said, her black eyes frankly gazing at me. She sat back and sighed. "We're educated to entertain our men," she said. "Some Southern women are like rivers in the outlands that flow along so smooth, and some are like creeks that are twisty and narrow, and some are like brooks that bubble and spurt and go prettily down over the currents, smashing at this and that, and I'm more like a pool with a waterfall tumbling into it. You don't know me very well yet, and I think even Woofer doesn't know how deep my soul is."

"Doesn't he?"

"I tell him my soul goes way down and to explore it with me, but he doesn't seem to know about that for more than ten minutes. He's a brook type of person, don't you think, bubbly and swift and pretty and sweet. He's a Capricorn."

"Oh, is he?"

"When were you born?"

"December 14th."

"You're a Sagittarius and are supposed to have a deep soul. You doubtless do. The stars are marvelous at knowing about us. Nobody ever takes me seriously enough to suit me, Colonel Wright, for I'm not a ball of fluff, or a playdoll with black eyes stuck onto the front of my face."

"I don't think you are either."

"Though I—do like to play more than anybody in this world. I do, I must say. I'm not so much for music as I am for words. Some people get so excited when they hear music, get to jumping up and down. Woofer does. But I don't care about music much. I'm a word person. I get so excited about people talking and saying things and exploring of one another, I get to jumping up and down, and even when my husband and his brother were being nasty to one another claiming which had killed their brother and which had made their father unhappy and how neither one had ever known a day of love in his life, I would get excited as I could be, for it was fine talk, it was, and all I ever said was, 'My husband knows love and don't think he doesn't for I love him myself and he loves me,' and Eli told his brother, 'She's telling the truth, and the finest hour of my life was marrying her, for she has taught me what love is.' Wasn't that nice of him to say?"

"Was it true?"

"Why, you better believe it was. When I married Mr. Crawford—I always did call him by his full name unless I used his nickname, which I hate to tell you—when I married him I found he didn't even know how to kiss. He knew how to peck my cheek. He never even knew how to kiss a woman's neck or anything."

"I think the war might have changed things a bit—"

"I knew how to kiss before we ever had a war, didn't you? He knew two things. Pecking my cheek was the first one and you can imagine what the second one was, and the second one followed on the heels of the first peck. I finally said to him, 'Mr. Crawford, I'm not a bottle of wine that has to have its

122

stopper pulled and that's all,' which set him to listening finally."

"I—I understand," I said, suspecting that I was red as a beet in my face.

"I said, 'Mr. Crawford, let me see can I put my tongue in your ear?' And when I did it the first time he got up out of that bed like I'd stung him with a pin."

"Well, he was old, I guess."

"His body had not a wrinkle on it, and he was full of life and was sweet as he could be. He was the most kindly, avid student I could imagine, and he got to waking up every morning at the same time and running to the toilet bowl, then he would come back to bed, bringing a glass of wine with him to wash our mouths out, and he would try and be so loving. And he meant it, what he told his brother, for he never even knew how pretty his own roses was until I held them up for him, he never noticed the difference in morning light and afternoon light on his own fields, he never did seem to realize how pretty a joe-pye weed is, or a seed opening. And so we had much to learn in our old age."

"Did he get more youthful?"

"Yes, he did. I thought I'd about overdone it on many a morning. He was old, you know, almost seventy when I married him, and he was seventy-one when he died."

"And you loved him?"

"I—loved him. But it was a disappearing romance, don't you see, because he was not going to live long and we knew that, both of us. Love ought to be nourished over a long period of time. Some men get it in their minds to come dashing in the house and say, 'I love you.' Well, love is steadier, don't you agree?"

"I do. Though maybe I'm not the one to ask now. Woofer knows."

"No, he doesn't," she said. "I tell him it's a long ribbon, life is, and has many colors to it, and even now at nineteen years of age I know one can get caught up and tied by it. I wonder if you understand me?"

"Yes. And Woofer would know—"

"No, I mean you, do you understand?"

I looked into those intense black eyes. "Yes," I said.

At once she smiled. "Then will you stay to supper?" she said.

It didn't much matter to me what we had for supper, for I was so taken with her. In the kitchen I was watching every move she made, every twist and gesture of her body. I said, "Have you got any meat in the house?" and she walked over to the larder and came out with a little joint of beef. She held it by the end of a bone, afraid to get meat on her hands, and I told her to put it on the iron spit before the fire and to put hickory or oak wood on the fire, and I watched her while she did that, and while she wiped her hands clean on her skirt, kept wiping her hands to get the meat off of them. A pretty face to make a sour face with, I thought. "Have you got any butter?" I asked.

She went out the kitchen door and into the springhouse and came back with a mold of butter, and I told her to baste the roast with it and put a pan under the roast to catch the drippings, so she did that, stooping and bending and modestly complaining with little grunts and groans about not knowing what she was doing, and I said, "Do you have pickled beans?" and she went into the pantry, walking around the table, me watching her, and got out a dipperful from a crock and came back, the dipper dripping vinegar on the floor, and I said to put them in a pot, and I said, "Have you got any potatoes?" and she thought about that, then went into the next room and came back with two, so I told her to cut them, and she put her tongue between her teeth and cut the potatoes into hacked off little pieces, the peel left on. I told her to put the potatoes in the pot with the beans.

We ate at the kitchen table.

We had two oil lanterns lit near our plates. We said nothing. I was reading the words of her breathing and she of mine, I suppose. Even when we heard Woofer approaching, neither of

124

us moved at all; we sat there looking at each other, chewing on our food, and when he came in, bustling with fine feeling, letting the cold wind into the warm room, tossing pound molds of fresh liver pudding and sousemeat onto the table, gifts gathered in Hobbs, we continued looking at each other, chewing our food, and when he got to telling us about Billy Furr's threat of another raid we sat there looking at each other, eating, and when he began to gush in praise of the happy fact that Sory and I had at last met, we sat there staring into each other's eyes. He never seemed to realize that we were trapped in a spell.

"You will talk to papa and Mr. Crawford for me, won't you, Owen?" he said. "Won't you?"

I said nothing. She and I went on with our supper.

"Owen?"

"Later, later," I said, a jumble of confusion inside my mind just then.

When at last I got up to leave, I was in such a somber mood I didn't know how to express myself. I said I would show myself out the front way, and she said she would come with me. She brought a lantern and left Woofer in the kitchen eating. I wanted to say something to her at the door, but I couldn't quite get hold of anything. She began to talk to me, patiently, calmly: "Woofer has often told me about you, about how Owen would do this as a boy or do that, how Owen went far into the mountains and tracked the big bears, how Owen shot the last panther to be found up here, how Owen had the prettiest horse and always jumped the pasture gate." She was watching me steadily, smiling, as she talked. "Owen won the foot race when he was only seventeen, and Owen left this valley, which his older brothers could not bring themselves to do, and has been in many battles and has won honors and has slain the enemy. I've heard so much about you and have wanted to be able to invite you to supper ever so many times, and it has been such a pleasure to have had you to supper tonight."

"If I come back and help you with the farm—" I began.

125

"Oh, would you?"

"Yes," I said quickly. "Yes. I will need to come back," I said, backing across the porch, finding my way into her front lawn and hurrying blindly across it toward the bridge, like a boy lost in first love.

The abrupt turning in my life can be measured from my meeting with Sory that night, and arranging other meetings with her at which she and I almost by contrivance managed always to have Woofer present. We talked about her farm, we planned with her workers, we got the slaves' houses cleaned out, we got her spring cleaned out—the first time in years, judging from the mud and dead leaves in the bottom of it,—we got her cattle and sheep put on to proper feed, even though we had to go off in a wagon and buy hay, we got her fences put back up, and yet our minds were constantly on each other, not on these other matters.

There was a place high on the mountain where there was a little vale between the shoulders of two peaks. One morning we decided to go look that over for fence breaks. We walked up there together, she and Woofer and I, and from along the path we could see just about all the valley. It was a majestic site, indeed. I would judge the pasture area to be five acres, and it was well watered. It would be wonderful for a few head of prize cattle in the summer, for it was about 500 feet in elevation above the river and would stay quite cool, even in August. She was radiant that day with excitement, for she had never been up here; she had no idea, nor did Woofer, what she owned, and none of it was marked, except here and there a small pile of stones was set up at a corner or a hacked-out mark was made on a tree. Anyway, we came to this vale, but it was on the opposite side of her snake fence, so it was on the neighbor's property, that of Abel Crawford, which we deeply regretted. We walked into his pasture and complained about his owning it. From there we looked down at papa's house and the church and Elvir Plover's place and the German's, and downriver for a mile or two at several twisty roads going off the main road here and there and reaching back into the coves for some more families, and up on the opposite range we could see several clearings, one of them the clearing I had made seven or eight years before. The sight of it depressed me, for it had been a shivering time of hard labor for me. The thud of the axhead and maul were still in my mind, the crackle of fire burning, the fallen trees and limbs. In the tired evenings my muscles ached, even in the second year of it, and Morla and I saw changes in terms of what last year's desperate plight had been or what next year's desperate hopes were, we measuring change by year, not days, but we worked each day as if we never would need strength to work another one.

I was sitting on the ground near Sory, telling her about it, watching her hair blow in the wind, wondering about her infatuation with me and when it would end, must end, and mine with her. Now and then she would glance at me and my mind would panic for an instant, for I could all too well read the longing of her glances and dared not see into her mind or my own. I even took comfort from the lingering looks she gave Woofer, and I noticed jealously but with delicious pleasure how she laughed at his jokes and funny expressions and stayed close to him, sat close to him even now.

"Woofer, you see anything out of the way about this field?" I asked him suddenly. "Do you, Sory?" I asked.

They made guesses about what I might mean, she poor ignorant dear guessing that "those green squirrels' nests in the border trees" were what I meant—those nests being mistletoe, not nests at all.

"It's that snake fence," Woofer said at last.

I laughed, pleased with him, then he laughed, too. He was bright as a whip or he wouldn't have guessed it so soon. We three made a tour of the other side of the field and found the place where the snake fence had rested before Abel Crawford had moved it. We saw where the bottom rails had lain on the rocks and where the weeds and little trees had got their start near them. The fence where it now stood had no growth around it at all.

Woofer went to fetch the two male workers, but Sory and I started moving the fence at once. A chestnut rail even ten or eleven feet long weighs only a few pounds; it's a light wood, indeed. So she could drag a rail with each hand, and I could carry a bundle of them. I showed her how to build the fence in a zigzag pattern, each rail slightly overlapping the ones on either side of it, and set at an angle to them. One has to build the fence a layer at a time, from the first layer on up to the fourth, and in some places the fifth. Sory had never made a fence before, and she was delighted with her success at it.

We sat down to rest after a while, and I noticed she sat off a little distance from me. It mattered to me at the time, for I was alert for any sign of interest. I hungered for such signs, and feared them desperately. She started asking again about my farm, which I suppose was an idle diversion, and I told her about my work, then she mentioned my wife and I told about her, and about burying her. "That was the last work I did on that farm. I dug a deep hole for her in the red clay, in among the sharp teeth of the rocks."

"What did you bury her in, Owen?" she said.

"I left her in what she had on. I was ashamed to undress her."

"I meant what coffin did you use?"

"I took the doors off the house and the shed and took those apart for their planks."

"If you used the doors ..." she said, and her voice trailed off in a moan and she sat there fretting, frowning at the place where the grave was. "Is the grave near that apple tree?"

"Directly below it," I said. "That tree has got grown since I left."

"I know what it is to lose a part of yourself," she said. "This past year many a time I would be sitting in a rocker and I would

be unhappy and lonely and realize I was waiting for Mr. Crawford to come home. At night I would be so lonely I would want
to break ever dish in the house and I would spank my boy over
most nothing."

"You had all those slaves to be with."

"Yes, they're company; they go and come and shut the
doors," she said. She broke a stick and threw the pieces away.
"You want to drag more rails?" she said.

"What about your first man, Sory?" I said, approaching the
subject casually, as if maybe I would soon forget I had asked her
at all.

"I don't even know where he is," she said. "He was a neighboring boy and he did what he wanted to and went away and
his papa said he didn't know what ever happened to Jimmy.
Which I suppose was not the truth."

"Did he cause a loneliness too?"

"He did. It hurt. I broke one cup when he went off, and I cried
for a day, that's all."

"But it's not like something missing, is it, from yourself, and
you keep meaning to find it again, and every so often the awareness comes to you that it's gone from you and won't come back
again."

"And can't be found again," she said quietly. We looked at
each other across a little distance. She didn't turn away, but
when I spoke her name she said nothing.

"Maybe it can be found for me," I said, watching her, but
when she said nothing, when she gave me no encouragement,
I tore myself free of her and stumbled across the field to the
fence and sat down there, my mind, my body weak from its own
conflict within itself.

She came to me finally. She stopped about ten feet away from
me. "Life gets crooked like a road sometimes, I know, especially
with friends," she said wistfully, "but we're neither of us ever
going to hurt Woofer, are we?"

I said nothing.

129

"It's all so pretty up here, Owen," she said. A long while she stood there staring off at the valley, I watching her. "Woofer takes so long to go do anything, you know it," she said. "He gets so engrossed in whatever he does." She was standing stiffly erect, her voice calm and simple, a flatness to the sounds of it. "I know you must get tired of waiting for him, for he can't seem to get anything done for contemplating the marvels of what he has to do."

"Do you love him, Sory?"

"I do love him, yes."

"Why do you mention his faults so much, why to me?"

"I love his faults," she said simply.

"But why to me?" I said.

"You're his brother," she said.

"Is that the only reason?" I said.

"I don't know all the reasons there are," she said.

"You know if there are others," I said.

"Yes, there are others."

"How do you feel toward me?" I said softly, scarcely daring to breathe.

"Why, I'm fond of you," she said. After a moment, she said, "I love you." And as I looked at her, she said, "Owen, I'm afraid I love you more than I meant to." She shook her head suddenly and abruptly began to talk. " 'If love is all one goes to bed with, it's a chilly night soon in that house,' my father used to say. Love won't hold up under more than a few tests by itself. It's all so sweet and hurtful to talk about, don't you agree? And I have already made all the mistakes a woman can make by nineteen." When she saw me about to come to her she walked out into the field several steps away. "We ought always to see everything from up high like this; it does level out the problems so much from up here, for nothing appears to ripple at all. It's chilly up here, don't you agree? I suppose it gets so cold up here even of a summer night that a body would need to be married to keep warm, or to have several babies one. I suppose we ought all of us to learn to ride the crest of it, Owen, to go with the current like dear Woofer does, don't you agree? Life is a river; didn't I tell you once it was a river?"

"It was a valley a moment ago," I said.

"I don't know what it is. I know it comes on me cruelly when I'm with you and is worse when I'm not with you."

Woofer came up the trail kicking at rocks and sticks and whistling. He had gone to fetch two men; he came back with all eleven Negroes, even the five children, with an oxcart and two oxen, and with bread and ham enough for everybody. Soon we were cooking and laughing—the others were laughing, anyway. I was in a despondent, solemn mood, and so was Sory. Now and then we would exchange glances, I from over to one side of the group and she from where she sat with Woofer, who was declaring happily that he had never felt any better than he did today, nor had he seen a prettier place than this field, which we had just reclaimed from our friendly adversary.

Each day I went to see her. Sometimes we would talk frankly about our predicament. We could see traces of human destiny in it, we decided. Man is sad by nature, I contended. Sometimes I would go alone down to the river, to the place where she had met Woofer occasionally; I would go to their trysting place and sit on the bank of the river and shiver in the cold, staring at that clear, icy water, lobbing pebbles into it to assuage my discontent. She never came to me, though once as I left the place and was walking into the beech woods, I heard a pebble plop into the stream, and I turned as if burned by fire. She was not in sight, yet there was a ripply place where a stone had landed in a pool—or a trout had jumped—who could say? There was at least a chance she had come to watch me, maybe to meet me, and in a fit of need I waded into that cold river saying her name; and when I got to the middle of it, the water up to my waist, my teeth chattering, her name almost frozen as it formed on my lips, I began to curse her profanely, a siege of anger overcame

131

me and I went charging across and up the other bank and stormed full of desire through that thicket, pushing saplings out of my way.

Until spent, weary, gasping I sank down on a rock in the sun at the edge of a field, my body trembling from my plight of the soul, and whether she was in that woods or not I didn't know. When later I mentioned going there she said nothing at all and only the tiniest frown indicated that maybe, maybe, maybe she knew more than she would say to me.

CHAPTER SEVEN

Captain Crawford and the conscription major, a peevish sort of fellow named Morgan, sent militia troops one place then another, and by the end of the first week I was home they had about fifteen men who had agreed to serve if their brothers would be left alone, or if somebody could be found to look after their stock or their mother or their children or whatever, most of them poor men dragging a living out of the begrudging soil. I added to the lot a few men who had volunteered: Elvir Plover, the fiddle player, and his son Victor, the drummer, and a man named McIlvenna, who played the bagpipes; he was over sixty years old—he had forgotten the exact number of years. "I don't think I'm too old for the war, if you don't," he told me. So we took him in and asked him to stand ready to go with us to Richmond in a week or so. I had talked with many other men and had got them halfway interested, men who would come by to see papa on business; many of them owed papa money. But papa would talk them out of volunteering before they walked to the road gate. Not much military business could be done around that house when he was about. He would wave them on their way and would come up the walk to sit down in the rocker next to mine, there on the front porch, and we would talk, never mentioning the army or the war, not often arguing, but each of us probing the other a little bit in difficult areas of the heart. "You know, Owen, I can sit here of an evening and worry, and not know what to do about it, or even what I'm worrying about. Now Hal King is home and courting Nell, and I'm half glad he is and halfway panicked by it, for she's my only daughter and I hate to have her gone from here."

"You can't run the lives of the whole world, papa," I said.

"Yes, I agree the world has about left me behind, but I lay claim yet to my daughter. There was a time when no major business was done in this place without my having a nodding acquaintance with what was going on; now the men ride out at night to bring everybody to one opinion, and nobody asks me for my own. Even my own sons."

"Even Jesse, you mean?"

"Even Jesse, who used to ask me about his ventures. And I saw you talking to Phillip about some secret matter or other."

"I was asking him why he always courts his girl away from the house."

"I wish you'd leave well enough alone, Owen. I do, I do. I get nervous seeing him with that Plover girl anyway. Did you have anything to do with this Hal King coming home?"

"No, no," I said.

"The Plovers and Kings. My Lord save us. Those families have no money. And why have you got Woofer over there at that widow's house all the time? Sory Crawford—my Lord in heaven. I saw him over there three, four times, sneaking through her back yard."

"It's not my affair to talk about, papa," I said.

"I tell you, when the chickens come home they fill up all the poles. I said before you arrived that you'd bring winds of change that would topple everything."

"I haven't done anything, papa."

"We've got raiders riding up and down through Hobbs, Andrews, claiming to represent both sides. Lord, what is this world coming to? Let the war stay in the outlands, for God sake." He sat there fiddling his thumbs, his hands laid on his belly, his eyes looking at the road where just now the miller's oldest son came hurrying along, his head bent low and his shoulders huddled down into his leather coat, a mist flailing him gently.

"I could die today, I expect, if I exerted myself to it, Owen.

134

I can feel it when it draws close, and I know I can touch it most any time I want to, but I would like to get everything in order first."

"I understand," I said softly. "Your brother Bee, what sort of man was he?" I asked.

There was a long quiet; not even his chair creaked. "His boy's in Ohio or Pennsylvania, last I heard, was engineering something up that way. I don't hear from him."

"Did your brother have similar characteristics to me, would you say?"

"Why in the world would you ask that?"

"You never got close to him, did you?"

He stared at me, impressed by such a bald confrontation. "I suppose it's true, Owen, that I never could get close to him."

"Or trust him?"

"I'll—I'll do my own talking. Or trust him."

"Or trust me?"

"Now I—I do trust you, Owen."

"But not like Jesse or Phillip?"

"Well, Phillip is a special case. I favor Jesse over you because I'm a fool for those who stay home, Owen, and don't go changing places about the countryside. Nothing grows without roots." He ran his fingers through his fine, thin hair, all the while his blue eyes studying me. "A family's land is the basis of aristocracy, the foundation of government, especially up here, and it wouldn't do to break up this farm. A farm like this bleeds if cut."

"But you have five children, papa, not one."

"I have one farm, though, one chance of letting one of them carry on some sort of order here."

"But even you can't do that from this farm, don't you see? Didn't you say the people don't ask your opinion now?"

"Well, a pendulum swings. It will come around again." For a long while he sat there considering that, then quietly he said, "My father willed the place to me, even though Bee was more —was brighter in many ways. Bee was hurt, but he was better able to do for himself, to make his way. All I knew then or know

now, Owen, is this one speck of the world. I experiment with it, but damn my hide, Owen, I resent changing anything one bit, so I experiment to prove the old way is best, don't you see? I'm too much one to hold onto what I know to be secure. But now it's breaking up, the family, the community. The country has split up somewhere hundreds of miles away, and the reverberations are splitting us here, down to the core of my house, down to the kitchen table when we sit to eat our supper together as a family." Very tired, quite heavy now his head. His eyes were more moist and rheumy than usual too. He blinked at me, somewhat apologetically, and abruptly he made a futile gesture with his hands. "I—will go see if your mama has got a roast cut," he said.

It hurt me to be set aside by him. I could imagine myself leaving the army, letting the conscriptors flounder, freeing myself from the war, even now, but there was no prospect for me here, that was the point of it. Unless, of course, I were to take Woofer's widow from him.

Next day the men at the mill were talking about a Negro man being hanged. He was a runaway from nearby, and the Rebel raiders captured him and strung him up. It was a needlessly brutal act. They were seeking brutality, seemed to me—a sign that the war's violence was taking hold here. One of the men had been at Andrews and he told about the hanging, repeating the story every time another person arrived. I sat out in the yard myself, listening to a tinker talk, a skinny, thieving sort of fellow who sold what he could scrounge; yes, and he could sharpen scissors and do such odd jobs about and around. Some said he could see visions.

"I wouldn't go back to that there war this year, if I was you, Cunnel," he told me. "Dangers multiply, if a man but watches the signs. All you need to do is read what they tell us plain as day."

Several of us were sitting around listening to him.

"Buzzards are flying over fields with no dead lying in them. They tarry o'er ary field they come to unseemly long. Chairs move theirselves of a night and voices on the peaks are clear to wail. There's been black clouds on ever moonlit night in January. No, I'd not fight wars this coming spring. Let them wait a year, till the signs are better for it."

I laughed, delighted with that proposition, yet not unconcerned about what he said. I suppose I never have been able to forsake completely a belief in spirits and such mysteries.

The miller and an old man named Willis, gray-bearded, gray-haired, began talking about politics; always there were men talking at the mill and the forge about politics and the war. "The Confederacy is needed to hold us together so we won't be attacked by England," the miller said. He was sitting on the tailgate of a wagon; no chair was ever big enough for him—he weighed over 250 pounds.

"What makes you think England is going to attack us?" old Mr. Willis asked respectfully.

"They done it once, didn't they?" the miller said.

"Well, England ain't within five hundred miles of here, is it?" a tall, lean man named Newman said.

"Neither is Washington," somebody else said.

"Richmond is," Newman said. "Richmond is not far—I mean as a bird flies, is it?"

"You know anybody that travels like a bird flies?" old man Willis said.

"Richmond is almost as far as Washington," somebody said. "Where is Richmond?"

"It's in Virginia," the miller said.

"Is everything in Virginia?" Newman said, cocking his head to one side, frowning critically. "Washington is in Virginia, ain't it?"

"It's next to Georgetown," the miller admitted.

"Look here, we got two national governments in Virginia," Newman said.

"Might as well join those two, I'd say," Mr. Willis said, a smile on his face, "and go on with the Union."

The miller snorted contemptuously. "What makes you think you can put the two parts back together, now that there is no Union?"

"Well, what makes you think you can make a confederacy hold together when a union can't?" Mr. Willis said.

"Listen at pop," Newman said. "He pinned you to the wall that time," he said to the miller.

"Pinned him to that there wagon bed," somebody else said, and laughed sharply.

All of which infuriated the miller. "It's part of God's plan for there to be independent states," he said in a flurry of anger. "There never was a united states, but always there was independent states and that's what the word united meant, was that the states had agreed to be united, although they was to remain independent."

"Well I declare," Mr. Willis said.

The miller waved his arm at him, dismissing him angrily. "The Confederacy is the accurate version of the United States," he said, "a confederation of independent states."

Old man Willis shook his head. "Well, are they any more confederated than they were united?" he asked.

"You have no more sense of patriotism than a dog," the miller said bluntly.

"Now, now, have we got so we can't talk any more, Charlie?" old man Willis said, all rather plaintively, I thought.

Murmuring about traitors, the miller managed to get to his feet and wobble off into the mill, which was clanking and grinding now, his son tending it. Mr. Willis looked after him, a sad expression on his face, his tongue tut-tutting in regret. "It's easier to talk over at the forge, I believe," he said. He took a big handkerchief out of his pocket and wiped his face with it. He belched. "Cunnel, does patriotism require that a man stop using logic?"

"It tends to hold anybody to a position, whether he understands why or not," I said.

"I suppose you need a lot of it in the war?"

"We have all kinds of men," I said simply.

"It's got so here a man can't talk freely. And even in trading, some men won't trade with me now, and on this past Saturday a group of young fellows come here to the field, and instead of running and wrestling with each other as usual, they split up along political lines. My boy come home singed, and I said what in the world happened to you, and it seems like they had got to fighting and some boys were thrown into fires, or fell into them. My, my. Friends, cousins, brothers, and I wonder if you can't use your influence to get us calm again, Colonel?"

He looked at me with such trust that I felt awkward about it, and guilty. I told him I didn't know what to do about anything as complicated as this or know what I could bring myself to do. "We all get trapped by one duty or another these days," I told him.

"Now not far away they killed that colored boy last night," he said. "Why did they do that?"

"Hateful, hateful," I said.

"We keep the blacks on the far side of the river; over on this side it's free—at least, that was the agreement made some time ago. Yet it was men from the free side that killed the nigger. You know the Bible says as we approach the last days and the coming of the Lord there'll be confusion in the land."

"It's about time for the Lord to come back then," I said gently.

"Oh my, yes. For there's hate abounding. I think, Colonel, we've played the fool to get mixed up with governmental differences, for we don't need much national government—about all it does is set the tariffs. I admit they set them unfairly for us as a region. And the North did get itself riding on a moral fever about slavery; some of the leaders couldn't wait for the crop to grow—they got like a farmer who plants corn the first Monday of May and begins to crop it the following weekend, which only means he plows it up again. Well, a man like that is a fool in farming, but he's sometimes a saint in politics."

"I understand," I said.

"No offense, Colonel," he said quietly.

"No offense," I said.

He was done apparently, but for a while longer he crouched there. The miller came back outside to take the sun. He stood in his doorway, just about filling it, and squinted at the fields and at a man named Murphy who had hung half a beef from a limb near the road, where he was selling and trading pieces of it. "You need that butcher in the army to be a surgeon, Colonel," somebody said.

I laughed.

The miller abruptly said, "There are many men who talk idly about slavery, don't they, Colonel?" He was frowning at Mr. Willis.

"I haven't heard anybody around here," I said.

"Abraham, Isaac, and Jacob was slaveholders," he said. "The apostle Paul sent a runaway slave home to his master, by the name of Philemon. And the same book of the Scriptures teaches the duties of master and slave, as well as the duties of parent and child, husband and wife—"

"Yes, well, it can be debated every which way," I said, interrupting, trying to stop the hurt he was inflicting on Mr. Willis. "If I thought this war was being fought to keep slavery, I wouldn't fight in it myself," I said.

The miller frowned at me accusingly, baffled by me, no doubt at a loss to know how to claim I was unpatriotic. He went on back into the mill, I suppose to debate it in loud arguments, for the clanking of his machinery would drown out whatever crude and angry comment he might make.

Mr. Willis sighed. He sniffed the air, the clean, fresh air, warmed just now by the sun. Somebody said, "If it wasn't slavery, Colonel, what was it?"

140

"Nobody thought the other side would fight," I said. "It all got started before anybody knew where the road went, and now we don't know where it ends, for it continues year after year."

"Are we winning it?" somebody said. Everybody was quiet now, as if we were talking about the dead, or some holy matter.

"We're winning the battles," I said, "but we're strangling. The Yanks have a navy larger than all the other navies of the world combined, and we can't seem to break it open well enough to supply ourselves, so we win battles and it gets harder and harder to breathe. Our machinery is busted, our supplies are gone entirely, and our troops are hungry men on the road. Every battle takes some of us away."

We sat there for a while, a gusty wind suddenly blowing in from the north mountain, which papa owned. Three or four men joined us, then wandered on into the building. A man named Fletcher arrived; his wagon had been dribbling corn all the way from home, as he found out now, and two chickens had followed him, so he wanted to sell the chickens or trade them. "They're corn fed," he told us, and everybody got to laughing with him.

"What is California doing, Colonel?" old Mr. Willis asked me quietly.

"I don't think the war's stirring much way out there," I said.

"How long would it take a man to get out there?" he said.

"From spring till fall," I said.

"My my, what a big country we have. It's no wonder we have differences. How far is West Virginia then?"

"Why, it's not anything like as far. It's a few days north of here. Maybe a week walking."

"Are there mountains up there, as I've heard?"

"Yes, though not as high as these."

"Is the water pure?"

"Yes, it is," I said.

"The people stand with the Union, I understand."

"Since the war started," I said. "When Virginia left the Union

141

those mountain counties up in there left Virginia, they seceded, too."

"Seeded?" he said.

"Seceded," I said. "So Virginia sent General Lee up there to get them back, and they beat him time and again."

"Not the same General Lee that now commands the whole army, is it?"

"Yes. They beat him every time, for he was lost in formalities, I suspect, and those mountain soldiers fought a better way."

"Can a man reach West Virginia by following the mountain ridge?" Mr. Willis asked.

"Don't go, don't go," I said. "People here don't offend you too much, do they?"

"They've always been patient with differences here," he said, "until here lately. Even when the first boys were brought back and buried, we all went to the service together, whether the boy was for the Union or the South. But now it's one thing or the other; some families are split down the middle like an oak log."

"Two different kinds of thread can be woven into a single piece of cloth," I said.

"But it takes a weaver," he said gently. "Maybe if you came home and helped, Colonel. It will take someone like you." He was done, apparently, but for a while longer he waited there, then rather plaintively, as he looked out over the field to the river, he said, "I admit to loving the Union, Colonel."

I was moved by the simplicity of the statement, and of course I knew what he meant. Even in battle whenever I had seen the Union flag, a nostalgia had afflicted me, and the first time I had fired at the Union army, a sudden awakening had come to me and I found myself even in battle demanding that I explain the nature of my allegiances. I had grown up respecting the government and knowing that the United States was my country, but when the Union had dissolved, I had clung to that part of it which was my own, the part which fell to me.

I spent an hour at the mill, then went over to the smith's and

142

listened to the men talk there; then I went toward Sory's house, debating with myself about whether I ought to go visit her or not. She was even closer to my feelings than was the war or politics or old men's dreams broken. I had a continuing, lingering need to consider her, to see her, hopefully to talk with her, touch her, and as I approached I saw her out by the stable—I believe she saw me for she put her hand to her brow to shade her eyes from the sun and looked toward me—but old Mr. Crawford and his son, the Captain, were sitting on their porch watching me, and the old man called out in a croaking voice for me to "come join, come join." So I had no choice except to join them and to listen to him explain why the Captain should be advanced to major.

Of course, I promised to consider it, and I praised the Captain's loyalty, which served further to embarrass him.

The two of them were troubled even more than usual, for they had received a report that last night, a Tuesday, a group of forty Yank sympathizers had raided in Avery County, stealing horses and cattle and had beat up an old man named Even Lance and left him in his barnyard unconscious.

"They kill him?" I asked.

"No. He recovered."

"Might be better to pass the rumor that they killed him," I said.

We sat quietly for a while. I looked at the river, remembering old man Willis, the patience in his eyes and voice, the hurt feeling that any animosity had crept into this valley.

Mr. Crawford was staring at me critically, curiously. "What do you say, Colonel?" he said, leaning toward me. "What say?"

"If we plan to conscript up here we'll have to make the climate suited for it," I said. "You can't use troops until the climate demands it." Poor man, I thought, poor old man; the winds are rising, he had said. "It's a pity," I said.

Old man Crawford squinted at me suspiciously. "You are a stern man," he said respectfully.

143

I said to the Captain, "You'll need to move it along, if you want to send troops in here to put down the violence." I said, "We have little time left."

"Yes, we can say he was killed, Skip," the old man said to the Captain. "The Colonel is entirely right about it."

And wrong about it, I thought, inside my damnable soul. I sat there for a while longer, and when they brought me a drink of whiskey, I drank with them. By now Sory had come down from the stable and was walking to the river with Eli; I watched her walk, knowing she knew I was sitting on the Crawford porch, knowing she knew I was watching her. I waited until she had gone back to her house before I left the Crawfords and went home.

I believe Jesse was active in some of the Yank raids, although he denied it whenever papa asked him about it. I think the smith was leading the Yank raiders and Jesse was second or third in command, but I'm not sure of it. The smith's brother was active, too, recruiting volunteers for the Yank army. So our family and the smith's were heavily engaged, and when Billy Furr's men finally rode into our valley they stopped first at our house and asked for Jesse.

I was with Woofer, having supper with Sory in her kitchen. We were in the kitchen by the fire, which was crackling hickory wood and spitting sap, for we had to burn half-dried wood at her place. I didn't hear the riders arrive, even though there were thirty or forty of them.

It was about eight o'clock at night, full dark at this season.

Papa told them Jesse was not home. The raiders asked him to take the oath to the Confederacy, but he said no, he wouldn't take any oath at all to anything, that he had given two sons to the Confederacy and that was enough. The raiders then told Phillip to take the oath, and Phillip considered it and said he would rather not, but when Sole McKinney shouted at him to take it or suffer the house being burned down, Phillip raised his

144

right hand and swore allegiance to the Confederate States of America without a qualm, for it didn't make much difference to him one way or the other.

Vaguely unhappy with his prompt compliance, the raiders rode on down to the smith's house, which was next door to the forge. There they were told that the smith was not home. No doubt he and Jesse were off converting some Rebel farmer to a Union disposition. The smith's two teen-age sons were there, and they took the oath; the oldest was fourteen, as I recall. Then the raiders found the smith's brother sitting in the bedroom, and they pushed him out onto the porch and told him to raise his hand and take the oath. He stood on the porch in the lamplight glaring at them defiantly, his big hands folded into fists; he was well over six feet tall and was a heavy man, overweight by forty, fifty pounds, and he had been a smith for about twenty years down near Marion. His name was Rog Roberts.

Directly four or five men got angry enough to come onto the porch and try to capture him. They subdued him, and Sole McKinney told the others to lead him to the barn.

The woman and one boy went into the kitchen and began to pray, and the other boy walked after the raiders' horses, berating them in a loud voice. I wish he had done something more productive. I wish he had sounded an alarm. I could have stopped them, I believe. But, instead, the boy harassed the raiders, that was all.

"Put him agin the barn," Sole McKinney said, which they did, and they brought their lanterns up close and shone them on Rog, and one of them said, "Repeat after me: I swear allegiance ..."

Not a word from Rog Roberts. He sucked at a tooth and spit. The boy came forward and took his place beside him, stood against the barn, but the raiders shoved him out of the way.

"I swear allegiance ..." they said.

No words from Rog at all, except that he said, "You let my hands go untied and you won't bother me," which was the truth,

I suspect, but it didn't leave the men in a more conciliatory mood.

Billy Furr said, "Why are we up here at the barn, Sole?"

"He's going to take the oath," McKinney said, "or I'll nail him to the side of his barn as if'n he was a skin."

"The hell you will," Billy said, astonished.

"They killed a man a few nights ago," McKinney said.

"Now, I'm in charge here—" Billy began.

"Hold up his left hand agin that log wall," McKinney said, and two of the raiders did so while from his saddle bag McKinney got a hammer and four long nails. He showed Rog the nails. "I've nailed many a bear and coonskin to my barn down home, and I'll nail you, and don't think I'm joking with you, for I'm tired of the smith and his family being agin this country. If you don't like this country, you can git to the North." He put a nail against Rog's palm. "Now take the oath. Give him the oath, Ernest."

"I pledge allegiance ..." the man named Ernest began.

No sound from Rog, so with a wallop McKinney drove the nail into the log, through Rog's left hand, and Rog roared in astonishment and pain, and the little boy came up off the ground like a tiger and had to be caught by two men and thrown back out of the way.

"Now, that's enough," Billy Furr shouted at McKinney, his voice trembling. Several others of the raiders said that was enough.

"Take the oath," McKinney said, his face up close to Rog's face, which was coated in sweat now, twisted with pain. "What say?" McKinney said.

Rog would not say a word. So McKinney backed off and walked about, caressing his face with his left hand, swinging his hammer, caught up in a moral fervor. "All we want is to have our own way of life and the smith's people take the slaves through to the North and recruit for the North. Now all I want is for him to take the oath, ain't it?"

146

Billy said, "You've done enough, Sole."

But one of the other men said the Yank raiders had killed a man, "and we've not killed one yet."

"Let him take the oath," McKinney said. "I'm not being unreasonable." He came in to Rog Roberts again, and Rog spit in his face, so McKinney told his henchmen to hold the right hand against a log, which they did. Billy Furr and many of the raiders said not to go any further with it, but without hesitation McKinney drove a nail through that hand too.

The little boy passed out. The smith's wife came screaming up to where her brother-in-law was standing, his face contorted horribly, blood flowing out of both palms and running down his great arms, and she turned on McKinney and began to tear at him with her fingers. She was pulled off and held, and by now everybody was in a turmoil and Billy was saying it was his orders that the men ride away. McKinney told him to ride wherever he pleased, but that he was not done yet.

The whole lantern-lighted scene was moving now into an incredible nightmare, even beyond horror really. Apparently McKinney told two men to hold one of Rog's shoes against the log, with the sole of the shoe against the log, and he leaned down and put a nail in place and shouted, "Take the oath," and when he heard nothing he drove the nail through the foot. The woman screamed hysterically and tore at the men holding her, and the other boy came out of the house, called by the screams, to try to see what was going on. In the confusion, basted with disbelief, the raiders saw two men hold Rog's other foot off the ground even as he shouted a clear, shrill bellow from a mass of pain, and McKinney drove a nail through that foot, too, then stood back to survey his handiwork, this big smith writhing in agony on the log wall, he stood there contemplating it even as Billy pulled at him and shoved him and got him mounted finally and led his men out of there, all of them terror-driven by their own daring, dazed, even McKinney frightened by his audacity.

Leaving the pitiful man wretchedly hanging, bleeding

147

and weeping, on the logs in the moonlight.

The woman, sobbing, crawled to him, tried to see if she could free his feet. The nails were in logs, not planks, and had been driven in all the way. The youngest boy, thirteen, screamed, disbelieving what he saw even as he stared in horror at it. The other boy managed to rise from the ground. He tried to lift his uncle, to lift his weight off the nails. Rog's blood flowed down over both of them. Finally, finally the younger boy went stumbling, running, screaming to the church and rang the bell, and we heard it even as we finished supper.

Hal, Woofer, and Captain Crawford were busy the next day with a frenzy of activity, for nobody in any valley was any longer opposed to conscripting the Rebel raiders, conscripting them by force and taking them off to the regiment. There was no public outcry from anybody even when the militia began taking both the Rebel and the Yank raiders, for we could not leave one here to prey on helpless people, the militia Major said. He had no opposition, really. He did have the problem of a dozen raiders who could not be found, and these he listed as wanted. One of them was Jesse.

His men also rounded up deserters, eight or ten—there were many more who could not be found—and put them in with the others and sent them off to Marion, to the railhead; and they took in twenty volunteers. I got packed to leave and so did Woofer, he in anguish because he had not married yet, and Nell was complaining, weeping even as she talked with me about Hal leaving. I told them the swirl of the war had caught us up and there was no way to subdue it, it had caught all of us, I said, and it was true even papa was in a state of confusion and doubts now. His house was quiet, as if in mourning, and whether it was mourning for the dead days now recognized to be gone, or for Jesse, or for that agonized man who lay in heat-sweat in his brother's bed not far away, I don't know—maybe for all of them. As for me, I was desperate to be gone, to keep myself from a

148

deep blunder which would suffocate me and harm others severely, and I was anxious to go before Woofer could marry her —I had myself delayed their wedding in every way I could; I could not stand to think of him marrying her.

What a pitiful bundle of inconsistencies I was just then. And the afternoon before we were to leave I even sent Woofer off to Andrews on a venture. It was nothing that needed doing. There were three deserters there of a single family, I told him, and maybe they could be found. My Lord, there were many more than three most everywhere. I sent him away, knowing even then what I was about, courting the inviting thought of it, and when he was gone I bathed in the washroom off the kitchen and put on one of Jesse's shirts and his pants to wear while Nell washed mine. I sat on the porch for a while, and one would think I had no plans for the day; oh, I had plans but I would not admit to them or debate them. When I walked down to the bridge I didn't admit even to myself where I was going. I moved casually, not asking myself if I was about to do what I found myself doing. I crossed the bridge and went on up through her yard and around the back of her house, looking at the house, the barn, the Negroes as they watched me, no doubt speculating about me and what I might be planning here alone. I let myself in at the kitchen.

The little black woman was in there creeping about in the dark. When I spoke gruffly to her, she picked up Eli and hurried outside.

I called Sory's name. How evenly and softly it rested on the lips and voice, I thought, how steady your voice this morning, Owen. I heard her on the stairs. She came barefooted through the dining room, wearing a long, plain white dress which clung to her breasts and hips. She stopped in the doorway, her black eyes somberly studying me, seeking maybe in my expression a further revelation about the matter which most of all concerned both of us. Her mouth was open as if in wonder or sighing.

"I sent Woofer away for a while," I said.

149

One white hand held to the doorframe near her face, and she leaned her cheek against it. "Owen, did you come to say good-by to me?" she said.

"Yes, and it will be for a long while, Sory, for I don't see how I can come back again," I said. At once I took her in my arms, and she came against my body and held to me and we swayed against one another for a moment, and I carried her up the stairs and to her bed, her arms around me, her face pressed against me.

The ways of love are numerous as sands; at least, I have never known two women who are alike, nor two acts of love which are identical, nor even moments of love that are the same. Our touching, holding, kissing, struggling had no pain of body to it, nor pain of heart or soul. There was unspoken understanding in her hand which touched my body, and my nerves came alive with her fingers and I held her face in my palm and touched her throat. Her breasts were under my fingers, she as close as her breasts to me, her thigh to me, she rising to touch and kiss me, to smell and lick me, to caress and hold me closer to her, as we made our decision, without mind or wonder, to come still closer together. We clung to one another, held each other, our passions rising in a wedding of our past lives; tenderly she received me, completely I took her to myself and owned her as my own dear wife and life for a moment, my dead wife and life, she compassionate, I as passionate as ever I had been before, she eager, inviting me, persuading me with her fingers, her lips, her teeth biting her lips, using her gasps and sighs, her cry, her cries, her black eyes awakening behind her half-closed lashes, her teeth moist, her tongue warm on me, in me, her voice soft on me, in me, her voice, her life and mine joined once, twice into unidentical knots which excluded everything else, others, even those parts of ourselves which could not come together in union, our embraces culminating the past and excluding future time, and there was no thought to wonder, there were no considerations, there was no judgment beyond this judgment which was from life itself in court assembled, no comment beyond her hands warm on my body, her body warm on my body, under my body, her arms and legs around me, her face close, her voice softly asking, please, asking please, and there was no next hour or even moment, for now, dear, was all time in a small place compressed, assembled.

A man can find himself in a woman, though not with any woman, not with very many, I judge, for the true mating of two people is possible only if one's mate knows one's own feelings, losses, regrets, wild exaggerations of hopes, fancies, longings. A man can find himself in a woman only if she has already seen the reflection of his life through her own. As a woman harbors a child's body in her body, so she can, if she has the ways and pities and instincts, harbor a man's life in her feelings. I have known myself, I have found myself in two women.

We lay on the bed spent. Sometimes one feels guilty, but I thought no, no, not here, not with her. Later I might decide that my crime was so immense that no small clattering of conscience would serve me at all; one does not strike down his brother and then compound his crime by murmuring regrets—let a man of guilt snatch out his heart, poke out his eyes, deafen himself if he must, rather than gnaw at himself, mumbling regrets. God knows, I felt no regrets just then, I think because in a perfect meeting of two people there is no room left for anybody else. I asked her if she had regrets and she said no, speaking at once without hesitation, and with a slight inflection of wonder which I took to mean she wondered why she did not or she wondered why I had thought it necessary to ask.

We lie together. We cleanse each other with a touch. We touch each other with our spit and tears. Our fingers entwine and leave no space between. We know no other, we have no brother, we have no father of her unborn child, we are once more seeking ourselves together and in each other.

151

I never did say good-by to her, not in words, but I remember being up in papa's field that evening, just before dark set in, lonely as a single bird in a tree, astonished at my own deeds, happier than I had been in years. I was walking, walking, and across the valley I saw her walk up into her pasture. I stopped when high up on my hill, and she did, too, each moving leisurely, and when I turned she came to me, and when she knelt in the grass I knelt before her and took her in my arms tenderly and kissed the loneliness from her cheeks. All from so far away. I took her in my arms across the fields; in the shadow of the mountains and the war, I held her for a little while.

◇

That night I dreamed most peculiarly. I dreamed that I was suffocating. I could not tear the pillow away from my face, and I was desperate, and I knew my father could save me, but he would not, and I knew Sory could save me, but she was unable to reach me.

When I awoke I was on the floor of my bedroom and Woofer was shaking me. "You were wrestling, but with nobody," he said.

"Get out of here," I said gruffly. "Get gone," I said. "Don't you help me," I said.

"I heard you from upstairs."

"Get out," I said, furious with him, wiping my arms where he had touched me.

Papa was sitting in the aisle of the stable next morning looking at the horse. He glanced at me as I approached him, then without a wrinkle of comment went back to watching the horse, which was in its stall breathing deeply and with pain. I stopped near him. "That horse was better for a while, I thought."

"She took a turn for the worse last night, Owen. I gave her volatile drops again."

"You going to shoot her?" I asked.

"She's Phil's horse."

"I have a pistol if you want to use it," I said.

"I see you have your uniform and hardware on." Little shafts of light filtered down from the roof shanks, and one shaft of light fell on the back of his head and spilled onto his back. "You expect those men of the smith's to fight in the war for you, Owen? How will they do, tell me that?"

"I don't know yet," I admitted.

"I don't imagine they'll do too well. You can't take a man of one view and turn him to fighting for the other side. If you can do that, what's to be said for humanity?"

"That horse is in pain I believe, papa."

"I remember once you had a sick horse name of Coal. Wasn't that her name? I came out of the house once and you were crying, and I said to myself, 'Well, Owen has to learn how to take what life has to offer, this being the law of the world.' So I told you you could use my gun. I suppose you've forgot about it by now."

"I suppose," I said, watching him, the round white head and rolled, slumped shoulders.

"I came on around the stable and was looking through that stall window there, and I heard you tell the horse about going to Morganton with him someday, all such as that, romantic notions, pretty sounds for the heart. You shot him finally. I was afraid you'd shoot yourself instead. And then there came a noise, Lord help me, a noise from that wounded horse's hoofs. Damn near tore out a board wall. Athundering he rode into death. But you don't recall, do you?"

"And I rushed down this stable aisle crying and got to the door there—" I said.

"You never were much on memory, not like me—"

"You caught my arm out in the yard—"

"Jesse was the one always could remember—"

"And you said, 'Don't forget to put your tools away.'"

"But one of the marvels of the world is that we're not all alike. Even brothers, we have our strangenesses, ever one of us does."

153

No profit gained by anger, I told myself. Let him have his views. "I'll be going on to Virginia now, but I wanted to say good-by to you."

"Uh-huh. That's a long trip."

"Yes, we'll be arriving there tomorrow night sometime."

"Several hundred of you, ain't they?"

"I expect there'll be a hundred fifty of us is all, but we'll report two hundred. Before I go I wonder if there's anything I could do for you out there."

"Lord, no. I don't need anything, except a box to be laid away in, and I can peg one for myself."

"Don't talk so simply about dying, papa."

"Why, it's on the same piece of string that birth is. When you get old you don't take on over death so much, Owen. My mother went to meet it, said she heard it singing, and she walked up on the mountain and we carried her back the next day."

"I remember. I was a boy then."

"She went to meet it. I find death easier to accept than I do change, Owen. Lord knows, I've got more change crawling over me just now than I can tolerate."

"Can you carry on the farm with only Phillip to work?"

"I don't know, and he won't agree to work anyway, unless I pay him. He says it's to be Jesse's farm, so why should he work for free? You arrived about two weeks ago, wasn't it, and since then every facet of this family has changed. Nobody but a genius could cause this much devilment. You've even got poor Woofer chasing widows. Is that woman pregnant, Owen?"

"I don't know."

"She looks it. It's too low down on her to be merely fat. Don't ever have any children, Owen. They grow up to disappoint you ever time. When I was a child I always followed my papa in his steps, learned what he knew, crawled when he crawled, ran when he ran, worked when he worked, and I took his place finally, but I don't have a boy who conforms as well as me."

154

"That's too bad, papa," I said. "I think you ought to forget him, if you ask me."

A while he sat there, his head cocked to one side, considering that. "Forget him?" he said.

"Yes, I believe I would, for you keep trying to hold everything like he had it. I had to forget my father, you know."

Slowly he looked up at me. "Owen, what's got into you?"

I offered my pistol to him.

He shook his head. "It's Phil's horse, I told you, Owen."

He walked into the yard and stood in the sunlight, blinking at the brightness about him. I followed him. "It has taken three generations to build this place, Owen," he said, "and what's to become of it now, with Jesse gone?"

"Is he the only son you've got, papa?" I said.

"My father built on it, then all my life I've worked on it, building, clearing, harnessing its streams, then Jesse—"

"Is he your only son?"

"We built that dye shed for your mama, Jesse and me, and for Nell, who said she was interested in learning to dye cloth. We raked those rocks out of the west field—"

"Did Phillip help at all? Didn't I help?"

"Jesse and me," he said, "and where is Jesse now, up in the mountains waiting for you to leave, or has he gone off somewhere? And how will I do for labor, for Phillip is talking marriage, and so is Nell, and both are saying they'll go to California if I don't help them. Everybody wants this farm divided, Owen."

"Well, what are you going to do?" I asked him.

"A farm bleeds if cut," he said, looking up at the mountains where maybe Jesse was. "So papa always said."

He helped carry my few odds and ends to the stable, and he helped me saddle the horses. At one point he said, "It's like meeting a stranger, Owen, coming across you after all these years. I resent it, in a way."

"Do you?"

155

"I always cling to the old attitudes. I like them best. It's the devil's own time for an old man to admit he might have played a lifetime error about a son of his."

We led the horses out into the yard and stood around, bundled up in our coats, waiting for Woofer and mama and Nell to come outdoors. He kept looking up at the side of the mountain, studying it, and now and then he moaned, and I suppose he was thinking about the family having been disrupted, the farm having been wounded in this strange way. Old age is lonely, I believe, having seen my father cloaked in it, standing in the litter of the plans he had made and worked for, all struck down by a far-off war, or fate, or God. I suspect a man who had fewer plans and dreams and had been less set in his ways would fare better in old age. I felt sorry for him. I did not hate him or love him or pity him, but for a little while, waiting for the others to come say good-by, I sensed the loneliness that was his closest company. My father, my father, my dear lonely father.

CHAPTER EIGHT

The worst time in the year to train soldiers is winter, and the worst place I can imagine is winter camp. The recruits came down with all manner of illnesses, and not a schedule could be made, not a march could be called that did not find a third of them on their backs in bed. In the first few weeks the scourges of lung illnesses struck several of them. Even Billy Furr fell sick; he had never been sick a day in his life. One man from Andrews died, and I had the task of writing his wife; he was the father of four, had been one of the smith's raiders. Another man died; his name was Cecil Sparks, Jr., he was from Hobbs, an only son. Diarrhea killed Sonny Thomas from Avery County. Sonny I had come to know, for he had a guitar and liked to sing, and I liked to listen to him; he was by nature a laughing fellow. One other new man died of diarrhea—I forget his name. All the new men had it, were inconvenienced by it, cramped by it. By this date early in 1863, in the third year of the war, more soldiers had died in our army from diarrhea than from enemy action.

The slush, the rain, the cold, out there sick, training every day, standing in water up to our ankles, without proper shoes or clothing. Where in hell was the clothing? North Carolina had more textile mills than the rest of the South combined, more than twenty mills, but we could not get suitable uniforms for our own conscripted men. No coats, no boots. I wrote Richmond, and they said the sovereign government of North Carolina and the Confederate government were negotiating. The Northern army went into combat looking like a supply train; actually they

157

were our supply train, but we couldn't wear Yank uniforms. Even our ammunition came from the Northern army. Our food. Listen, we once captured an entire Yankee supply depot in Virginia which was so vast the whole of Stonewall Jackson's corps could not carry it away, and I got all the caviar I could carry—this is true—all the fish eggs I wanted—they said it was fish eggs. I ate three pounds of it and threw up. I ate it with my corn bread. I never cooked it. Somebody said not to cook it. It was a different food to what I had been accustomed to, I'll say that. We captured butter, wagonloads of butter. We dug our hands into it.

Anyway, I had shoddy clothes and shoes for my men. Some men cut up blankets and bound their feet with the cloth. That muddied up, however, so that they were trying to lift ten pounds of mud on each foot. I saw one poor fellow stuck halfway up the hill, unable to move. Men made sandals from pieces of wood. One poor devil started slipping near my headquarters and crashed into a wall.

Then I would get an order from General Manger: Drill each day for six hours.

Drill? Without shoes? Six hours?

And another: The men will be taken on a ten-mile hike on February 6 at 1800 hours to prepare them for night marches.

Prepare them? I would lose them, that's all.

I wrote back and asked when we would get around to military maneuvers or have an issue of ammunition and muskets.

Colonel Penny replied, sent me a list of three books on military training, all emphasizing drill and advance-in-ranks tactics, so I asked him if in two campaigns we had not learned more about fighting our own war than the Prussians had ever anticipated on our behalf thirty years ago.

Also we would receive word that General Heth or some other general would review our troops on such-and-such a day. We would clean everything, bury all the waste that had been left around or had blown into our street. We would find our banner

158

and wash it. "And wash your lousy shirts." My men had lice crawling on their shirts. Even a general could see them. The men would cut their hair, shave, trim beards and mustaches. We had to find among us a regulation uniform apiece, so we stole and loaned and borrowed as best we could. We hid our civilian clothes and our fur coats and caps. Some of the sick men I hid in neighboring huts. Two men with skin mange I hid. Three or four drunks I hid. We even raked the road, got the big rocks off it. And on the 23rd day of February, one day I recall, at four o'clock in the afternoon, we were standing in our regimental street, each man by his hut, each hut neat ...

We stood there for two hours and forty minutes waiting for General Heth to arrive, he and some congressman—I never caught his name. From near Salisbury, I believe. He wasn't even from our Congressional district.

"It looks like you're doing an excellent job, Colonel," General Heth told me ten minutes later as he left.

Then, of course, the regiment fell apart around us. Junk that had been hid was uncarted. We had our sick and scrawny to gather in. We had to give clothes and shoes back to their rightful owners. We had used the last of the soap ration for February; we had not a pot of soap in the entire regiment. We put on the rabbitskin coats, the fur hats, the scarfs our wives had made for us. We let our hair and the lice grow untended.

Every mail that went out of my camp told of the conditions.

Dear Papa,
    I wish I had what you are feeding to the dogs, 'deed I do ...

Dear Mother,
    I get hongry. When you can do it, send me an apple and an irish potato ...

Dear Mama,
    The conditions here I don't think they can get much worse, but there's no use in saying soldiering ain't tolerable

cause it is. A man has to live one day at a time and make-do with what he has ...

My dearest ones,

How are my little boys? I miss all of you. It is lonely here, there's nothing but people as far as you can see and not a one of them means a penny's worth to me. I only hope I can make up for it when I see the enemy and can take a shot at him, for I will never forgive him for taking Sgt. Horace Willis away from his three sons ...

I put my full energies into training; I bled myself into the routine of the army. I couldn't bear to think of Sory. I couldn't bear to wonder about the crime I had done Woofer either. I didn't want to be with Woofer, I resented the kindnesses he showed me, the considerateness he held for me. I needed his affection, I needed his attention, for I was more lonely than ever I had been, but it was beyond even my power of compromise and falsity to accept him, to present myself to him as a friend. I was in a turmoil because of this and even considered confessing to him and hoping, on the other side of that dreadful moment of truth, to find a new relationship, a close relationship with him.

But I decided the secret was not mine, and I was not sure I had the courage to tell him anyway.

Each night I wrote Sory a letter. I mailed none of them. I got no letter from her. Every time the chaplain arrived I would seek him out, find something to talk with him about, hoping there would be a letter for me. Nell wrote me twice in February, and that was all, and in neither letter did she mention Sory except in one brief note—did Nell know, did she suspect? I wondered. Fearfully I wondered. In one brief note she said, "Sory came to church and sat alone, lonely."

God, if I could have sat with her. If I could have touched her elbow with my arm. If I could have touched her hand. If I could have seen her eyes once more. The tilt of her head was

160

dear to me. The smile she had for me.

I swore I would never go home. Was I to go back there and watch as Sory reared Woofer's child? Was I to shadow them all the days of their lives together? I hope not. I decided I could not. Let it all go. Let me turn my life into a soldier, only that. Let me go back now to being what I was before Woofer arrived, except I would be a soldier even more exclusively, more fervently. Let me dedicate myself.

And let him not be killed, lest I know I killed him. Please, God, do not let him be killed. Would she ever believe I had not killed him?

◇

I sought out General Jackson on two occasions, but neither time did I dare mention General Manger to him. I didn't know how General Jackson himself would take to my ignoring the chain of command he had established or to my criticizing officers he had put into positions of power. Also, I didn't know whether he would mention my complaint to Heth or Manger, which would endanger me, particularly when assignments for battle places were made.

However, my ambition fed on my discontent. I must move on to higher rank, I felt. Whatever I did would be justified, I told myself; the conditions in the camp were intolerable, the training schedule was impractical, and I noticed that Colonel Penny was signing more and more of the papers. I girded up my courage and sought out Jackson again, this time at an inn where he was to spend a week or two. I was sitting in the lobby near the log fire when he arrived, accompanied by two officers I didn't know, who viewed me suspiciously. Jackson himself seemed pleased to see me. He was a bearded man, raw and rough in appearance, but mild and courteous in manner, and he always had liked me very well, perhaps because I had never in battle disappointed him. When I told him it would be helpful to me to talk with him privately about a matter, a deeply sympathetic, even studious expression came over his face. "Yes, yes," he said, and he took my arm firmly and walked with me to one corner of the big room. "What say?" he said. "What is it, Colonel?"

I had not intended to tell him all I felt, but his attitude was so receptive that I found myself relating far too many details and I became even more emphatic and critical than I had meant to be. I exaggerated too. I mentioned to him as certain knowledge that General Manger was ill, that he was dying, and of course I had to tell him about Colonel Penny assuming responsibilities.

"He's not somebody who would want to kill Yanks on Sunday, is he?" Jackson asked me.

"No, sir. I suspect not. Nor any other time."

"I wonder if any of us should kill Yanks on Sunday, Owen."

"Sir, I don't think the Sabbath commandment considers killing Yanks to be work."

"It's not hard work, is it? And it might be we'll find that the Yanks we kill on Sunday add more to our credit in Heaven than Yanks we kill on a weekday."

"Yes, sir," I said, laughing, although he was solemn, even yet.

"I sometimes pray, Owen, for God to allow me to kill Yanks on a Sunday for His greater glory."

"Well, if we are permitted to get an ox out of a ditch on Sunday, we ought to be allowed to get ourselves out of one," I said.

"But God hasn't given me a sign." He gave my arm a steady shake. "They're going to come on us right heavy this spring, Owen, with over 120,000 men. But I don't worry about numbers, not as long as God is with us and we have 120,000 cartridges."

"Yes, sir," I said. I found it devilishly hard to tell when he was joking, for he was solemn most all the time. I felt I was being evaluated, that his casual statements were being made to judge me by my reactions, and the judging process required that Jackson not help me decide how to react.

"I didn't know General Manger was sick," he said suddenly.

162

"I remember we heard rumors of it a few months ago and General Heth asked him about it and Manger denied any problem."

"I—well, I think he will do anything to save his command. But he is risking my life and my men's to save it, General."

"You want me to put you in his place?"

"Sir, I am not here trying to gain an advancement," I said.

"If I set him out to pasture, and it kills him, I'll feel sorry about it."

"So will I, General."

"Will you?" he said bluntly.

"Sir, I think I will. I tell you, it has taken me a month or more to get the nerve to come tell you all this, and I have had so much suffering from the matter already that I've come to dislike him."

"Why did you wait a month?"

"I hesitated to hurt him."

"What made you stop hesitating?"

"Seeing Colonel Penny's name signed to more and more papers. We not only have a sick general, but we have a cavalry colonel sitting beside him, holding his pen."

Jackson's gaze was steady on me. He was studying me, weighing the matter carefully. He pursed his lips. "Colonel, if I ask him myself if he's well, will he lie to me?"

"Sir, I don't know. He'll fight for his life. Any man will do that."

"I can't commission a surgeon to examine him, and I can't send him an order to open his mouth and let us see inside it."

"He was coughing up blood, General."

"Did you see it?"

"Yes, sir."

"Are you certain?"

"Yes, sir."

"Well, I will talk with him. Now, then, if he knows you have come to me he will be angry with us both, so I ask you not to mention this conference to any other person, and I won't either.

I will tell my two aides something or other."

"Very well, sir."

He grasped my arm again and shook it. "Leave it in my hands," he said, and as he rejoined his aides he said, "We must try to get Colonel Wright fifty uniforms, gentlemen, for he's got the worst worries about nakedness of any man I ever listened to." And off he went up the stairs, his heavy boots banging sharply on the hardwood floors, not even glancing at me.

◇

We never got used to drill. I never did anyway, for I never could understand why so much of it was necessary.

I recall one day it began to snow; it snowed hard too, and at noon we went out into the snow to drill. After an hour of it, my feet and hands numb, I got hit back of the head with a watery snowball. I whirled around, saw that the smith had thrown it, so I went after him myself. A cheer went up, and the first thing I knew every man in the regiment was throwing snowballs at me, or at other officers or sergeants. This simply wouldn't do, so I shouted, "Charge!" and started across the field toward Colonel McRuder's regiment. My men sent up the Rebel yell and came after me, and of course his men sent up a Rebel yell and came to meet us, and pretty soon snowballs were in the air so thick you'd think they were ticks on a sergeant's mattress. It was the best training day we ever had, everybody agreed. McRuder and I agreed anyway.

Another day, bright and sunny, the entire regiment in passing health now, we were out there drilling, my men pivoting and turning and squaring off and acting as if they could march very well. Even General Heth, who sometimes would view the drill sessions from his horse, even he watched respectfully as we went parading by. I saluted him and he saluted me; we were as grand as any Virginia regiment, when before us appeared this rabbit. Not a damn reason for it to be there. There it was, and in one mad, yelling charge my regiment attacked it. If I had not been nimble I would have been trampled.

164

McRuder's regiment and Reid's regiment saw what was going on and came at the rabbit, too, and the clash of the three regiments of Manger's brigade created an incredible melee.

Where was the rabbit? I didn't know. I didn't care to know either. It disappeared. I got an invitation from General Heth to attend him, and it took all the jokes I could muster to get him to see any humor in the incident. I don't know what happened to the rabbit. That's what he kept wanting to know. "Why did they want a rabbit anyway, Colonel?" he would ask me. Did I tell him the men were hungry? No, for he was the one who had to issue potatoes and corn and cabbages for us. They never got to us, of course, but somebody in his commissary department—

Oh, let it go. I've said enough about the food. I begin to bore myself.

I suspect it was Sory's slaves who passed the word to other slaves and they to whites that she was pregnant. Also they said that it was Woofer's child, but that I had been alone with her at the river and in her house.

One night Captain Crawford came to me pale as a ghost and haltingly asked if Woofer had been with his aunt and who had told the men that Woofer was to be his uncle. He insisted I was seeking revenge on him because of some imagined affront. He was deeply concerned about this, as was plain. And what had been my relationship with her, he wanted to know.

I left him and went at once to Woofer's hut, where I found several men crowded at the door. They grew quiet once they saw me, and appeared to be embarrassed. Inside the hut I found Betsy sitting on his bunk, and crouched by the fire was Woofer, staring into the flame.

"It's not so, what they say," I told him at once.

He looked slowly up at me, then his face contorted in anguish too profound for me to bear. "Is it, Owen?"

"She wouldn't have done that to you, and I wouldn't have."

" 'Think of yourself first,' you always told me," he said.

"Ahhhhh, no, not with a brother, not you."

"Your brothers mean nothing to you."

"Listen, you matter to me."

"Does she love you?"

I hadn't expected the question and couldn't answer readily. "I don't know," I said. "Woofer, I—don't know."

A hurt beyond pain gripped him and he leaped at me and delivered a hard blow which I took on my shoulder, even as Betsy came forward and grabbed him. Woofer at once broke like a long-stemmed flower, bent double, weeping.

"Woofer, I never touched her," I said. "I want you to know that. It's not true, whatever it is they claim."

He walked hunched over to the far wall of the room, butted into it, and stayed there close to the wall, bent low, weeping, staring at the floor of the room. "Get out, Owen," he said, sobbing.

"For God sake," I said.

"Get out."

Outside I saw Martin Luther running down the road toward us, and I told him to bring Woofer to my place when he could. I sludged on up the road, miserable in my soul. God knows, I had never felt so cruel. I had gone maybe a hundred feet when I heard somebody laugh, a high, intense giggle, and a voice called out, "Keeping it in the family, Colonel?"

The street was empty. Not a man was in sight, but other voices began calling and laughing from the huts up and down the road, a torrent of questions and sounds, bombarding me with obscenities and contortions, which tore into my conscience like knives in flesh. "Did all you brothers get her in the same bed, the same night, Colonel?" "Did one of her niggers put it in for you, Colonel?" Vicious—there is nothing meaner than self-righteousness among soldiers.

There is nothing forgiving or relenting about a regiment of soldiers either, not when they have a blood lust on them like this. They weren't about to let me ignore my horrible predicament, nor Captain Crawford his ludicrous one. "Is it your baby too?" a voice would call out to him.

"Don't think Captain Crawford can be the father, seeing the swish on his ass."

"Poor Captain Crawford, they've took his aunt away."

I sought Woofer out each day, desperately in need of his forgiveness, but it became obvious to me that he would not forgive me and that I had become a liability to him. As sometimes happens in one of these regional regiments, the men had found a way to punish their officers and exercise their sleepy sense of moral indignation at the same time; the accused were permitted no defense. Woofer, because he was my brother, was exposed and helpless. There was nothing to be done about it, by him or me, except live it out. The men would tire of their righteousness soon perhaps but, of course, they could not set our lives straight again or heal me in my soul, nor him. There was no salve to heal my soul just then.

Preparing for battle, I divided my regiment into three battle sections of three companies each. Lieutenant Hal King was over A, B, and C Companies. Lieutenant Stan McGregor was over G, H, and I Companies. And the three companies in between, D, E, and F, were under Captain Skip Crawford, who was not accustomed to being given a battlefield assignment. Into his D Company I put the smith's raiders, about forty of them, and I made the smith the sergeant in charge of that company. Captain Crawford told me that would prove to be an error, but I decided to follow my own judgment. E Company I put under Billy Furr in the same way, that company being composed entirely of his raiders, about forty-five men. In F Company I put my musicians, including McIlvenna and Plover and his son; I also put in there the other conscriptees of various persuasions, most of them young men, and I put them under a Sergeant Red Raper, who was an experienced soldier. As you see, I had all my conscriptees under Captain Crawford, which he surmised to be the

167

beginning of my effort to unseat him from rank.

As is true with the instigation of any plan in the army, there was confusion. Some men make a policy of trying to overturn everything orderly if it is dictated by somebody in authority over them. Even so, many soldiers wanted to transfer companies. Officers were displeased; old ambitions were aroused in Lieutenant McGregor, for instance, who complained that Crawford was a captain and he, with equal responsibility, was not. His sons—he had two sons, he told me—an increase to captain would matter ever so much to them. "I don't care one way or the other, as for myself, Colonel," he said.

"Yes, yes," I said, I suppose wearily, for I did get weary during this period of adjustment.

Even Sergeant Smith came to see me, to complain about his commission. He said his name was Horace Roberts. "I'm not Sergeant Smith," he said.

"You're not Sergeant Roberts, surely," I said. "I never heard anybody call you anything except Smith."

He became angry. It was as if in robbing him of his name I had committed a personal affront.

So I changed the commission, which was devilishly complicated to explain, especially to Colonel Penny; one would judge I didn't even know the names of my own sergeants. In time we obtained a duly registered commission made out to a Sergeant Roberts. After that he was always called Sergeant Smith, but he was content.

The winter camp was now blessed with the arrival of several of the army's select units, men passionately dedicated to the Southern cause who had wintered elsewhere in greater comfort. They arrived with much baggage, with beautiful horses and saddles, with slaves. They were decked out in all sorts of special uniforms. The members of the Granville Rifles of North Carolina wore black pants and red flannel shirts. A regiment of Zouaves were dressed in bloomers bound at the ankles with white gaiters. A special outfit arrived from Texas wearing whitish suits.

"Getting married, fellows?" my soldiers called to them.

"Come out of them graveclothes, I see you're alive in there," they called.

"You hellcats planning to go into battle in your shrouds?"

The cavalry under General Jeb Stuart's command rode through. There was nothing frayed or torn about any of them either. They made my own regiment resemble a band of impoverished strays who had come together for self-protection. The artillerymen also were more active. Locksmiths and miners, shoemakers and wheelwrights, stonecutters and tinsmiths, teachers and college students, landlords, glass blowers, city grocers, barbers, barkeepers and innkeepers were in camp now, and farmers—most of the men were farmers and planters. The camp by the middle of March was so crowded that there wasn't room for a single other hut. Even so, more trains arrived day and night, bringing old men and boys of fourteen or fifteen, and men of every age in between.

Food became even more scarce. Men with money bought food from sutlers. Everybody wrote home begging for food parcels. Foraging parties would go out into the countryside; one man actually ran down a fox, caught it with his bare hands. I know it's hard to believe. Tobacco was scarce. Virginia and North Carolina were the world's tobacco centers, but what we had in camp was a dollar and a half for a plug; cigarette tobacco was even more exorbitant. Coffee was $1.50 a pound, tea $15 a pound. A soldier's pay was $11 a month, whenever he got any at all. (Mine was $200.) Writing paper cost 15 cents a sheet. Men were writing on the backs of letters they had received from home. They wrote on wrapping paper, even wallpaper. Clothes were scarce, as I have said. One soldier in my regiment patched his pants seat with a flaming red patch shaped like a heart, and that created a springtime fashion sensation which swept my regiment; all my men had hearts, eagles, cupids, angels, and apples on their ass soon afterwards.

For me it was back and forth to headquarters now, getting orders. And once I went to Richmond. So far as I could tell,

Manger suspected me of no treason. He was polite with me, even confided in me that he was hoping Colonel Penny would find another place for himself in the army. "He knows nothing about battle, or women, so what's the use of his company?" he said. On one occasion he told me, as he had often in the past, that he had me in mind to succeed him, if anything ever happened to him.

Penny was polite to me, although aloof, and he did resent my criticisms of his training schedules. He also knew I had taught my conscriptees on my own how to take cover under fire, how to crawl and creep, how to tourniquet their own limbs and treat their own wounds. Penny had got reports on all changes in his schedule that I had made, no doubt from Crawford. I said nothing in argument. I would be done with both of them soon I had no doubt.

I mailed Sory a letter. I could not deny myself the joy of touching her, even in this way. My letter was written just before the spring campaign began. I was careful not even to mention Woofer or to refer to his plight with the men or with me. God knows what he had told her by then and what the state of her mind was.

> Dearest Sory,
>
> All my instincts are brighter, now that it is spring. Even my sorry prospects appear better. The colors in the grass and sky are brighter, everything excites me: the trees, the budding of the bushes, even the roosters strutting about the roadside. Our woebegone trains begin to look as if they can run for another few months.
>
> I awake each morning refreshed, and I awake wondering how you are. I imagine myself walking down to the road and seeing you.
>
> Excitement is everywhere, Sory. Especially in Richmond, a great city, one able to show many faces. It can change its expressions with the seasons, to conform to the

times. In the streets are more carriages now, swift horses, galloping and neighing, many blacks trying to calm them, more shopkeepers closing their doors half an hour early and going out into the sun. Policemen are sweltering, sweating in their winter uniforms. Men are singing songs in the streets.

It is time for even reserved men like me to admit to love and submit myself to a playful woman. All days are pretty, like soft poems. I am yoked to my love in my imagination and never want to be free.

The sweep of great events propels us forward; my own life races forward. I have no time to mourn. I meet the warm days, welcome the bright days, as I prepare for war. At last winter is over and we are going forth to slay our enemies, and my blood runs ninety-eight degrees in the shade ...

CHAPTER NINE

The Northern army was in motion beyond the river, and our part of the Southern army moved out and camped at sundown. The men cut roasting sticks and roasted fatback over open fires, and balls of dough which they made of flour and drippings and water. Those who had coffee boiled a portion of it in their tin cups.

Some men scooped out places to sleep on the ground. Others slept in the warm ashes of a fire, or put up canvas shelters, or cut boughs of trees to sleep under. I lay down in the open, with my blanket to keep the rain and dew off. Woofer lay to himself, also in the open, I noticed, not far away from where I slept. God knows what was in his mind, what hate and revenge he felt for me.

The guards tried to keep the men from getting up during the night, but there is no controlling the bowels and kidneys of a regiment. Many of the men were sick with the runs again, anyway, for they had drunk the creek water. The army was so immense it had contaminated the streams for miles around. The three corps of our army, which marched along separate routes, must have numbered 60,000 men.

The generals directed us not to throw away any equipment or clothes, but next day the fences and bushes on both sides of the roads were decorated with haversacks, overcoats, blankets, underwear, socks. Impoverished civilians came to collect them, bringing oxcarts and wagons, or sleds drawn by calves or milch cows. Among the gatherers were children and old

172

women, scavenging for them, burdened under them.

My soldiers would send up loud chants. "Food, God damn you, General Manger," they would say, "Food, God damn you, Colonel Wright." And so it went down through the chain of command to the lowliest sergeant. They were issued four ounces of sowbelly and a pound of corn meal a day. Once in midafternoon I sent word to them that a steer would be provided to each three-company section that night—I had to buy them myself. The men began to talk about what they would do with a steer, how much they liked beef, what part of a beef they liked best, and when they camped and the steer was brought to each section, they slaughtered, severed, hacked, and ate it before full sundown, sometimes uncooked and in most cases without salt, for we had precious little salt.

I recall that night the rumor went through the regiment that Company A had found two rows of buried Irish potatoes. There was a stampede instantly. On another hill Company D, the smith's men, camped at an apple house, literally surrounding it, and hid it from sight, and by the time Company E arrived not even a core remained. That was the night a young fellow caught a gander. It had been scared out of a barnyard, and it came through camp. This boy simply got it, that was all, and held to it in spite of the efforts of men to take it from him and of the gander to escape. He had caught the prize of the regiment that day. But since looting was quite definitely against General Manger's orders, I felt obliged to mention this to him. "Where'd you get that goose, soldier?" I asked. "You been looting?"

"No, sir," he said, scared to death, clutching his prize. "It's fair game, Colonel. He hissed at the flag, sir."

I had to laugh at the damn fool.

The chaplain must have been advised by Captain Crawford not to allow me to see the men's mail. Or perhaps the chaplain was irritated with me on another count, for when I found out he was charging the men a penny to post a letter for them, I dubbed his service "one cent by God," which caused him much embarrassment in the brigade. I managed to see only a few scattered letters.

Dearest Anna,
The Northern Army is on the road ahead of us we hav herd tell. God hep us. We wil not giv quarter. they are twic our number and hav a new genl named Huker. He is no matc for Lee and Jackson, nevr fer, but I dont dout the yanks ar a matc for me ...

My dear father,
The Yanks are moving toward us, to endanger Richmond. A battle might be anytime. The leaves here in Virginia are breaking green, buds are popping, we are men walking through a God-blessed land, rich and sunny ... God forgive us for the use we make of his gifts.

Dear wife, my ink is pale; my pen is frail; my love to you shall never fail. God bless you. Kiss Mark for me and think of me as often as you can, for I will never see more pleasure in this world than I have when I think of you ...

Dear Harry,
If I get shot in the stomach, I don't know that I will want to come home at once, and if I get hit in the face, I might not come home, so do not allow Martha to spend all my money merely on first report of my death or disappearance ...

Dear Rose and Sims,
Being of sound mind and in the presence of two witnesses I declare this to be my last will and testament. To my dear wife, the bed she sleeps on and its covers and the remaining furniture in the house and use of the house so long as she lives; to my oldest son, Charles Bridgett Sims, that portion of my land beginning at the white oak tree at the Thompson corner and going northward with the fence to the spruce pine from under which comes a bold spring, and eastward following Elf Marsden's boundary to the top

174

of the mountain at the red oak tree where in 1846 he killed a sow bear, and along the crest of the mountain to a major white oak with three marks cut in its bark ...

My regiment was assigned its regimental surgeon and his medical staff, along with their wagons and ambulances. The chief surgeon's name was Carter. Lieutenant King got the name wrong on first meeting and kept calling him Dr. Cutter, which I had the good humor to let go without correction. He became Dr. Cutter to us all, officers and men.

General Manger came to call on the same night, another sign of the proximity of the battle, and I invited Hal King to join me at supper with him and his two companions, Colonel Penny and a Lieutenant Something-or-other. Colonel Penny wore a Richmond-tailored uniform, infantry, not cavalry. He wore a silk shirt. He had on new leather boots, as fine a leather as I had ever seen. He had on a diamond ring and a gold watch and chain. Quite a sight, I must say, especially when compared with me. I was muddy and dirty, my uniform patched and battle-worn.

General Manger was wheezing, and now and then his mind would wander. Maybe I saw symptoms of illness in him because I wanted to find them, but I did decide he was losing strength.

Colonel Penny was talkative. I poured him more whiskey and let him talk. He was critical of my food. I told him battlefield colonels have no cooks or extra rations. He was also worried about the Yank artillery, which he said was better than ours. I couldn't tell whether the food or the artillery worried him more.

"We'll have their cannon soon enough," General Manger told him. "Give us one battle, and you'll see how much artillery we have."

"When will we meet them?" I asked.

"Tomorrow or the next day."

"We have no ammunition," I said.

"Oh, my Lord. Penny, where is the ammunition?" Manger said.

"We're not near the Yanks yet," Penny said.

"We're not near them my ass," the General said. "I want you to issue cartridges to the regiments. I told you, damn you."

"It's—not far away," he said, incensed to be criticized so bluntly and openly.

"If I were a Yank general, I would attack this army now, at night," I said. "I doubt if we could defend ourselves."

"They don't fight that way," Colonel Penny said, and it was with some pride he said it, as if in the art of war there were a few gentlemen who could be counted on to fight according to the textbooks. Of course, I was utterly prejudiced against him and maybe make him sound even dumber than he was, but he was not a soldier, not a Jackson type of soldier.

"My people up home only had one battle before this war started," I told him and Manger. "We generally fight the way we hunt bears, as we did back then, and there are no rules or ceremony to it."

"Kings Mountain," General Manger said reminiscently. "That battle won the war, Owen, I believe, won the American Revolution, for Washington was bogged down in winter camp all forlorn and disheartened and the British had taken South Carolina and were moving north."

"I don't know what it won," I said, "or even if my people knew what the war was about. I think they had got an insulting message from a British general, so they left off work grubbing laurel and walked down out of the mountains to settle with him, and they met near what's now called Shelby."

"Shelby was their general's name too," Manger said.

"Weighed almost three hundred pounds," I said.

"Not at that time. That was later," Manger said.

"I don't know all there is to it," I admitted, "but those men didn't fight by the rules. They fought from rocks and trees and gullies. I remember men telling me what words Shelby shouted out before they went up the sides of the mountain. Do you recall?" I said to Manger.

176

"God, no, damn you, I'm not one for memorizing obscenities," Manger said with a blunt, sharp laugh. He was drunk on
brandy by now; he always carried a few bottles in his general's
carriage.

"They were down there in a meadow cooking their corn-
bread," I said, "and the British were up on the ridge, and in
between was a big woods, and Shelby said to put out the cook
fires and come along if they were going with him, so they began
to throw water on their fires. They got their guns loaded,
mostly homemade ones, I imagine. All volunteers, no officers to
speak of, hunters, farmers, tough lean men, mountain men, and
this officer they had elected got up on his horse and settled his
three hundred pounds of fat in the saddle, for he couldn't walk
anywhere—"

"It was later he weighed that much, Owen," Manger said.

"And—it's not the way I heard it as a boy," I said to him, "and
he shouted out across that field six words that won our part of
the country from England: 'Every man is his own officer!' "

Of course, that statement represented a world away from
what this fellow Penny thought an army ought to be, and Manger too. I knew that, which is the only reason on earth I was
anxious to tell the story in the first place. Penny obviously was
baffled, was irritated by it. The statement of Shelby had nothing
to do with drilling soldiers endlessly on a parade ground or
allowing officers to lord it over them; it had nothing to do with
conscription either.

"The mountain men killed and captured all that general's
army that morning, eleven hundred men, and killed him and his
redheaded mistress and left their naked bodies to rot in the
sun," I said, feeling mean about it, even now. "What do you
think of that, Penny?" I said.

"It sounds like—a rather despicable act, I would say."

"Maybe you would have been on the British side," I said,
"which most planters were."

Manger snorted angrily. "You needn't insult us, Owen. Why

177

do you remind us of what will only split us apart, Owen?"

"Our army has come to be too officer-ordered," I said, a devil in me making me go on like this. "It's too disrespectful of the men themselves. They are the army. We're not. We feed them fatback and corn meal and let them scrounge for themselves and pick lice. I liked it better when they elected their own officers—"

"Oh, God, don't start on that, Owen," Manger said.

"I liked it better when all the regiments were like mine, the men coming from a common ground, and they elected the men to lead them and decided for themselves how to live. And they went home if they wanted to."

"Oh, God knows, Owen, why do you want to turn the clock back? Why do you insist on angering me, damn you?" Manger said.

"We're getting too far off from our roots," I said, "and we'll starve ourselves before we're through."

"You can fight a one-battle campaign with volunteer remnants and every man being his own officer," Manger said, "but not a war, not three years, for God sake."

"They have no voice at all any more. We've become the lords and rulers. But they're the ones who are supposed to be free citizens, owners of the country."

"Don't let him have anything more to drink," Manger said. "He's getting so sentimental about his men that he'll melt into a puddle of sugarwater."

I had to laugh, for it was the truth. I do get sentimental when I drink, especially when I've not had much food during a day. But what I had said was the truth anyway.

When the General was leaving, as we came near his big, black general's carriage—only Heth's generals had carriages in our army—I realized that several of Billy Furr's men had surrounded it and were taunting the two Negro drivers. The two Negroes were looking straight ahead, outwardly as undaunted as ebony statues. I said good evening to Sole McKinney and the other soldiers and suggested that they get out of the General's way. I told the Negro drivers to pull the carriage out onto the road, which doubtless they were pleased to do, though there was no sign of relief on their faces. This further infuriated the Company E men, who would not, simply could not tolerate seeing a black man who was unafraid of them.

"I'll not be equaled by one of them," McKinney shouted at me, interrupting General Manger, who was trying to say good-by. "Because they're free up north don't mean a damned thing down here. Niggers acting like people, sitting up there like Jesus Christ ..."

Colonel Penny was taken aback, to say the least, but we got the carriage onto the road and the three officers inside it. McKinney murmured to me, "When the fighting begins, we'll see how tough our officers are."

"And our soldiers," I added, which silenced him at last. He watched sullenly as the great carriage came to a stop on the road and General Manger called me over to the carriage window.

"It's when they get nigh a battle, the fever gets to them, don't it, Owen?" Manger said. "They begin to feel their own blood."

"Some of them," I said, "the more frightened ones."

"I don't understand the nature of your authority," Penny said critically to me.

"Well, how does an officer enforce his authority out here?" I said. "I can't threaten to put a man in jail and deprive him of the pleasure of being shot at tomorrow."

"How then do you command?" he asked, his voice taking on a characteristically waspish quality.

"That's about the last thing you ever want to do around mountain people," I said, and smiled at him, for he did appear to be dismayed.

"Leave Owen alone," General Manger said. "He'll lead those men, that crazy one and all the others. You'll see." He clicked his tongue and the black drivers put the four horses into motion, and the carriage with a gold star on its side moved off toward

179

the northeast, where we would find the enemy. I kept looking at the carriage until it was out of sight, wondering how long it would be before General Jackson made his decision concerning that carriage and me. ◇

We came upon the Yanks near a little town—scarcely even a town—called Chancellorsville. We heard the rattle of muskets way off, and General Manger, who was mounted on a huge white horse, stopped the brigade on a ridge crest from which we could see out over a vast expanse of pine woods, mostly second-growth timber with the trees growing like wild thickets, maybe ten, fifteen years old, growing close together and darkening the earth, killing everything under them, as pine woods tend to do when they are young and scraggly.

Two raggedy-clothed Virginia boys were standing beside the road looking wide-eyed at all they saw. "What do you call that woods, fellows?" I asked them.

"The Wildness," the younger boy answered.

"Is that its name, that big woods out there?" I said. The forest billowed on the hills for ten or twelve miles, dismal and uninviting in a drizzly rain.

"Wildness," the boy repeated.

The older boy, who was maybe eleven, said, "He can't say it, mister."

"You say it then."

"The Wil-der-ness," he said.

I heard a scattering of shots from the bowels of the Wilderness and judged them to be about two miles away. Musket shots at that distance have the sound of peas being dropped on pigskin.

Nearby was Company B and I could see Woofer clearly, sitting beside the road with Betsy. I waved to him, said we had met the Yanks at last, and Betsy raised his hand to me in a friendly gesture. Woofer said nothing. He was nervous, fretful. We heard another volley, and I saw two long, thin rows of blue smoke rise from inside the woods. The smoke continued rising. It looked like the Wilderness was emitting little puffs of air from two series of punctured wounds, like rows of puffball. In several places I noticed the dark pines were dotted with oak and hickory stands, and here and there were several fields, like pockmarks on a man's face. Many miles away was a snaky river.

Captain Crawford came slodging along the road, his head bent as if his thoughts were uncommonly heavy. He sighed when he saw me and flopped down on the grass. "They think they've caught the Yanks in there, do they?" he said, trying to appear to be calm.

"They crossed the river and were coming up through that woods, I imagine," I said.

"How can they get an army through there?"

"They must have been risking our not catching them is all. They can't maneuver in a woods like that very well."

Caissons came rumbling toward us, a captain shouting orders to unlimber. Men swung a 20-pounder Parrott rifle into position while my men watched, pretending disinterest. A shell was brought from a wagon and was shoved into the mouth of the cannon close to me.

The cannon had a marvelous full voice. I had my hands over my ears, but even so the boom fairly deafened me. The shell exploded over the center of the woods, exploded rather high and far in, about 2,500 yards away.

Lieutenant King came running up the road toward me. "What is it, Owen?" he said.

"They caught that new fellow Hooker trying to sneak an army through a jungle of little pines."

"I'll say this for the Yanks," he said, flopping down under a dogwood that was in bloom, "they got nerve to keep coming back at us with one fool general after another."

Plover came over to say hello, his fiddle with him. He was tuning it. "I've got the runs so bad, Owen, I don't know that I can go into action," he said.

"Fight with your pants down," I told him.

"My bowels have moved eighteen times in three hours," he said. He was a sorrowful sight, scruffy, heavily protected by wool clothing, amply supplied with two haversacks, a knapsack, and a big blanket roll. His son stood nearby chewing on a grass blade and staring at the artillerymen.

"Can't you get on without me?" Plover asked me.

I had to laugh. "You'll get hard bowels when the Yanks start shooting at you," I said.

A cannon went off just at that moment, and I must say the noise frightened him.

"I believe we might get splattered sitting this close to a man with the runs," I told Hal. We both moved off a few yards from him, laughing like damn fools.

Manger's wagons were rolling by, striking sparks from the rocky places in the road. A wagon broke its wheel and the two drivers got down, cursing, throwing their hats in the dirt and spitting tobacco juice. "How 'bout a hand?" they asked a group of my men.

Two of my men slowly got up, spit on the road, threw their hats in the dirt, then sat back down, so the two drivers began to unload their wagon themselves, mumbling about infantrymen. Other wagons, loaded with medical tents and supplies, passed by. "We're even behind the ambulance corps now, Plover," I said. "You'll have to move forward to reach the hospital." Along came my surgeon, with his litter-bearers, many of them convalescents from my regiment, and his four assistant surgeons, of whom one seemed suspiciously wobbly to me. "You reckon that fellow's drunk?" I asked Hal.

"I wouldn't let him touch me with a knife," he said. "Or a saw either."

Plover shuddered. "I don't mean to lose ary arm, for I can't play music if I do."

Hal and I laughed. "You're crazy as hell," I told him. "What sort of prime reason is that? You couldn't plow, couldn't cut

182

food, couldn't sew a coat, or peg a chair, or shuck corn, or shoot, or lay a fire. But you come up with a fiddle reason."

A cavalry troop rode by, big plumed hats, jingling spurs, hoofs throwing dust all over us. They didn't care one damn bit, either. My men cursed them thoroughly. I moved out of the dust and into a field, to a point of rock where I could better watch the Wilderness breathe below us. A white smoke cloud from shells exploding lay half a mile wide and a mile long, about a hundred feet above the trees. When the cannons weren't firing, I could hear the musket fire. Two thin blue lines of smoke, one from each army's riflemen, were rising along a two-mile-wide front. That smoke infiltrated the white smoke from the shells. The woods were dressing themselves in new rags this afternoon, all right.

One of the lines of riflemen began to move back toward the river. It was the Yank line. Soon there was only one blue line, the Rebel one, for the other had ceased firing, and after another few minutes no blue smoke was seen at all, the musket sound had stopped, and the day was so quiet I could hear birds singing.

I stretched out on the grass, my head resting on my blanket roll, and watched the blue sky which the smoke hadn't got to yet. McIlvenna started playing his pipes. The two Plovers lazily joined in. Several men gathered. Even the doctor came to join us. He sat down beside me and patted my arm and said, "You're going to have a fight today, are you, Colonel?"

"Think so," I said. "Or tomorrow."

"Not nervous?" he said.

"My hands are nervous," I said.

McIlvenna began playing "Billy in the Low Grounds," and I thought: Here I am a king of some country, with about 500 loyal and disloyal subjects, with musicians to play for me, with food served me by my government, fatback anyway, with a surgeon to care for my health. What more perfect life is there than to be a colonel in the Rebel army?

"I've found eight this week with syphilis," Dr. Carter said to me.

"Plover, how come your bowels have stopped moving?" I asked him.

The doctor said, "Did you know that better'n eighty-five out of every thousand Yank soldiers have syphilis?"

"Who counted them?" I asked, which tickled him for some reason. He was a fine man to laugh when prompted.

About five o'clock we got word to move forward. We had not received an ammunition issue even by then, so I sent Sergeant Silver to inquire of General Manger. I led the regiment, my companies followed in alphabetical order, the hospital corps falling in behind. Many of my men were carrying their tin cups to keep them from rattling against their canteens, a needless precaution up here. One young Company A man who had entered the regiment with Woofer, a Hobbs boy named Few, was talking with a companion about the Yank army being beaten already. "Maybe the battle's over by now," he said hopefully, this while we were approaching the edge of the Wilderness.

Once the darkness of the woods closed over us there was no talking at all. There were occasional sighs or coughs. The place was dark except where cathedral-like shafts of light filtered down through the pollen and dust. There was not enough light to see more than a few men ahead at a time, yet one could in certain places see a long way off, where a spot of light lay or where a field was. I heard a distant whippoorwill's call, all lonely notes in here.

We came to a long line of litters with wounded men lying on them; they were men of General Longstreet's corps. There was a hospital tent thrown up in a crack in the woods, and we could see four tables inside, and the assistant surgeons of some regiment were busy at them, cutting and sawing. We went past that as quickly as we could. We enjoyed a pleasant walk along the edge of the woods, along a narrow, rutted road, and much sooner than I had thought likely somebody came run-

184

ning up to me to say we were to make camp.

I put a few guards out, then set the men to work pushing over the pines and piercing paths through the thickets. A weird-looking sight these aisles were, too, for they crossed one another and none of them was straight. Somebody would call out, "There's water over here," so several canteen men would clear a way to that spot, converging on it only to find a trickly spring. Most of them at once would go off into the woods again, clearing paths in every direction, forcing their way through, pushing over dead trees.

An ammunition wagon arrived at last, here at the very jaws of the enemy. I went about cursing Colonel Penny. Also two food wagons rolled into camp. "Sergeants onto the road now," I ordered, and that word moved through the woods. At my headquarters site I had two rows of pines pushed and axed down and a fire built, one about twelve feet long and two feet wide, laid in a pit. "We'll issue heavy rations tonight," I told the sergeants. "The men ought to cook them all, for we might not be able to cook tomorrow. The rations are to last three days. Cook both the bacon and beef. Also, we have the ammunition at last. Colonel Penny finally parted with it. He makes any responsibility he's given last as long as he can. Issue sixty cartridges to each man."

For a sleeping place I crawled under a pine and curled up where I could see the fire burn down. When Captain Crawford came along the road asking for me I kept quiet, but one of the sergeants told him where I was. He crept under the tree on all fours. "Hey, hey," he said. "Colonel, now that the battle is set, I hope you'll relieve me of my section."

"No, you carry on," I said.

"I—always in the past, you've relieved me," he said.

"You lead them this time, Captain."

For a long while he was quiet. Finally he said, "If—if as in the past I find the brigade headquarters, find where

185

General Manger is, I can stay in contact with him—"

"No, I'll have Sergeant Silver do all that."

"This is my third campaign, and I must admit to you that I'm not steady just now."

"Are you asking to be relieved?"

He thought about that. "Would it go on my record?"

"It would go on your record, yes." I lay there waiting for him to decide, my eyes closed.

"Colonel, I've done what I could to help you, to keep you out of trouble with the army. For God sake, I—I need some consideration."

A long while he crouched there. Now and then he moaned. Finally I heard him shuffle out of that place. Later I heard him near the fire say to a soldier, "Well, tomorrow'll be the day for us," his voice trembling like a recruit's.

Before dawn I was awakened by a vibration, not by a sound so much as a trembling of the earth and the air that must have been caused by the wheels of many caissons on the road. I crawled out from under the bush and stretched; the fire had burned down to red and gray ashes. Somebody came dashing swiftly through the woods, and Sergeant Willis jumped, scared to death. "Who was that?"

"It's a deer," somebody said.

"Or General Hooker," somebody else said.

I warmed by the fire. Near me a middle-aged soldier was groaning in his sleep, huddled up with his blanket roll pulled into his stomach like a baby. I tapped him on his shoulder and he awoke with a start. He was the miller from Surry, a man about forty, a veteran soldier. "You were talking in your sleep about some woman," I said.

A courier from General Manger came along whistling. He crouched down where I was warming my hands.

"What are we doing?" I asked him.

"Generals Lee and Jackson want to try to keep them in here, Colonel Wright. Jackson plans to take his corps around to the right flank of the Yanks. It's about a ten- or twelve-mile march to get to the flank."

I scratched at my arm, where I had many bugbites from the night before. "It's always interesting fighting a war for Lee and Jackson," I said. Of course, it was risky, moving a corps across the face of the Yank army. While we were on the march we would be stretched out and thin, and Lee would be left with only 15,000 men to hold the main body of the Yank army, should it strike. "I hope God told them to do this," I said.

In the bleak, early light I went to find Woofer. I had a small supply of bacon that Sergeant Silver had cooked for me, and I offered him a piece. It was streaky, not altogether fat, and his stomach growled even as he glanced at it. I laid the piece on his knee and sucked at another. "It's settling time with the Yanks," I said.

He was looking off through the woods, tense as a drawn string.

I belched. "My stomach gets nervous before a fight," I said. "My stomach and my hands." He said nothing. "Don't try to win the battle all at once," I told him. "They generally last three days."

"We going to lead in it?" he asked.

"Jackson generally likes to have us up front, but I never volunteer for anything." I showed him my watch, a London silver watch with a verge movement. "If I get caught short, Woofer, you can have it."

He looked at it as if he couldn't focus on what it was, then turned once more to stare out through the woods.

"Here, eat this," I said and poked another piece of bacon at him. He was extremely nervous, I noticed. "Every man goes into a battle differently," I told him.

Sergeant Smith came through the woods moaning and groaning. He said his men were not going to fight. I said to tell Captain Crawford, not me.

"I've told him ten times," he said.

187

"Well, tell him to tell me," I said.

"Will you talk to them, Owen?" he said.

"He will," I said. I left Woofer for a little while, went to ask Crawford to talk to all three of his companies, and he did so, but he told them next to nothing, so I spoke to them for a few minutes, walking up and down the road between their columns, the men sitting down or leaning against the trees. I started with a cartridge, which I usually do at such a time. I held one up for them to see. "It's a piece of paper with a lead ball in the smooth end and the gunpowder in the crinkly end; you bite off the crinkly end and put that end first into the muzzle of the musket, is that so?"

They nodded dumbly.

"Then you take the ramrod and push down the bullet and its wadding to hold the powder in place, so that the powder can be lit. Then you do what?"

"You shoot," somebody said.

"Well, you just shot your ramrod at the enemy, soldier," I said, and everybody laughed. "Which most of us have done from time to time," I said. "Now listen, don't fire until ordered to, and fire only when you see an enemy clearly. Fire deliberately. Take your time, don't rush. The war is going to take most all spring."

"A-men," Sergeant Raper said.

"Don't shoot high. Shoot low. Yanks don't live in Heaven. Shoot at the officers first. Aim to wound, not to kill; a wounded man is more of a problem to an army than a dead one. Don't huddle. If you're in a second or third rank, keep behind the man in the first rank to make a single target. You can't shoot anyway until he drops to fire or load his gun, or falls—for whatever reason. In battle when you are signaled forward, follow in random order, that is, about one third of each company moves forward while the others cover them. Stay with your company. If I or Captain Crawford or a sergeant signals for you to fall back, do so in an orderly way. More men are lost retreating than attacking. Don't stop to help the wounded, no matter who he is, except in retreat. Don't stop to help me, for instance. Don't stop to help your brother or the man who bunks with you. The best service you can be to your friend is to push the Yanks back, for they will kill him quicker than your mother would wring a chicken's neck."

I backed off the road to let an ambulance pass, then several mounted men rode by, all going to our left flank as we faced the enemy. The withdrawal, the Lee and Jackson strategy, was beginning now. With half as many men as the Yanks, they were dividing their army. It made no sense, of course, especially to the enemy.

"Don't pick up spoils during the battle," I said to Crawford's men. "If you see a diamond ring as big as an egg, call out and tell me where it is, and you go on."

The men fell to laughing. They were nervous, anyway, and susceptible to humor.

"Now, the hospital corps has convalescents to help with the wounded, and they have litter-bearers and assistant surgeons, and if you get wounded you will see them coming along. You'll find that one of your big needs is water, for you'll be sweating from tension. Don't drink all that you've got in your canteen. If you get wounded in the stomach, don't drink water at all. If you get lost, ask somebody where Manger's brigade is, or ask where I am. We're in Heth's division, Jackson's corps. We're going to be rounding the enemy most all day and that can be dangerous, for we'll be a thin line. If they attack, we're not going to try to hold them. If you get captured, say I told you to go home."

Several of the men laughed.

"Anybody want to go home?"

Nobody said a word. We stood there looking at each other, most everybody smiling except for the smith's men.

"Now, I do want to say one more thing, and those who know me know what it is. I've been put on the honor roll eleven times for past battles, which is a creditable score, and I have four medals, but I didn't get decorated all those times by being a hero all the time. Pick the occasions carefully when you are willing to risk your life."

"Tell 'em, Colonel," Sergeant Raper said.

"If we don't do anything today except find out how to protect ourselves so we can fight tomorrow, that's all right, because I expect there's going to be a fight here tomorrow. So you men who are not sure you want to fight in a sorry place like this can wait out your chances. We don't expect men to fight all the time. It's your army, and you'll find in good time that it's your war. Nobody who fights likes his enemy for very long. Keep your head down, keep your ass down, stay low, love the ground. Crawl if you can. Fire from the ground—I'd rather have that than have you stand out there like a queen's guard and be shot down. Nobody on earth can accurately fire a musket standing up anyway."

"A-men," Sergeant Raper said.

"You'll see some of Jackson's other regiments marching forward, erect and in order, and it looks impressive as hell, but we use a more frontier way, not theirs, not the army-manual way. That's why some of us have eleven honor roll citations and are still around. Now, any questions?"

"I got my cartridges wet last night, Colonel."

"Use your bayonet," I said. "Anything else?"

"Colonel, I got them wet, I tell you."

"Sell him a few rounds, Sergeant Furr," I said. "Anything else?"

"When we going to get our mail?"

"Let's say it'll be tonight," I said. "How the hell do I know?"

"Didn't you once promise we'd have us a band, Colonel?"

"We got one," I said. "It's right down there. One fiddle, two guitars, two banjos, a drum, a bugle, and the bagpipes."

"Seem to be playing for you more'n us."

"Now I notice that some of you still have pets. Is that a dog, Meadows?"

"Yes, sir."

"Well, can she shoot?"

"No, sir. But she can retrieve." He laughed nervously.

"What are you going to do with her?"

"I'll tie her to a tree, sir."

"I think you better give her away to the cavalry, where she'll be safe."

Several men laughed.

"I want to offer a prize of ten dollars to the first man to show me a dead cavalryman of either army," I said. "Last year nobody was able to collect. This year I'm offering the same prize."

"My brother is a cavalryman," a young soldier said defensively.

"Well, once he gets home you'll need to buy him a bigger hat and a wider chair seat."

"Sick call," a man said, "what about that?"

"No sick call today. Most days we're only pretending to be soldiers, but today we are soldiers, and it's a clean feeling, it'll heal you."

"We going to use these bayonets, sir?"

"If you get close enough to a Yank for that thing, take your rifle barrel in your hands if it's not too hot and beat the bastard with the butt of it."

"What do we do with the bayonet?"

"Throw it over your left shoulder as far as you can when Captain Crawford's not looking. Now, put your name somewhere on your uniform, pin it to your jacket, inside or out. Nothing to be ashamed of to admit you've got people who'll want to know if something happens to you."

They fell to work at that chore, and I noticed most of the smith's men were preparing the name slips, along with the rest, though they glowered at me moodily, grumbling at me whenever I came near.

When our time came I led Company A down the road, back the way we had walked yesterday, down between the double lines of Company B troops. I saw Woofer standing in his place between Betsy and Martin. He was looking straight ahead, stiff of back. Betsy was picking at his teeth with a stem. The road itself had probably not been used very much over the years, and since yesterday the wheels of our wagons had cut deeply into it, had mired in, had had to be pushed and pulled out; horses had mired in, too, and now thousands of men were walking through it. The road was soggy and bleeding. It had no bone left unbroken in it any longer. It was all mud and water as we sloshed along. I suppose the Yanks thought we were retreating, for Jackson had his hundreds of wagons clearly in evidence.

About one o'clock, at a swollen stream, the artillery pulled across a few caissons, which of course mired up to their hubs and had to be pushed out. Sitting on an old nag nearby was General Jackson, long-legged and lean, mounted on a worn saddle, a tough-looking man today, wearing a torn gray uniform, no markings on it at all. I suspect he had been up most of the night, scouting and conferring and planning. He made no sign of recognizing me, but I waded through the mud over to where he was. "Evening, sir," I said.

"Colonel, I've suggested that you be given that command, and Heth was to arrange the details of it," he said, his gaze still on his troops, not on me. "I thought he would have done so by now, but I notice you're still wearing a chicken and not a star."

"I've not heard a word of it, sir," I said. "Of course, my interest was not in getting an increase for myself—"

"I suppose Heth found General Manger opposed. He told me he didn't look forward to challenging that old war horse one bit."

"Yes, sir."

He signaled for a courier, who came alongside at once. "Ask Heth to arrange the Colonel Wright matter before we get too deep into this battle." When the courier left Jackson nodded briefly to me. "Where is Manger, anyway?"

"I thought he was up front, sir."

"He's in a wagon if he is, or I would have seen him. Go on up that road with your regiment. The Yanks are over to your right. When you go about a half a mile, you'll be told to turn into the woods. Lay your men by there for our attack. No delay, no delay. We've almost got them."

There were Reb troops on all sides of us, moving along swiftly now. I saw General Manger standing on a wagon looking about, and he reminded me of nothing so much as a farmer out looking for cattle that had strayed. When he saw me, a jolting, fiery anger swept into his face all in a moment, and he swung away in a fury. Colonel Penny got up from a rock where he was sitting and turned to stare at me. Neither of them said a word to me, but I was conscious of their hatred, and not unconcerned about it either.

I turned into the woods. There was scattered musket fire many miles away, probably as far away as General Lee's army. Between us and that gunfire lay the Yank army, like a lamb's gut full of cheese. I placed my men six feet apart, each company forming three lines, each line about ten feet behind the one in front of it; thus my Company A, with about fifty men, had sixteen men in each of three lines, each line being about forty-five feet long. B Company took its place to the right. In all, my regiment occupied the front for a distance of about 400 feet, with Lieutenant King in charge of the left section, Captain Crawford of the middle, and Lieutenant McGregor of the right. Another North Carolina brigade fell in to my right flank. On our regimental left were Colonel McRuder's men.

I checked my lines. Sergeant Smith was so disturbed he couldn't understand a five-word question, even when I spoke slowly to him. Billy Furr and his men, on the other hand, were eager to be off; it was as if they were expecting to have a race and the starting pistol was about to be fired. I asked for Captain Crawford and found him behind a hickory truck, sitting on the ground, Sergeant Red Raper with him, and he was telling Raper that he wasn't going to accept ever again the sort of insults several of Raper's men had heaped on him that morning.

On my far right I found Lieutenant McGregor's three companies in perfect order. You would think he had used a ruler to measure the distance between his men. He had a command post set up, had even sent a sergeant around to be certain every man had kept his cartridges dry, that the nipple on his musket's firing pin was dry, and that nobody had mud stopping up his musket barrel. He had hot coffee, a canteenful of it, and I drank half a cup, which was all any one person was allowed, he said. I mentioned to him that we had not since dawn had a single message of any sort from General Manger and it appeared I was ostracized for some reason. "If a courier from Heth arrives, I am to be found at once," I said. "It makes no difference what stage the fighting is in."

The men had card games going by now. Several men were trying to read their testaments, even in that dark woods; others were singing softly to themselves. Many were writing letters. One elderly man was eating a piece of corn bread; he had no teeth and the crumbs kept falling out of his mouth. Another was chewing on a raw piece of bacon, which I suppose wasn't good for him, but there's no point in telling a man waiting to go into battle that it's unhealthy to eat raw pork.

I saw Woofer. He saw me, too, but he made no sign. He was sitting on the ground with his back against a little scraggly pine, whittling on a stick. He had a vacant expression on his face; there was nothing lively about it. Betsy came toward me and led me away. "He's wondering just now if he can fight, that's all," he said. "He's never even killed a pig, and he's sick."

"His stomach or bowels, or what?"

"In spirit is all."

"Can you keep him in line when we move forward?"

"I will or I'll crown him one."

"He's not going to flee or anything like that?"

"No, he talks reasonable enough. He gets mad, says you told him to be mean, so he will, he says, but he can't do it."

"Betsy, I never wronged him with this woman."

"Uh-huh," Betsy said absent-mindedly. He didn't believe me apparently. "It wouldn't do any good to talk to him about that, Colonel. It would make it worse, wouldn't it, for he needs to get mad enough at somebody so he can kill Yanks."

"I don't want him mad at me," I said.

"It's late to think of that," Betsy said.

A while I stood there staring at the boy. He was about twenty feet away. A lifetime away, I decided. A woman away. "Don't let him get into any special danger," I said.

A band began to play, a Yank band. Not far away either, and my musicians perked up. The Yanks were playing "The Girl I Left Behind Me." Betsy laughed out loud; music tickles men whenever a battle is brewing. I sent word to my three officers to advance their sections slowly to the first field. I crept forward with Company A, with Hal King. Usually I kept to the center of my regiment, but I wanted Crawford to feel the full weight of his responsibility. Ahead of me I could see the little scraggly field. Most all my men were crawling now.

We stopped at the edge of the field. It was about a hundred feet wide. On the other side of it a Yank officer climbed onto a breastwork he and his men had made the night before. It was facing toward our old position, not our new one. We could see other breastworks in a line going into the woods, all facing wrong. To outflank a company or regiment is often done in a battle, but to outflank an army is remarkable and says precious little for their perceptiveness. I suspect their generals were so far removed from the actual battlefield, and their Yank organization so complex, that they didn't know what changes were taking place and they couldn't evaluate what they did know. Jackson, on the other hand, stayed with his men and did much of his own scouting.

A Yank soldier, blue uniformed, wearing good shoes and a peaked hat, walked casually down to a creek and got water in a cup. He returned to his fire.

195

"That apple tree's going to be pretty in a few weeks," I said to Hal. "It's budding."

"Must have been a homestead here once," Hal said.

A deer appeared, moved out into the field about 150 yards to our left, where McRuder's men were quietly moving to the edge of the woods. Another deer appeared farther down the field. The Yank officer, his hands on his hips, studied about that, looking thoughtfully along the line of woods.

Hal said, "What would you do, Owen, if you were that Yank officer?"

"Get ready to run," I said.

Victor Plover came forward. He had his snare drum strapped over his shoulder. He was a child, really, and was so dumb or scared he couldn't understand what was being said to him. Several of Hal's men on his nod put their muskets to their shoulders. That poor Yank officer was still standing up on his breastwork studying our woods fretfully. You better get down, mister, I thought; you'll soon be food for Virginia tumblebugs if you don't mind.

The drum roll began way off, the long roll, and moved swiftly toward us, and in that instant the muskets fired and the Yank officer was flung upward and backward. My drummer boy was striking his drum now and Hal's men rose with a yell, that infernal Rebel yell, a mingling of challenge and blood-terror, a hunter's sound meant to frighten. His men moved out into the field, walking quickly.

One of them fell. He scrambled to his feet, started back toward where I lay, his hand inside his jacket, a young man, about nineteen, a veteran soldier named Vance. He took his hand out of his jacket. His hand was red and dripping, and he said, "Colonel, what does this mean?" and fell dead.

The yell sounded again. As far as one could see were gray men moving through the woods and all about were the shattering noises of our muskets firing. At this close range a ball goes zip. There is no whistle or shriek or whine. It goes zip, with now and then one singing off into space with a villainous, greasy slide. My men were in perfect formation, except as I moved to the right I found that the smith's men were lingering in a mass back a ways.

After a while Yank musket balls began to whistle and whine, and now and then to shriek through the air overhead. They flew past us sounding like swifts. Others sounded like bumblebees.

A man twenty feet away crumpled to the ground. I decided he was acting, that was all. "Get up, mister. On your feet," I said.

He got up slowly, not looking at me.

"Go slow, no hurry," I told him. "Those bees won't sting you." I saw my bagpipe player moving ahead, his pipes on his back, chewing tobacco and spitting and peering forward, hoping to catch a sight of the Yanks. We had crossed the field and were once more in pine woods, where low branches had already been broken by Yanks, so we had to avoid the sharp pointed stubs that were left.

The shelling began, our own artillery opening fire on the body of the Yank army, which was no doubt in confusion enough without this added excitement. Big shells flew overhead, sounding like locomotive whistles, and exploded over the woods ahead of us, scattering hunks of metal. The shells had been made of iron from the rails of old North Carolina railroad track, I suspect, and lampposts taken off the streets of Charleston and Atlanta and Memphis and other cities, and black iron cookpots from Alabama, Mississippi, and a thousand other places. The South was breaking iron this afternoon, trying to free itself. Sergeant Smith's men panicked at the noise, started running toward the rear. I decided to hell with them for now. I couldn't outrun them, after all.

"You want to play a tune?" I asked McIlvenna.

"Don't I have to be quiet?" he said, astonished.

"Quiet?" I said, and laughed.

He struck up a tune. He was grinning with such happiness he could scarcely make a steady sound. There he went walking

197

through those pine woods, playing "The Highland Laddie," which tingled in my blood. The Plover boy came running, ready to join in. The sound of the artillery seemed less dangerous now.

When we came upon wounded Yanks, we walked on past them. To step over wounded men adds to the feeling of omnipotence which a soldier gets in battle; the more wounded men a soldier sees the less likely he is to be afraid of being hit, for each one is a credit to his infallibility. We didn't hear most of their cries, anyway, because of the rapid musket fire around us and the artillery shells overhead, and my band playing.

Colonel McRuder came hurrying through the woods, proud and big, puffing for breath and patting his huge belly. "Owen, where did you get that bagpipe player?" he asked. "Damn me, I want him. I'd rather have him than my own cannon."

"No, no," I said, "you'll not get him, Mac."

"I'll give you two scouts that can find their way home blindfolded."

We laughed and listened to him play, and walked along in the deep woods, neither of us having lost many men yet—though I had lost a few to the rear apparently.

We were coming to places where shells had exploded earlier, and there were many Yank casualties about. A wounded Yank was pinned under a shattered tree limb, and Betsy and Martin and Woofer had stopped to help. I said, "Move on, soldiers," and they turned, astonished, to stare at me, for the Yank was in pain. "Move on," I said.

Betsy and Martin obeyed, but Woofer stood there staring at me incredulously. "Owen ..." he said, trying to begin his plea, but he would make no request of me, it seemed, and of course he had reason to know how callous I could be. "G-g-god damn you," he said, and turned, white-faced, and ran through the woods, following Betsy, shaking his head furiously.

Captain Crawford came up to me. "They—it's getting late, Colonel," he began, almost incoherently, "and the men want to attack." He was shirt-ripped and had powder marks all over his face, marks daubed on by his fingers, I could tell, not put there by biting cartridges. "Billy Furr wants to advance," he said. "He wants to go forward faster."

"Every man stays in line, Captain," I said.

At once he nodded and started away, staggering, so frightened that his legs were wobbly.

Our cannons were still lobbing shells over us and we were moving forward steadily. There were scores of prisoners. The Yank army couldn't get organized to turn to meet us, and time after time pockets of men would have to surrender. We would disarm them and wave them toward the rear. All was going well, but I suppose Billy Furr was afraid the battle was going to end before he could get in the thick of it, so he and his men spurted forward in a charge. Sergeant Raper and I tried to overtake them. We saw them stop at one point, baffled, confused, for they had thought in a battle there were two lines, one always pushing at the other, and here they were, having exposed themselves, offered themselves for combat, but where were the enemy? They began running forward again. Raper and I went chasing after them as best we could, I shouting at them. The tree limbs were raking at our uniforms, but we tore our way through. We got quite far out ahead of our own line, which meant we could conceivably be cut off and captured, but how does one stop a runaway company gone merrily to see the enemy? They were losing their canteens, their cups; I saw one man cut his haversack's straps to let it fall so he wouldn't be delayed by the trees snagging it. "Come back here, you fools!" I shouted at them.

"Forward!" Billy Furr shouted.

"Damn you, come here," I demanded and fired my pistol over his head, but it might as well have been a robin peeping in this noisy place.

A Yank appeared. Billy let out a Rebel yell and went tearing toward him, to choke him to death, I suppose, and the Yank retreated right smartly, Billy's men following along a little trail about eight feet wide. Six Yanks appeared, blocking the road, and fired down the road at Billy Furr's company, almost in their very faces. Billy's men reeled, stunned, screaming, some of them hit, of course. Even as this happened another group of Yanks began firing on them from the woods to our left. I shouted for Billy's men to get into the woods to our right. Raper and I ran here and there, trying to collect them, few of my brave Company E being able or even interested now in returning the enemy fire. They were so shocked, scared that all they wanted was to run the other way, and off they went tearing through the woods, as swift in retreat as they had been in attack. Only a few of them helped Billy Furr answer the enemy.

I left those few to fight or retreat as they chose, and took half a dozen less belligerent men back the way we had come, Sergeant Raper joining us with ten men. We entered our lines almost sheepishly, and I saw Lieutenant McGregor watching us, his hands on his hips, a big grin on his handsome face.

"What do you call that maneuver, Colonel?" he asked me.

"Charge and retreat," I said.

"You've got two or three fast runners there," he said.

"I think so," I said.

"You fellows get a look at Washington, D.C.?" he asked them.

Billy was still out there firing away.

I sought out Captain Crawford to ask him to resign from the command. I found him squatting on a path, trembling, and he said for me not to say anything more to him, that he was sick. "I never been so sick," he said. Even then he tried to vomit, and I said he could at least get off the path, which he did, moving like a turtle, his pants down around his knees, and he kept gagging.

"You want to write out a resignation, Captain?" I asked him. "You've lost severely from two companies so far."

He went on gagging, but nothing was coming out of him at either end. Abruptly he looked up at me, almost overcome by revulsion and bitterness. "Ah, God damn you, you'll strip me down to a coffin as you have the General, as you are him. The lust you got! Until you are General Jesus Christ!"

"Where did you hear anything about a general?"

"You think I don't know what you're up to?" He gagged and spit on the ground, his stomach heaving. "I'm sick," he said huskily. "God, don't you care if a man is sick?" He looked up at me pitiably. "Go taunt your brother and leave me be," he told me furiously.

Dusk. The air smelled of sulphur. The moon was covered over with a thick cloud of smoke and gas. The Yank artillery was bombarding us now, but far behind our lines. Many of the men were walking about dazed, even coming from other regiments, glassy-eyed, unable to talk except in monosyllables. Many of them were lost, others were claiming to be lost whenever they were asked why they were here. A dwarf came through; some regiment's drummer boy, I suppose. Now and then a wounded man or a dead man would be found and the men would argue about who was going to go through his clothes and pack, and to whom his watch belonged if he had a watch, and his spoon, his knife, his shoes. The men shared the Yank hardtack they found and the Yank coffee.

Billy Furr was back, somebody said. He had brought back seven of his men with him.

A Yank came through, walking about; nobody said anything to him. Doubtless he was addled by the scenes he had witnessed; I had never been part of any army which had disintegrated, but I suppose such a situation would produce terror in the bravest man.

I asked Lieutenant King to bring Woofer to supper. I had some eggs, I said.

"Eggs out here, Owen?" he said, incredulous.

"Oh, yes," I said, "I have a dozen eggs with me."

201

He went to invite Woofer, to try to persuade him to come with him. Directly both of them came pushing dead branches off of pine trees and cussing the stingy, little bark particles which scratch and nettle the skin. They sat down at my fire, which was about the size of my hands and was in a creek gully. "Where are they, Owen?" Hal asked. "Show us."

"He hasn't got any eggs," Woofer said sullenly.

I had in fact the day before broken a dozen eggs—or Sergeant Silver had broken them on my instruction—and had poured them into a spare canteen, so now I poured two of them out into a tin cup and scrambled them over the fire, and both men's stomachs began to growl, just as mine did, and a big smile came over Hal's face. "It makes the war worthwhile," he said.

"Oh, everything's judged by contrast," I said. "Any little pleasure is a mountain out here. Two eggs can make a difference in a war."

"Only two?" Hal said.

"We're not done with the battle yet," I said. "We'll keep half of them for tomorrow."

"I don't plan for tomorrow, not in a battle," Hal said.

"You shoot anybody?" I asked him.

"No. Did you?"

"No," I said.

"Did you shoot anybody, Woofer?" he said.

Woofer grunted and shook his head.

"Woofer doesn't have any enemies, except me," I said.

Woofer said nothing, but his eyes were sad as he watched me.

"I want to tell you both something," I said. "It's not for the others to know." I handed my first cup of cooked eggs to Woofer, for he looked so hungry and forlorn, and I took his cup. "You going to eat them with your fingers?" I asked him, surprised.

Hal cut him a pine stick, flattened it with two strokes of his knife, and gave it to him.

202

"I'm a general by now," I told them. "I have General Manger's command."

The look of perplexity that came over both their faces was a wonder to see. Then a smile appeared on Hal's face. "Lord help us," he said. "We're eating dinner on a silk tablecloth, Woofer. You see the white cloth?"

"You a g-g-general?" Woofer said, perplexed and hurt and pleased.

"What do you think of it?" I asked. "Papa's going to split his britches."

"Jesse will, you mean," he said. "You a general?"

"I had to do it, didn't I? You can see that. All day out here without one word from him."

"How did you do it?" Hal asked.

"Never mind that," I said. "Manger would have strung me up if he had caught me at it. But I had to take the chance."

Hal laughed softly and poked playfully at Woofer. "He'll be next to Jackson soon."

"Oh, hell," I said, laughing with him, and I gave him two cooked eggs and waited for a while to cook my own, for the excitement had got my stomach upset.

"Who'll take your place?" he asked me.

"You, I expect."

"No, no, Owen. Let me tell you something, I'm a watcher. Do you understand? I watch people and comment to myself."

"You're too modest, that's your trouble," I said.

"I'm not being modest when I separate myself from others this way. That's not modesty, is it?"

"You'll have to lead this regiment," I said.

"No, you give it to McGregor. Heth prefers officers who run errands."

"I don't run errands."

"He doesn't much like you either," Hal said.

"My trouble with McGregor is that he's too military to be an army officer," I said.

Woofer let out a laugh. He lay back on the ground laughing at me.

I said to Woofer, "What are you laughing like a fool for? I'm not military, I admit it. I don't like officers who go around with their right hand holding a war book and their left hand flipping a riding crop against their boot. Mountain troops aren't soldiers."

"You don't like Lee?" Hal asked.

"I like the way he wins," I said, "the way he and Jackson win."

"Is it Lee or Jackson who wins?" Hal said.

"It was Jackson in the Shenandoah, for Lee wasn't there. It's hard for me to know which one decides on battles since then," I said.

"Maybe both of them, maybe both of them together," Hal said.

"Owen's wary of officers when they dress up and ride a good horse," Woofer said bluntly.

Hal laughed, trying to relieve the bitterness of the statement, and then I got to laughing, for it was true. Hal said, "Owen will be up there on high with them soon."

"Well, I tell you," I said suddenly, "it's something powerful to be with an army that always wins, and you have to ask why it is, ask who is responsible. God knows, we are a sorry lot, but we always win, we beat the Yanks, while out west the Westerners usually beat our people."

"Our men don't have Lee and Jackson out there," Hal said.

"I know. That's what I'm saying. It's the two of them together, maybe that's what it is, and we think it's Jackson because he's the one we can see from here in his ranks. I don't know yet, but I might know soon, once I get higher up."

"When they going to announce all this?" Hal said.

"Tonight or tomorrow," I said. "It's decided. Manger knows, but it's not nailed to the tree yet."

"How do you know it's done?"

204

"That fool Crawford." I lay back on the ground, happy with my lot, even excited by the jealousy Woofer was showing, that and the happiness he couldn't hide.

"Owen's a general," Hal said, savoring the words. "You're eating supper with a general, Woofer, and you don't have clean hands."

"Yeh, I'm God Almighty with a star on my ass," I said. "I'll take Sergeant Silver with me, Hal," I said.

"Tell McGregor," he said, "not me."

"You will take the command, won't you?"

"No. My one ambition is to go home, Owen."

"Yeh, you got something to go home to." I saw Woofer turn to stare at me. "You and Woofer," I said. I closed my eyes to hide the sight of him, a pain shooting through me. Sory, Sory—what if Sory were waiting for me, all dusted and powdered and smiling for me? What if her house were our house, open to the nighttime breezes, and the fields were ready to be planted and the cellars were full of wine and food, and the wood were cut? How is it in life that the perfect dreams get twisted?

"I see a star," Hal said. "That's your star, Owen," he said.

"I know it is," I said. And she can see it too, I thought. We can hold the stars in common. "I'm lucky in the war, I admit it," I said.

"I would give a prize to know how they got up there that way," Woofer said. He was lying on his back, staring up into the heavens.

"Looks like they were flung there," Hal said. "Maybe God was out sewing with golden seed and they flashed fire at him."

"I don't know another thing he did that way, with so much space left between," Woofer said. "Usually God filled up space, whether with trees or laurel or what not, but he sowed lightly up there."

"He might have had a reason," I said.

The wind shifted slightly and the odor of sulphur came in stronger on us. Far off shells began to burst over the

205

treetops, shattering them, I suspect.

"You suppose he sees us?" Hal said softly.

"Why, I know he does," Woofer said. "What would he make us for if he didn't want to watch us?"

"What does he want us to do, that he watches us for?" Hal said.

"To do right," Woofer said.

"Oh my," Hal said, and he laughed softly.

"And who's to say?" I asked quietly, watching the sky.

"Maybe he knows that too," Woofer said. "Maybe he's studying it out all the time."

"Who do we do right for?" Hal said.

"He helps us decide," Woofer said. "And he orders natural things, the seasons and all, and the storms."

"And the wars," Hal said.

We rested there on the ground, each man reflecting on what he thought and what he saw on the great domed ceiling of the world, on which we are such small parts. Even soldiers.

After supper I found Sergeant Red Raper sitting in a circle made up of pots and pans he had confiscated from his company. He had several decks of cards too, which he had decided to destroy, lest God retaliate against him. Two guitar players were playing, and we listened to them for a while.

"How many injured do you have?" I asked.

"We got pine-stung is all, though five men faded away to the rear," Raper said.

"The army might bring them to us by morning," I said.

"Two are already back. What do I say to them?"

"Tell them you missed them."

Sergeant Smith came through the woods. Of course, he was resentful of the ridicule being heaped on his company by the other men, and he was anxious to know what might be expected of him tonight or tomorrow. I told him to keep his company in the line, that being the secret of it. I crept to where Billy Furr's company was and found him stretched out on his belly looking toward the enemy, his loaded rifle in hand, his eyes squinting into the woods.

"What the hell do you want?" he said to me. "I tell you, let me say right now if you don't like the way we've been fighting, Owen, you can get a new sergeant and company both."

"How many men are you missing?" I asked him quietly.

"You gave us that Captain Crawford to lead us, and he's got no balls. All my men are cussing him. Then we walk through a pine woods all day without so much as a breath of clean air to breathe, with our feet out of our shoes and our bowels running, stepping over Yanks. Christ, what a way to hunt game."

"How many men are you missing?" I asked him again.

"I can't find eleven of them yet," he said.

"That's more than a fifth lost," I said. "Four more days and you'll be out of a company."

"You lead it tomorrow then, damn it," he said. "You can go to hell for all I care. We're the only company that had guts enough to charge the—"

"You see something move over there, Billy?" I asked softly. He hushed.

"Near that mother pine?"

"Huh?" he said. "Might be one of ours. There's a man or two of mine out there looking through Yank pockets."

"Is McKinney out there?"

"He's out there. He goes and comes."

A far-off shell lighted the road for an instant.

"Is he as mean as he appears to be, Billy?"

"You better believe it. He—he—he is more trouble than all my other men combined. He won't listen to an order, won't wait for nothing, and he's not saved one bit. That man when he dies is going to Hell the fastest way. I saw Sole once kill a nigger ever so clean. He didn't even hesitate."

"Killed him for what?"

"Escaping along that mountain trail where your brother Jesse used to take them. He cut his head off. The nigger's body stood there on the trail, spurting, then it wilted at the stalk."

I said nothing. I was too horrified to form a statement, really. We lay there side by side, looking into the woods. Way off another shell burst in the air, ours I think it was.

"We winning this battle?" he asked me.

"I think we are," I said. "We are sending back enough prisoners, anyway."

"How you tell who wins one of these?"

"They tell you afterwards," I said.

"How many days will it go on for?"

"Three days."

He grunted. "Why's that?"

"Father, Son, and Holy Ghost," I said.

He grunted. After a while he said, "Think of that."

"Yes," I said. "It's all in the Bible, as you know."

"Uh-huh," he said.

The damn fool, I thought.

He aimed his musket at a bush across the road.

"Don't fire that thing in my ear," I told him.

A man came crawling out onto the road. He stopped, sat bolt upright in the road. A flash of shell-light fell on him.

"What you doing so quiet to be shot for?" Billy said to him contemptuously.

In another shell-light we saw that Sole McKinney had a Yank's head in his hands. Even Billy— Neither of us knew what to say, and when the next shell flashed, McKinney was holding the head up before his own face, so that its blind eyes were glistening at us. "Hee, hee, hee," he giggled. "Hee, hee, hee."

I was moving carefully along the road back toward Company A where Hal was, when I heard a number of riders approaching. I stepped into the woods and challenged them. They reined in. The flash of a far-off shell lighted six officers of our own army, and I said, "How you doing tonight, mister?" On the front it's as well not to identify an officer, especially a general.

"Whose men are you?" he said.

"Owen Wright's," I said.

208

"Where is he?" the General said. "I'd like to see him."

"Not far away," I said, and stepped onto the road.

"I mighta known," he said. "You're sounding gloomy tonight. I thought you might be celebrating."

"I've been stung by pines all day and have lost several men."

"Pray and be comforted," he said. "Our minds should be more on the Lord and less on the matters of this earth. I have lost a thousand."

"Yes, sir."

"May God judge us."

"Yes, sir."

"We need to press right on now. Gather your men and proceed. And be assured I talked with General Heth today, and he has talked with our friend. We have got it done, and I can justify it within my own conscience, for we must make soldiers' decisions in a war. I hope you never have regrets."

"I hope not, sir."

"Has Heth sent you word?"

"No, sir."

"He will," he said, and with a brief nod he quietly added, "General," and spurred his mount, and the group of riders, staff officers and couriers and signalmen, went noisily along the road following him.

I stepped back into the woods to hide myself, to cover my elation, for surely I could not share it. I was even more affected than I had been earlier, with Hal and Woofer. I tell you, when a man has been a failure until the age of thirty, then later receives a title of high nobility, it redeems his failures, doesn't it? I had to sit down by a tree, I was so weak in my legs. My God, I thought, my God.

A shot rang out down the road. I scarcely was aware of it. Then a volley of them, cruel and sharp in the night here close upon us, and a nauseous clot came into my throat. "Not now," I said.

I dashed down the road, ignoring the challenges of my own men. "Don't shoot! Don't shoot!" I said, as I ran as fast as I could, past Billy Furr's company, past Red Raper's, past the three companies under Lieutenant McGregor, until near the union with the other brigade I came upon several men standing on the road, milling about, asking each other what had happened.

"Who the hell was they, mister?" one man said to me. "Come riding through a battlefield ..."

I stumbled over a dead horse on the road. I recovered my balance and bumped into General Hill, Jackson's second-in-command, one of the officers who had been riding with Jackson.

"Who shot at us, Colonel, do you know?" he asked.

"Where is he?"

"In there. He rode in there," he said, pointing to the woods.

Some soldiers said, "They rode down the road and I thought they was Yanks. How the hell could anybody tell they wasn't Yanks?"

He was from the other brigade, he was not one of my men, for which I thanked God. Thank God. Thank God.

I entered the woods and tore my way through the bushes. I came upon two men kneeling beside the body of a wounded man on the ground, the man lying on his back. Distant shells were lighting the sky in momentary breaths, so I couldn't see very well, but the wounded man was talking, murmuring a prayer, and I knew who it was. Helpless now, fallen, one of the great generals of the unbeatable army, hero of two fabled years of victory.

A staff officer, Captain Wilbourn, was kneeling beside him. "Lieutenant, go find a surgeon," he said, and the other kneeling figure rose at once and hurried off into the woods. I took his place beside the body. I watched, cold with fear, as Wilbourn loosened the General's field glasses and haversack and put them over his own shoulder, then began to cut the cloth from the General's arm and shoulder.

General Hill came through the woods. "I have been trying to make the men cease firing," he said. He knelt beside Jackson. "Is the wound painful?" he asked him.

"Very painful," Jackson whispered. "My arm is broken."

Hill gently removed the General's sword and belt.

"You will inquire whether the surgeon is competent?" Jackson asked.

Captain Wilbourn tied a handkerchief above the wound as a tourniquet; the blood had begun to clot by this time. "Do you have any other wound?" he said.

"In my right hand, but never mind that; it is a mere trifle."

An assistant surgeon of Pender's brigade arrived with a litter. A soldier appeared to say the enemy was only fifty yards away and was advancing. General Hill went out into the road to try to organize the troops to withstand an attack, should one come.

Wilbourn and I helped Jackson to his feet. Over my shoulder he put his right arm and bleeding hand. His feet dragging, he stumbling, we helped him back to the road and along it slowly.

"Who is that?" the men asked. "Who is it there?" they said.

"It's only a friend of ours," I replied.

One soldier darted in close enough to stare at the pale, bearded man. "Great God," he cried, "it's General Jackson."

"No, it's only a Confederate officer," I said.

The boy said nothing in dispute, but he looked again at Jackson and turned away in silence.

The surgeon called for the litter-bearers and we helped the General to lie down. Four of us took up the litter just as the road was swept with a hurricane of canister, grape and Minié balls. One bearer fell, wounded, and two other bearers laid down their handles and dashed into the woods, leaving Jackson on the ground. Over us the projectiles were shrieking. Horses—there were several of them, all from the General's party—were running about, frantic with fear. Another officer and I stretched ourselves out on either side of the General to protect him as best we could. He in a daze started to get up, but I held him on the litter. About us grapeshot and Minié balls were striking the stones of the road.

When the Yanks began to fire shells, two of us picked Jackson up and carried him into the woods, another officer following with the litter. Once in the woods we got him onto the litter.

211

General Dorsey Pender found us. "General, I am sorry to see you have been wounded," he said, dismayed. "The lines here are so much broken that I fear we will have to fall back."

Jackson raised his head, his eyes flashing. "You must hold your ground, General Pender. You must hold your ground, sir," he said.

We raised Jackson. We managed to get the handles of the litter on our shoulders and started through the woods, but one of the bearers caught his foot in a vine and fell head foremost. The General fell heavily, landing on his shattered arm, and a great groan came out of him. We managed to get him once more on the litter. His eyes were shut, his face was bloody, his breathing spasmodic. "General, are you in deep pain?" I whispered.

"No, Colonel," he said steadily, "don't trouble yourself about me," he said.

We began to move through the woods with him again. I knew by now that he was dying. I knew he realized he was dying. The Yank artillery was still firing along this part of the front, breaking the trees over us. My uniform was covered with scattered pieces of tree branches. They were scattered over me, just as all my plans in the war were scattered, too, scattered over me.

CHAPTER TEN

There was a siege of rain, I remember, and we were camped out on a hillside and the mud was cold and it stuck to our clothes and skin; it was not the most of my misery, but it was a division of it. This was sometime later, several days. The battle had lasted three days, and by evening of the third day the Wilderness was aflame and my men were exhausted, yes, and many of them were dead and a large number of us were torn and bleeding. I recall we had pushed the Yanks back across the river—a mighty victory, or so it was said, but we were not victors in our souls. God knows I was not.

Though on that third night in the moonlight as General Lee came down the road, riding his great gray mount, his aides following, even my men, tattered, exhausted, tortured by the loss of powers and blood and the sights we had seen, when they saw Lee they took off their caps and waved them, and from their bodies, even from the wounded lying on the ground, came calls, whispers of praise and adoration. And he, majestic, handsome, the symbol of victory in battle after battle, accepted their cries and favors and bowed to them, waved his hand and hat to them. I was reminded of the confusion that sometimes entered the minds of people of ancient times as to whether a general was a man or a god.

When he rode on, we were left with our moans and the doctoring of ourselves, and I was left with my fateful misfortunes, which had accumulated like bad weather in winter.

Hal King approached, sat down nearby, clutching his fingers

213

in a strange, incredible, painful way, and I said, "Stop it, Hal."

He lay back on the ground and looked up at the dark sky, the smoky sky, and we listened to the distant musket fire. "Who won the damn thing, Owen?"

"We did, I believe," I said.

"Did we win the war, do you think?"

"I don't know yet. Did you see Woofer since sunset?"

"I saw him." He was still grinding his fingers together.

I got up, weak and sleepy, and started on up the hill, the men following, and soon I heard Hal behind me say, "Owen, I can't do any more of these battles."

We walked up the same road we had used on our approach. It must have been ten o'clock when we got to the artillery position of three days before. I paused there to look out over the fire-lighted scene. Never did a painter paint with blacker swaths and brighter splashes the colors of a battle scene, the fiery disarray and chaos here.

The artillerymen were unable to get onto the road because of the press of traffic. There were swarms of Rebel soldiers still coming out of the caldron, and there were scores of black ambulances, their horses heaving, their drivers swearing. And there were the swift, prancing members of the cavalry, whom we all cursed as they rode by. "Where the hell you been?" the men shouted at them. "What the hell you good for?" There were Yank prisoners, too, thousands of them, well and wounded men, all of them downcast and miserable. One of my men shouted at a group of them. "Going to give our niggers the whips and you the plows."

"You'll like Libby," the men told them.

The Yank prisoners studied us with their deep-set, baffled eyes, saying nothing, while above us the clouds, where war and fire smoke had rolled together, looked like Calvary.

Let it be a funeral pyre for weeks, I thought, then let it be strewn with salt and lime to rot the bodies; burn its soily flesh so that never can a pine grow there again. Never let a line of

214

men move through a dark woods on this place again, where Jackson fell and my regiment was so victorious that it cannot stand to be saluted in the moment of its victory. Let us lime all the dead. Let us not bury anybody else in America. Lime the dead. Let us lime them before the stink alters our politics. Look down at that fire—smoke rising so high in the sky that not a hawk is able to rise over it—roast the hawks as they fly.

I stand here heated by the fire half a mile away, and hear the thin rattle of the muskets firing as Lee brings down more Yank soldiers. Lime them. Lime the dead. Do not break out their gold teeth either. Lime the dead. Do not bury all the thousands who have fallen here.

I sought the ground. I felt my mother, the earth, my friend, the bosom of the ground.

I could see him—I dreamed I could see him. I drew closer. His jacket was torn open down the front and in his hands was the bleeding head of the Yank soldier, which McKinney must have given to him and told him to suckle. This head Crawford held against his own tit, and he was singing to it a lullaby of sorts, a weird mixture of sounds and words, sobs and groans. Sweat was on his face like oil. Blood was on his hands and arms. The dead eyes of the Yank face were open. His own eyes were stark, wide, staring, yet blind, if awareness is a judge of sight. His voice a woman's, his words a woman's choice, his voice breaking like a woman's in sorrow, his hand smoothing the matted hair of the Yank head in his arms, he comforting it as a woman comforts a hurt child.

I kicked the head out of his hands. It went rolling across the floor of the woods. He began to cry and to reach out for it. "It's not for you, Skip," I told him.

Dearest Sory,   ◇

I have not heard a word from you, and I must criticize

you for that, since I need now the comfort you can give. Does it cost a woman anything to comfort a man? Have you not written me because you dare not approach the wall which has separated us? If I were with you I would not admit to a wall, not tonight, for I am in more misery than I can tolerate alone. What is to be our fate? For God sake tell me.

We have won the battle here. We have captured their supplies and sent them fleeing. We have got the notion in our minds that we are invincible. Yet we are lying on the ground with pain—not I so much as the others, for my wounds were made inside. You have heard by now that Jackson was shot down, and though he lingers even tonight in life, he is dying. My God, what is that loss, what in heaven or hell or earth will it mean?

Before he fell wounded he raised me in rank to a general. Think of that, dearest Sory. But since then nobody has mentioned the matter to me, and when yesterday I saw General Hill and asked about it he said that subject could best be determined after Jackson's recovery. Which I take to be a sign that I will not be tenderly handled by Hill and Heth and Manger when Jackson dies. Already I feel the wrath of Manger, for whenever I see him he smiles with deep bitterness and says to me, "You will be pleased to know that I am feeling better, Owen."

Also he has raised Crawford to major, over my objections, and in spite of my official criticism of his inefficiency in battle.

Dearest Sory, I am deserted even by this army. When I entered it, a man could more easily make his own place here and fight the war on his own terms, but now it is all rule and design and conspiracy. I am lonely even here among my men, and I fear for them as I do for myself. We are prisoners of our own army. We have created a machine larger than men can competently control.

Why do I write you full of sadness? Is it that I believe you have known sadness and loneliness and can pity me? I am not made to pity others, for I find pity weakening. Maybe men are often of that sort. I am not strong enough to risk pitying another. I can sense somebody else's suffering. I can sympathize, but I cannot pity them, and I believe this is a fault in myself. You can pity me. Please pity me, Sory. Pity me because I am forever separated from you, and also pity me because I am separated from the army in which I have put my life, and because in that army my life is now controlled by an old man, evil and sick and dying. God knows, pity me, even though I cannot pity even myself ...

And so my letter to Sory spun itself with woes, and I would not have mailed it except that the chaplain came by and was collecting mail and even had an envelope to sell me. I mailed it, then regretted mailing it. I wrote her next morning, telling her I felt much better and please to ignore my slobbering emotions of the night before. "I was exhausted and should not have admitted to any feelings," I said. "The rumor is that we will push now into the North, itself, and I am looking forward to seeing the enemy on their own soil and feel better."

I told her I could not account for the despair I had expressed, except that the loss of Jackson had crumpled me painfully. "It is not you, Dear Sory, it is not the two of us, and there is no need for you to be wretched on my account, for the sunlight leaves me warm and more cheerful."

Then on the next day, or the day after, I received a letter she had weeks before written to me, in reply to my first letter, and that was a dear possession to read again and again and to carry on my body, to recall now and then that it was there, to take it out from time to time to read, to cheer myself with it, to longingly wonder what meanings I could read into it.

> ... and so we got the spadin done and prepared the rows and planted, and I thought of you and said to myself that Owen wuld be plesed to see it done so well. All of us worked on it, tho some mor than others. Mr. Crawford was

217

most critical, for he said he had never seen a woman be a gang foreman before. He complains if I go to help myself, for he wants me to turn the place over to him.

When you went away, Owen, I missed you, but the throb of pain is now less than it was. I say this so that you will not wory about me unduly.

I am also cleanin the house and we are daubing the chimneys whenever we have time. The men say it is not spring work, but I tell them to com on and get it done, and all of us do it, women and men. My hands are red with work, Owen, but it helps my mind to think of other things.

Yet I do wory about you, yes and Woofer too. I feel I want to wory about you and to know the detals of what I must wory about. Pleas tell me, for I cannot so easily wory about big and general matters, such as the war itself. I cannot wory about you and Woofer unles I know what the danger is in detail. Pleas tell me, for I want to hold close to myself the fears I have for you and even to weep for you. I want to weep for you.

I don't want to weep for myself for that is silly. Do not worry about me one bit, Owen. I am working and am taking hold of this place as best I can, and two of the women are helping me, though the men are casual about it.

I am enclosing a leaf from a tree, so you will have something from home.

I am writing Woofer today, so you need not tel him of this letter or about what I am doing to occupy myself. No, it is not true that I am merely occupying myself, for in fact I am trying to stand on my own feet for the first time. That thought comes to me even as I write it. I am not dependent on any man just now and even find the men here critical of what I am trying to do. Well, a baby will fall many times in trying to stand. I can report that the stable is cleaned out, the garden is growing, the corn fields are hoed, the house is being cleaned and repaired, the stock is well fed, and I can report that even Eli seems now to understand that I am the mistress of this place. You will not know me if ever again you see me, for I am thinner and my clothes are worn and dirty and my hands are coarse.

Dear Owen, the leaf is from a tree I love . . .

◇

We marched north through Northern Virginia. Our army extended as far as I could see, even when we were high on a hill, and what a sight it was, too, a stinking, scrawny mass of humanity, the worst for filth and wounds I ever saw. We had no gear to speak of; we had in my brigade only eight supply wagons assigned to us, except for the surgeons'. We had few tents or shelter halves. When we camped we flopped down on the ground, or appropriated some Virginia farmer's barn if one was nearby and if he permitted it. He would offer to sell us chickens, pigs, or other food, but we had no money. All this was in Virginia, as I said, but once we had crossed the border into Pennsylvania, we were able to take food from farmers and sleep where we pleased.

What a curious lot of Pennsylvania people stared at us. I suspect to them we were the worst form of impoverished humanity. They were sullen, unfriendly, even insulting—often crude comments were hurled at us from garret windows by crooked crones, but we were busy just then cleaning out the village bakery and cornering chickens in the back yards and going off with the lady's milch cow on a line.

I marched my men through fields, preferring them to the dusty roads, through rich fields with violets and daisies mingled with the sweet grass, and sometimes we were forced by circumstances to walk through wheat fields, the grain nearly ripe, and farmers would come screaming after us. Beyond the field was a hill I needed to climb to see what enemy lurked beyond the field and where the fattest cattle might be hid. I sang to myself a song of my grandfather's, about a fox who ran forever through a field of ripened wheat with a red rose in his mouth.

All this looting is merely what the Yanks had done to our farmers in the Shenandoah Valley, mind you, but our doing it did give the Pennsylvania farmers a lurch, and they got to shouting at us as if we were not a conquering army at all but a band of urchins.

I appointed special companies for special duties. I assigned Sergeant Raper's company to raid beehives and smokehouses. Company B, which Woofer was in, was assigned to raid for onions, potatoes, turnips, and cabbages. We had a company for cherries alone. We had a duck, goose, pigeon, and pheasant company, known as the rare-bird brigade. We had a cider and whiskey company, a flour and corn meal company, a beef company, a milk and eggs company, and a sausage and sauerkraut company.

We would do most of our marching at night. I suppose this was meant to conceal our movements, but I fear it was no secret as to where we marched. The Yanks could smell our army from miles away. Usually about dawn we would stack arms in a field or along the road and settle in with our night's loot. My regiment, which had built one fire for each company in Virginia, built several fires for each company in Pennsylvania, for fence rails were plentiful. We would make wheat bread for breakfast, and if we had no yeast or baking powder we would put in many eggs and make a sort of bread pudding. Then after a morning's sleep we would sit around the campfires and eat again and pick lice off our shirts and write letters home about the hard life of soldiering.

At dusk, after supper, we would douse our fires. All about us other regiments would be dousing theirs, thousands of little fires would be steaming. Then we would go north, strolling through the lush countryside, portions of yearlings and hams dangling from our musket barrels. The Southern army had arrived, stinking and torn and damn near broken down, in the land of milk and honey.

I recall when we reached the fork of the Mt. Summit Road, we overtook General Longstreet and General Ewell as they sat on their horses, conferring about the pleasantness of the evening air, and another time we came within sight of General Lee, his nobility obvious in his carriage. I saw him dismount and ask a soldier to help him put the rails back up in a farmer's fence, where a group of soldiers had left them down. Often we saw General Heth, who was riding about on a black mount. He was coolly polite to me and was careful not to fall into conversation with me privately. He had never mentioned to me the matter of my advancement, nor what he and General Jackson had agreed to, and I didn't mention it to him. Nor had I ever mentioned to him the dangers of Manger's animosity toward me.

The preachers were particularly busy now. Every afternoon hillsides would fill with men from many regiments and evangelists would try to convert them to Christ. Every day about four o'clock I would hear the men of first one meeting and then another start singing the chorus of the invitational hymn, "Just as I Am." There was more religious fervor now in the regiment than there had ever been, even before Chancellorsville, because we all knew the battle ahead for us would be hard fought, that the Yanks would surely make a stand on their own land.

Colonel McRuder came by. I believe this was on Monday. He sat his big butt on a log near my fire and speculated about the importance of the approaching battle, which well might be decisive, he said. "Owen, we can't go into battle with Manger like he is, can we?" he said.

"No," I said, pleased to have him come to that conclusion, though it surprised me that he would admit it to me.

"It endangers us. I have heard he's ill."

"I've heard that," I said.

"We're having a meeting tomorrow, as you know. Colonel Reid has recovered enough from his arm wound to be there, and I will be there."

"Yes, I know about Manger's meeting," I said, suspecting I knew what McRuder was leading up to, and being eager for him to say he would support me.

"You'll be there?"

"Yes."

221

"I suppose you know Manger and Penny have marked you for an example."

"I suppose I do," I said, smiling at him, "and I need all the support I can get."

He sat there on the log in the dusty sunlight, crushing lice on his sleeves. "What are you going to do?"

"What are you going to do is my question," I said.

"Well, Owen, I fear that Manger will be pushed out by Penny soon."

"Pushed out?" I said, surprised.

"Penny's gaining on him, is making him move over now."

"Why, I'd rather have Manger than Penny, hadn't you?"

"I would rather have me, hadn't you?"

It was abrupt, rough, startling to me, for I had seniority over McRuder both as an officer and as a colonel, and I had expected he would support me.

He sat there on the log and moaned, and looked off at the dusty shafts of sunlight. "Owen, if Penny is getting Manger out for health reasons, all we have to do is block Penny, don't you see?"

"Well, yes, you must do what you can," I told him.

"If you would go to Heth and slash up Penny, take Penny out of it for me, then I will be free to take command without any charge of ambition."

There was reasonableness in his request, I could see that, but I was unwilling to help him get the place I wanted, even though I was in danger, as matters now stood. I was jealous of him, I suppose.

"You won't be chosen, Owen," he said.

"I'll consider it," I said, knowing I would not, could not bring myself to help him, even though I should.

Later that evening six citizens came up the hill to see me. They had a sturdy wagon pulled by a beautiful team of draft horses and in general they looked like prosperous people dedi-

222

cated to the Lord and angry with looters. Sergeant Silver and I went on with our cooking. Finally one of them, a man dressed in a waistcoat and coat, came forward. "We have a complaint against three of your men," he said.

"My men never looted a thing in this world," I told him, basting the hen Silver and I were roasting.

"Colonel, this morning three of your men raped a woman of this town."

"Oh, I don't think so," I said, astonished. "My men?"

"We followed them to this hillside, to those woods down there."

"I don't believe it."

He told me the raped woman was thirty years of age, that she had been sweeping her front yard, that the three men had jumped the fence, had taken hold of her, had torn off her skirt and underpants, had upended her and had crammed into her two openings as much dirt and trash as they could.

"And stones," a woman added grimly.

"And stones," he said.

"I don't believe it," I said. "Do you, Sergeant Silver?"

"No," he said.

"I have never known any violence to any woman anywhere by a soldier of this army. I don't believe there has been any."

"It's quite true, nevertheless," the man said.

"Well, did they rape her, too?" I said.

"They ravaged her in the way I have said."

"But did they rape her in any standard meaning of the term?"

"I don't know about standard and unstandard rape," he said.

"I think you do, and since we are talking about a serious offense, I need to ask specifically if they had sexual intercourse with her."

"I don't know how Southerners have intercourse," he said.

"Nonsense," I said. "I assume you are telling me they did not, but that you wish they were guilty of it anyway."

He didn't much like that, but I waited him out and finally he said, "As I say, I don't know how Southerners do."

"Yes, yes. Silver, do you think my soldiers would have done this?"

"No, I don't believe it," he said emphatically.

"She's a Negro," the man said.

It was so abrupt and unexpected a blow that I froze in place. I was stunned by the meaning of it, and so was Silver, I could tell, and watching us coldly were these three men and three women who had come to make their complaint, their charge against the Southern army as a whole, yes, even the South as a whole, and three of my men in particular.

"She is afforded the rights of citizenship in this state, Colonel," the man said. "She was assaulted and we ask you to take action."

"My God have mercy," I whispered. I had learned to be cautious whenever the racial issue or sex was mentioned. The two together were immensely dangerous, it seemed to me, and I explained this to the six civilians, but they remained adamant, stiffly, starchly pure in purpose. "Sergeant Silver, go down and get those three men," I said finally.

He got up slowly, looking around cautiously. "What three are they?"

"I expect you'll find they admit to it," I said.

He slowly went on down the hill. About five minutes later he and three men came up the hill, and behind them came about forty other men, curious to know what was going on. Several men from other companies saw them assembling, so they came along too. About a hundred men were soon approaching us, and I noticed that the six citizens began to wilt somewhat. I asked the three guilty men to step forward, which they did proudly, big grins on their faces, and I said, "You three put dirt in a woman today?"

"Do what, Colonel?" one of them said, pretending astonishment.

"Put dirt in a woman."

He shrugged.

"She got pert with you, did she?" I said.

"She was so damn cocky it made you dizzy, Colonel," a boy named Milford said.

"So you got angry and lost your head."

"No, sir, I didn't lose my head. I'll do it ever time I see one that's uppity."

"How many have you stuffed?" I asked.

He smiled embarrassedly. "One."

"Yes, I thought so. And you, Scott, what did you do, hold her or put in the dirt?"

"I dirted her," he said.

Somebody in the crowd yelled out, "What you got against them, Colonel?"

"What the hell's the matter with you, Colonel?" another man said.

"I did it, Colonel, I did it," somebody else yelled, and in a few moments that got to be a chorus, a score of men admitting they had helped violate the woman. I climbed up on the citizens' wagon to regain control of the group, but enough of the men were frenzied and vocal, making all manner of catcalls and mule brays, that nobody could gain order. A dozen of them were holding up their hands, volunteering to be found guilty along with the three men, and Sole McKinney was telling me I was a nigger lover and that he wouldn't fight the war with me any longer.

"Well, all right, I'm a nigger lover and you're nigger rapers, is that it?" I said.

"I'm a nigger raper," several men began to shout, holding up their hands, so enraged and delighted with themselves that no wedge could be driven into their confidence, the hillside bubbling with their chanted admissions of guilt—until abruptly they fell silent, stood stunned, staring blankly at me. They even began to make warning sounds in their throats, gurgling and moaning noises, more ominous than their previous cries—well,

I had not seen its equal. "What is it now?" I said to Silver.

He pointed behind me. I turned, and standing in the wagon was a tall Negro woman, a blanket pulled around her body like a Grecian robe—I suspect she was naked, or partially so, and she was facing the mob with the proudest, damn most confident, arrogant look I ever saw—Jesus, she must have been a queen of Africa.

I got away from her. Instinctively I jumped away from her. By now about fifty men were making guttural noises, out of anger and lust; they were going to subdue her, they would tear that woman limb from limb if they needed to.

Martin Luther was near the front of the crowd, his Bible in his hand. I suppose he had preached somewhere. He started calling for mercy. "We must love all God's children, all God's children!" he shouted.

"I'll love her, let me love her first, by God!" this big sweaty son of a bitch said as he came pushing through the crowd. But even he, mad as he was, stopped under the steady gaze of that woman. He stood there trembling like a leaf in the wind, frustrated—my God, it was terrifying, for the pressure was ever-increasing. Martin Luther threw back his head and began to sing in a full-voiced bellow: "Just as I am without one plea," the redemption song of most all these men, and as Martin started the next line I began to sing with him, and I motioned for Sergeant Silver to begin singing. Others began to sing, many of us did, and soon that hillside was singing, the hate-filled noises were defeated by the memories of this song, and that fellow who said he was going to assault the woman fell to the ground in a fit, he was actually convulsed by the duel between repentance and lust, and that dear Martin—Lord, had I ever underestimated the power of preachers, and of this one in particular—took hold of the horses' harness and started leading them away, singing all the while, the woman still standing in the wagon, glaring about her with the same immense show of pride and dignity. Martin led his pilgrimage through the field to the road, a hundred of my men glaring after him, a hundred of my men

226

following behind him, and I heard them singing as they moved toward town: "Sweet Lamb of God, I come, I come."

$$\diamond$$

Somebody had passed along the rumor that there was a warehouse of Yank shoes at a town nearby. Shoes were the only part of a Yank soldier's uniform which a Rebel soldier could wear, of course, and the rumor was of interest to many commanders, among them a young General Pettigrew. He left that night to get them, but came back next morning with the report that he had encountered enemy fire and, since we had been ordered by Lee not to engage the enemy, he had withdrawn. He said the soldiers he had met were militia of Pennsylvania, not regular army soldiers, and that it would have been easy to overwhelm them.

That afternoon when we had our meeting with General Manger the main subject of our premeeting discussion was this skirmish at Gettysburg and who was going to go get the shoes.

The meeting was held in a stone house, in a ground-floor room which held two cots, a small table, and a bench. There was one little glass window and it was vine-covered, so we left the door open to get light to see by. Hal had come as far as the yard with me, and he was sitting on a fence in the sun talking with the farmer whose place this was, who was hoeing in the garden, his wife helping. I rather wished I was out there, hoeing with them, instead of being administered to in a meeting.

Colonel McRuder was being particularly jolly and friendly, preening himself to take over the brigade, I suppose. Colonel Reid had arrived, and I offered to shake hands with him before I realized he had had his right arm removed since Chancellorsville. He extended his left hand and grasped mine warmly. Colonel Penny was present, of course, with a detailed agenda, and he had his own aide now, a young lieutenant I had never seen before. General Manger called the meeting to order and told us General Heth might be along later. Manger told Penny to give us information about where we were located. Penny told us we were fifteen miles east of Chambersburg and five miles

227

west of Gettysburg. He told us the Yanks had changed commanders again; General Hooker had been relieved and General Meade had been appointed.

Manger then began talking about the whiskey wagon, which was divided into compartments for each officer, in which he could lock up personal possessions of all sorts.

"When are we going to get our issue of ammunition?" Colonel McRuder asked, interrupting.

"I'm talking about the whiskey wagon, damn you," Manger said. He informed us that our decision in the last meeting had been reversed and that the wagon driver was to have a key to each officer's chest. McRuder tried to object, but Manger silenced him by saying Penny would now report to us about the ammunition.

General Heth had issued the ammunition to the brigade, Penny said, but the ammunition would not be issued as yet to the regiments. Colonel Reid spoke up and asked who had decided this matter, "not that it matters greatly at the moment about this decision, but this is contrary to the way our brigade has always functioned, where everything is discussed with the regimental commanders—"

"I decided it," Colonel Penny said.

There was a long silence before Colonel McRuder ventured forth with the question, "And who the hell are you to decide it?" He gave me a look of death, as if to say he had warned me about things like this. Irritably, abruptly he left the meeting and went outside to stand by himself on the road, and both General Manger and Colonel Penny went outside to try to calm him.

Colonel Reid, who was sitting near me, began to laugh. "I lay in the hospital, Owen, and got a perspective on all this, how silly our meetings tend to be." He moaned sadly. "We better start reading our Bibles more prayerfully, I fear."

The new aide cocked his head.

"Especially the Book of the Revelation," I said.

He laughed. Then he did an extraordinary thing for a soldier:

he reached over and grasped my arm warmly.

I was quite moved by the gesture, and I said, "Thank you, Colonel, for your concern."

"When you have but one hand left to touch with, Owen, you find you want to use it more often," he said.

The new aide sat back in his chair, studying us suspiciously.

A carriage pulled to a stop and General Heth got out of it. "The ball of light on the road to Damascus," Colonel Reid said to me.

Colonel McRuder returned to the room. He was in need of a drink, he said, but the aide didn't even rise. The aide stood when Colonel Penny and General Manger came in, however. Then in came bustling General Heth, a tough-skinned, tough-faced man, a handsome man and a competent field commander. "Sit down. Sit down, gentlemen," he said.

There was no place for the aide to sit, nor room for him to stand comfortably. "Go outside," Heth told him, and out he went as if propelled by a spring.

"Now then," Heth said, adjusting himself to the bench and patting General Manger's knee a time or two, "let me cover a few matters briefly. Gentlemen, General Manger has come down with the croup, and this even as we come to the big battle before us. We must arrange some sort of administration for the brigade. Now, how many officers do you have in readiness under you, Colonel Wright?"

"Lieutenant McGregor, Lieutenant King, and Major Crawford," I said.

"And Colonel Reid, how many officers have you?" he asked at once.

Colonel Reid reviewed his situation, which was about the same as my own. Colonel McRuder was asked next, and his voice trembled so much that General Heth had trouble understanding him; McRuder had three officers in good health. "One of whom I have groomed to take command," he said.

Heth paused to let that slide by, then he said, "Gentlemen, any one of you has authority from me to come directly to me

229

with any questions at any time. I am not going to relieve any one of you of your regimental assignments, since these are the critical ones just now."

"If three regiments were combined into two," Colonel Reid began, "maybe Owen could be—"

"I will appoint General Manger to serve as my assistant in the coming battle. He will be my second-in-command. He will consent, I'm confident. I will ask Colonel Penny to coordinate the three regiments, to work out details of this temporary administration of the brigade. He will consent, I'm sure. Are there any questions?"

McRuder was as red in the face as a fall apple. Reid was smiling at the sheer hopelessness of our new plight. I was stunned to an anger, stung to hatred actually, but thank God I said nothing, did not reveal it.

"You forgot about the shoes," a beaming Colonel Penny reminded Heth.

"Oh, yes, yes. We need shoes," he said, "and I have asked for permission to move to a town nearby to get them. We will leave during the night. God help us all." As he stalked away, Penny went hustling after him, seeing him to his carriage. I noticed that the dust of his carriage clouded Hal and the farmer he was helping to plant potatoes.

Colonel Reid went outdoors to stand in the sun. Colonel McRuder sat on a bench, shaking his troubled head and murmuring to himself.

I said, "General Manger, I hope your health has not taken a turn for the worse."

Manger's red eyes moved to me. They were rheumy with hatred. "I'm sure you do, damn you," he said.

Colonel McRuder went outside, walking irritably, nervously. I stopped near him, and he told me we would need to do something to free ourselves from this new danger. What we could do was not clear to him just yet, apparently.

I asked Hal to keep his mouth shut as we started back to our hillside. I was in a ponderous mood, my thoughts were unwieldy. "I'm getting damn tired of this army," I told him. We had about two miles to walk. I had a horse assigned to me, but I walked wherever I went, which was papa's way to do. And today I talked, told Hal what had happened, told him I would have to bring Penny down somehow, in order to protect my men from him. "And he'll be trying to get me," I said. "It's dangerous, war is," I said. When we got near the hillside where my men were, I said, "I can't leave and let Crawford take my regiment into battle, him and Penny."

We saw that a big, sweaty fellow was preaching to forty or fifty men sitting near the road. He was in shirt sleeves and had a Bible in his left hand, and his right hand was threshing the air emphatically. We paused on the road, in the road dust from passing wagons, and listened to him shouting out the truths he had gleaned.

". . . God will give us the victory, the victory in Christ, a-men. My Bible tells me that the Lord will be jealous for His land and His people, yea, the Lord will answer and say unto His people —'Behold, I will send you corn, and wine, and oil, and I will remove far off from you the Northern army, and will drive him into a land barren and desolate, with his face toward the east sea, and his hinder part toward the uttermost sea, and his stink shall come up, and his ill savor shall come up.'

"All this God has promised us, His people, praise His name, if they but prostrate themselves before Him and give Him the credit for it. He wants us to glorify Him, don't you see? He is a kind father to us; we are His children. Think of that, beloved. And He will drive away our enemy into the sea and destroy them as He did the army of Pharaoh. Do you recall? He divided the Red Sea and drowned them, men and horses. What great victory God gives. And He has promised a victory to us, His people, one greater even than Fredericksburg, greater even than Chancellorsville. It says in the Bible: 'the Northern army.'

Think how clear God can be to His people. And knowing our Bible, studying the Scriptures, we can realize that the sea is the Atlantic Ocean. That great body of water will be turned into a writhing bath for a hundred thousand men and all their horses and cannons and wagons. Oh, it's a sight to think of. That salty sea right around Philadelphia or Washington will be the drowning place. And out of that victory God will send, as the prophecy says, plenty to His people. We will have our corn, our wine, which I interpret to you to mean milk, and our oil, which I interpret to you to mean butter and fat. Our fields again will be crop-planted. We'll have cribs full of grain, cellars full of fruit, springhouses endowed with butter and cream, we will live in a land of milk and honey. That's the promise. Do you see that it's all here in the Word? It's promised to us and I've only been interpreting it to you. My, don't it make you feel good to know that God is on our side? Don't it help you to know God will stab the wounds on your behalf, that He sides with His people, is very mindful of us, and don't it make you want to glorify Him, to kneel and put your face to the ground and say, 'Father, Father, we are only children and cannot know your great plan, but we put our trust in you and ask you in Jesus's name to deliver us from our enemies and destroy them, dear God, kind Father, destroy them, destroy those who torment thy people, destroy them ut-ter-ly ...' "

◇

The meeting with Manger had left me colder in my heart than a stone jar. I had never felt more out of sorts. Yet I felt closer to my own men than before. I wandered about among them, remembering the names of most of them, asking about their families. It is amazing how misery helps the mind to recall and the heart to care.

I came at last to the men of Crawford's section. They had not a semblance of military order in evidence, and I had never seen such a variety of animals and fowl—it was remarkable, really. "Well, you have stunk up the countryside and have now started

232

hiding your herds in the woods, have you?" I said.

The men went on cooking and lounging about, though they were attentive to me, and most of them were at least mildly respectful. I walked among them, kicking over empty cracker boxes and the like and shooing chickens out of my path. "What do these Pennsylvanians think about a flea-covered clutch of farmers without any barns? Are those your ducks?" I asked Plover.

He nodded sullenly.

"Well, you are a sorry soldier for a fact. What's behind you?"

"It's his horse, sir," Sergeant Raper said.

"His horse? His horse?"

"Yes, sir," Raper said.

"Where is your saber?"

"Sir?" Plover said.

"Would you like to join the cavalry? You can mount that horse and take your ducks and go find the cavalry for all I care. I understand General Stuart has taken it to Maryland to visit his family."

"I'll go home if I can," he said.

"I'll see you hanged too. Now you clear out that flock of birds and that decrepit nag." I waded into the flock of ducks, and they went flurrying about all over the area. "This is called an army," I declared, "even if it's not any longer much of an army. We are the ragtail ass end of the army, boys, for the legs have walked off and gone home, the arms have got shot off, the head is going blind in Richmond, and the full body never has been put on the fields. You are the ass end of the army, and you have no horse to ride on." My sad gaze came to rest on Plover. "Except this man has. This warrior here. What's your name, soldier?"

"Plover, sir."

"Clover has," I said, smiling at the other musicians. Hell, I knew his name. "Clover—what a happy face for a flower," I said. "You do have a rosy face. What a kind man to be a soldier.

233

What a soft-living man you must be back home, no doubt with your slaves and herds—" I stopped, for back of Plover, as if on my command, appeared a Negro man. Then I saw other Negroes who dared to venture out now. "You men going to take slaves home with you?" I asked.

Nobody replied. Several soldiers suddenly busied themselves with their fires.

"You're not going straight home, you know, boys," I said. "We're going to have an entertainment first. You are invited to stay for it. Do you like to see plays, Clover?"

Plover nodded dumbly.

"Do you recall how in plays actors march across a stage which comes by imagination to represent the fields at Agincourt or some such place? Well, sirs, kind sirs, we have a play set in Pennsylvania, and we're going to have real soldiers in ours. Think of that. The armies are composed of men just like you. God pity me, they are just like you. God forgive us for our audacity, but it's true, they are not a whit better than you. You sorry bastards are the characters in the play. It's a different sort of play, you understand, for it's not about Uncle Robert on his gray horse, or even old General Longstreet, or dead Stonewall Jackson, or that near-blind president in Richmond—no, it's just about you. And you don't have a steed and you don't have slaves." Deep sadness enveloped me, as I reflected on their sorry lot. "You can give your slaves to the generals and they can put them on their plantations at home. All the generals own slaves. But you don't get to be planters, you see. Oh, you sorry bastards who aspire to own slaves! But hear me now: the generals of the army, who own slaves, have decided to make it up to you and let you play the leading parts in the new play, once the action gets under way. Think of that. You get to shoot real guns. A few of you can be sergeants. You can be a fiddle player, Clover, and you can be a pipe player, McIlvenna, and those who aspire to high drama can get your guts shot out, and all this for the generals to watch from the hills. You see how important the parts are that are offered you? And the lines to

234

be learned are only a few. The Rebel yell is the main one. You throw your head back and gather all your hate and puzzlement and anger together in one mighty blob in your throat and hurl it out with a great AAAAAAaaaaaaahhhhhhhhhh-YYYYYYYYYYeeeeeeeeeeeee!!"

There was a long silence. Even I was quite stunned by the yell. The men watched me uneasily, glancing about cautiously.

"Are those bare feet, sir?" I said to Private Hayes.

"Yes, sir," he said, looking down at his toes.

"Where are your shoes?"

"They're not here now, sir."

"Uh-huh. I believe the play will require that the actors wear shoes."

"I left them some'ers, sir, in a loft some'ers."

"In a loft?"

"Yes, sir. I was reaching the cherries, sir, and there was hay there, and I lay down and went to sleep."

"And took your shoes off—"

"Yes, sir. I always do when I go to sleep. Then night came."

"Night has a way of creeping up on you, does it?"

"Yes, sir. So I come out of that loft when I heard a noise of a snake I think it was."

"A particularly noisy snake?"

"Yes, sir."

I looked about at the other men. "You there, you lost your shoes too, did you?"

"I have them in my blanket roll, sir."

"Saving them, are you?" They were in all manner of dress—some of them in shirts they had that day taken from a farmer's chest of drawers or from some wash line, wearing all manner of pants and hats. "Men, I want to announce that this entire drama might unfold tomorrow, so tonight in an hour I want to have an inspection of these three companies. You hear? Everybody had better be ready in an hour. Now I don't know that a battle will occur tomorrow. I suspect, knowing the army we're left with, that it will come when we stumble onto it unaware. But tomor-

235

row it could be, for I'm told the Philadelphia newspapers don't like the way you're terrorizing the populace—and indeed you are, for they have not seen your like before."

Somebody back in the night shadows laughed.

"Now an inspection is a simple thing, and the one of you who comes in with the poorest showing will be honored in a special march through the countryside on a rail." I was looking specifically at Plover.

There was quiet for a long while.

"You blacks get to your homes now," I said. "See to their safe passage, Sergeant Smith. You men give your horses to the artillery or to the farmers. We won't ride to the play, and I fear we won't ride home, once the play is over, either. We have heavy parts to play, do you know that? I won't bore you with my thoughts. I believe it's going to be a tragic piece, for we've come onto their holy ground. No point in asking what the theme of it is to be, for life works out its own themes. I once thought I understood our cause, for all we demanded was independence from them; I even thought I could trust our army. Now it's all complicated and beyond anybody's reach, and I believe I only understand this regiment. You men are my family and I am part of yours, and I want to say in closing that there will be no inspection tonight. I don't want to measure out punishments to my boys. I would give my life for this regiment, and I know you will certainly do as much for each other, and, God knows, you will at least put on your shoes for me. So get these companies in order, get the ducks and chickens and hogs out of the camp. And thank you so much for listening to me. At somber times I talk a great deal, I know, but I mean well and I wish you well. It's only that I am sad tonight." I stood there feeling like a fallen hero for a while longer, before without any further comment I walked on off along the hillside, my head low, my shoulders stooped, my mind reviewing the dangers of our predicament and the wonders of myself, and my performance in what I knew to be the prologue of the play.

236

CHAPTER ELEVEN

Hal and I were up well before dawn, washing ourselves in the creek and drying ourselves by our scraggly, gasping little fire. I felt somewhat better. I had got so low in spirit the night before that this morning by contrast was a shiny, promising one to me. I even told myself God had peeked through a cloud and said, "Owen Wright, today you will be a success in all you do." To hell with Penny, I told myself.

In my blanket roll I hid a canteen full of eggs; also I had two pounds of corn meal and a number of hunks of cooked fatback. I sent my jacket to my whiskey chest in order that I would look less like an officer. I carried a pistol, of course, but not a sword. Why carry a sword? Almost all the officers had them and would flourish them in battle. They got shot sooner, that was all, the best I could tell.

I walked down to the road that led to Gettysburg, followed along behind Colonel Reid's and Colonel McRuder's regiments, my place being in their dust, as usual since Jackson died. Colonel Penny was riding on a coal-black mount, accompanied by his shiny aide. He shouted to me that we would be accompanied by divisions other than Heth's on the march. What divisions and how many was apparently none of my business.

What had happened, as I learned from Lieutenant King, was that General Heth had got worried the previous evening about maybe meeting an enemy army by himself, so he had petitioned help from General Hill, who had by now taken Jackson's place as corps commander. Hill had assigned for support the division

237

under General Dorsey Pender from North Carolina, the division under General Field from Virginia, and since everybody else was going, why not send the brigade which had just yesterday gone to get the shoes and had come back with the report of enemy militia, that of General James Johnston Pettigrew from North Carolina? Yes, and why not send the artillery battery under General Peagram? So our General Heth found himself this morning royally cursed by all the other generals of our corps for dragging them out on a shoe march, especially young General Pettigrew, who said he easily could have got the shoes yesterday if we were not under orders from Lee to avoid engaging the enemy, and here this morning he was walking down the same road again, walking behind the whole damn corps, following Heth, for God sake, whom he didn't much like anyway.

As I say, my premonitions had told me it would be a successful day, and I did rather enjoy seeing thousands of men and a full brigade of artillery doing what would have been done by a troop of cavalry, if General Stuart wasn't off raiding or visiting in Maryland.

I had my pipes player and drummer beat the rounds, and got a swift reprimand from General Heth for it. He came riding back himself, red in the face. "Stop that damn noise," he said.

With it stopped, the sound we heard was of 15,000 men marching, 400 or 500 horses trotting, and a brigade of caissons rolling along, with Lord knows how many supply wagons. "Is that better?" I asked, smiling up at him.

"Where's your hoss, Wright?" he said, disgruntled.

"Shot out from under me," I said.

"You need a hoss," he said.

"I always walk," I told him.

"Where's your sword at? And your jacket. Here, bring this man a hoss!" he thundered. "And a sword! And a jacket!"

His couriers brought me a sword and jacket and a nice big roan horse, and I told Heth I was sorry as I could be, but I always went into battle informally. He ordered me to put the gear on and mount, so I decided what the hell. I mounted the hoss and sat there receiving the catcalls and critical observations of my men, which so astounded Heth that he started waving his hat at the men as if they were a swarm of flies. "Hush, hush, hush," he shouted.

Hoss, hoss, hoss, I thought, and I dismounted and led the hoss, a pretty hoss, and went along the road with my sword dangling. General Heth turned red as a beet and galloped on up the road, stirring up dust for my men to walk through, and for me to walk through, shouting to his aide at the top of his voice, "God damn that mountain crew."

I let Woofer ride the hoss and I threw away the jacket, for it was another bright day. I was being blessed by God today, I tell you.

We were by dawn all out on this road to Gettysburg, which wound through the beautiful, peaceful country, most of it cleared and productive. We were all out there, 10,000 or 15,000 of us trying to be quiet and sneak up on the town, I leading my hoss, when Penny comes galloping back to where I am and begins talking to Woofer, thinking Woofer is in command since he is mounted on the hoss, finally gets it straight that I am in Woofer's place and he in mine, and he says, "General—that is, Colonel Wright, I am putting out our regiments to help skirmish for the corps, and you are to set your men on the extreme left flank and move along that hillside."

The hillside was a long, low, slender ridge half a mile away from the road. I had never heard of such a skirmish line, but it was dusty here on the road, so quite happily I led my men through a pasture and toward the ridge. I passed close to Colonel Reid, who was to have his regiment skirmish just left of the road; between him and me would, of course, come Colonel McRuder. The three of us met for a fleet moment on the field, and McRuder began to tell me about catastrophe approaching in this cursed open countryside, especially out here on an exposed, thin flank, with a novice, Colonel Penny, in command.

"We'll all feel better," I said, "once we get the shoes."

I put my Company A on the top of the ridge, and my Company I in the valley, so all of us were walking along the side of this big pasture, presumably to be sure there were no enemy soldiers under the cow dung or hiding behind the tree trunks. Five men could have done it all. Or better yet, two cavalrymen. I kept brandishing my sword at apple trees and sticking it into tufts of dung. Finally I tossed it near a creek, hoping a boy would find it someday. Woofer was riding the hoss up and down behind my regimental line, which kept slowing down in the right flank as the men along the creek stopped to pick blackberries. Every once in a while here would come General Penny telling Woofer or Crawford what to do, and Woofer would come tell me—to keep my line straight was one command. From the ridge crest I could see a skirmish line made up of all the brigades under General Heth, a total of twelve regiments, and he was dashing up and down behind them on a hoss with a fleet of aides on hosses, and there were four other generals, one for each brigade, each mounted on a hoss with one or two aides, and these bundles of officers were riding up and down behind a so-called skirmish line which extended from the top of this ridge, down across the creek, across the road, across the far field, and up onto the other ridge where a stone building was, a seminary, but what shone the most were the rifle barrels of all these men and of the thousands of men behind us walking along the road and through the fields close to the road, with Peagram's artillery in the rear; what a tremendous sight, with banners flying—I didn't have mine up yet, but most of the others did, and all the men were walking in formations, the masses of men undulating with the undulations of the earth, turning with the snakelike meanderings of road and creek, yes, and railroad, for Colonel McRuder now had a railroad cut to walk along, a partially graded one, not finished, no track laid, running parallel to the road about a hundred yards to the left of it, on our side of it.

I was, of course, still up on this ridge, but my pasture was now giving way to woodland, so I sent four men forward to skirmish for me, and I told Woofer to get off his hoss lest a Yank shoot him. I climbed to the top of the ridge and walked along there with Sergeant Silver, making certain we were not advancing on some Yank artillery position. This would be an excellent place for one; artillery up here could destroy much of our corps before it could unlimber a cannon of its own, for the corps was all down there in clear sight, in the open, lined up and exposed.

Now the valley narrowed, and General Penny came thundering up to me with orders to keep the full width of our line, which meant I must move my regiment over the ridge crest onto the other side, which I did even though it cost me my view, and after another little while Colonel McRuder's regiment was over on that side too. We could look up the hill to our right and see Colonel Reid riding along the crest, so now he had the view of the corps, for which I envied him.

About 7 A.M. the first shots were fired by the Yanks. I waved my men to wait until we could determine what we were encountering, but Penny waved me on, so I began to move my men forward a company or two at a time. As best I could tell, 800 yards ahead of us, too far for accuracy in their shooting, a group of state militia were behind a fence. They were firing carbines from positions about 30 feet apart, so I judged that there were not many of them. We were in some danger, however, so I told Hal to keep himself and his men close to the ground, and I moved to where the smith was and encouraged him to keep a tight check on his men. Then I ordered Lieutenant McGregor to send a company of men around to the left through the woods to flank the fence.

He said he would lead it himself, which I agreed to, then I ordered my other men to move forward cautiously, distracting the enemy while he was completing his maneuver and gaining his position.

This, however, was not satisfactory to Colonel Penny, who

came riding furiously down upon us, ordering my men forward, ordering me forward with them—a most disagreeable fellow for a reasonably agreeable day.

"You see that fence?" I asked him.

"I know about the fence, but my brigade is falling behind the others," he said. "Get them moving forward, Colonel."

The ridge to our right was petering out now; we could hear heavy musket fire on the other side of it, and I wondered about that too. I assumed they were our guns firing, but at what I didn't know. On our side of the ridge we moved forward steadily, as Penny ordered. Lieutenant McGregor had disappeared, and I supposed his men were waiting until we were within firing range of the militia to reveal themselves.

Then I saw why they were waiting. We came to the petered-out end of this ridge to our right, and I found that my men, as well as McRuder and Reid's regiments, were not only advancing toward the little string of militia behind the distant fence but also had come upon the right flank of several regiments of Yank soldiers who had not realized we were behind the ridge at all, and who were setting up formal positions to face our army in the valley itself. I was totally unprepared for this, I simply had not thought the little bit of resistance we had encountered was a major portion of the army of the Potomac itself. I saw Colonel McRuder, who was mounted, wave to me, wave me on grandly. I turned to the woods where Lieutenant McGregor was and waved for him to bring his section into action, hoping he was in position flanking the fence; he was, and he charged effectively, his success making it safer for me to swing my regiment and begin firing into the exposed flank of the main body of the Yank corps. McRuder and Reid's regiments swept forward sounding that infernal Rebel yell, Penny waving them on. My men advanced more slowly, but the blood-lust was on them too. We advanced firing into the ranks of Yank regiments, which were falling back in confusion. A fervor, a mighty chorus of yells and screams, gripped us all. We were wading toward the Yank columns, firing and bludgeoning. Even the smith's men were caught up in it—many of them. Even Woofer was caught up in it, the best I could tell, so that once I saw him, when he was perhaps thirty feet from a young Union officer, raise his musket to his hip, not even to his shoulder, and fire, and the officer fell, this being but a moment in time, a glimpse among a thousand sights all coming over me in a minute or two, with men firing and loading as fast as they could. I stopped my regiment's advance now, for we would be advancing into the line of fire of the main body of our own army; we were kneeling or lying on the ground and firing as fast as we could load while the Yanks withdrew, when I saw the Yank cannons. They were being wheeled about to fire at us. I saw Woofer standing erect, he and all of Company B, and I ran toward them. Hal knocked Woofer down even as the first cannon fired. Canister, hunks of metal, ripped into the ranks of Company B. I saw Woofer as he rolled over to look dazedly about him at his fallen friends. He saw me, and he lay there frozen, staring at me. "Get gone, get gone," I told him, realizing he was out of his senses. Hal crept to him and shook him, even as the cannon fired again.

Colonel Penny came riding up, brandishing his sword, saying "Forward!" A fever was on him and he was anxious to have this victory made secure. "Forward!" he shouted. I saw that he had sent McRuder and Reid's men far out into the open field, and now he would have my men go too. I shouted at Penny to see that Reid and McRuder's men were in danger of being shot down by other units of Heth's own division, by General Archer's brigade particularly. He swung around on his mount to study this, and maybe he realized the dangers those men were in, I don't know.

"They'll be lost," I said. "Go help them come back this way, Penny."

He hesitated, terror afflicting him.

"The passage to them is closing," I said. "You'll lose your command."

Abruptly, with a loud growl, he tore himself free from his fear, kicked his mount's sides, and rode toward where Reid and

McRuder's men were battling, he shouting, calling for more frenzied effort. The men were no doubt surprised to find him riding a horse into such danger, as well they might be, for quite soon a number of Yank riflemen had him in their sights and fired at him, and he was lifted off his horse by the impact of their bullets and was hurled to the ground amidst his men. I watched it, I saw it all acted out as if on a great stage, I shivering as if from the cold of a winter's day.

Reid and McRuder's men began a retreat, leaving Archer's brigade exposed. Almost at once Archer and his men began to surrender. I ordered my men to stay close to the ground and hold steady. "Where is Woofer?" I asked Hal.

"He's all right," Hal said, and went down his line shoving his men to the ground. Out in the field I saw Heth appear on foot, shouting fiercely, trying to consolidate what was left of his brigade, which was dangerously confused. He began ordering men to get down into the railroad cut. I now had the only undefeated regiment left in this vicinity. I saw two Yank cannons wheel into place near the front lines of the Yank infantry, but to my surprise they turned their aim not toward us but toward the railroad cut, and began firing into the cut, firing canister directly into the men of McRuder and Reid and Archer. When Heth saw this, he being still on the bank, he shouted in a great voice full of agony and ordered his remaining men to charge the cannons. I was unwilling to sacrifice my men in so hopeless a situation, so I ordered them to retreat, gathering all the prisoners we could, and led them around the little ridge we had come along, and before long we began to trot freely, safe at last. I led them up to the top of the ridge, and from there we could see below us the mighty battle before Gettysburg's town streets. Across the entire valley the Rebs were pulling back. The proud Third Corps of Jackson was withdrawing. And from the ridge I could tell that about all that was left of Colonel Penny's brigade was my men and me.

We wandered dazedly along the safe side of the ridge, picking blackberries. Now and then I would sit down, my body weakening, my mind dizzy. I saw Woofer and he didn't recognize me and I said hello to him as if he were a stranger. I met three little Pennsylvania boys and bought their stock of blackberries from them. They told me where the best berries were to be found, and I led my regiment that way. I knew that Penny was shot, I suspected Heth was shot, I knew our brigade was broken and scattered, our division was defeated, our corps was retreating, and that we were left, survivors walking as if dead, picking blackberries in a field near a little brook with sheep grazing on the hillside nearby.

One of my men shot one of the sheep. As the flock began to run, other men shot them. The sheep ran back and forth in the pasture until all were dead. Viciously my men vented their fury, their guilt and anger on them.

Major Crawford came up to me, distraught. "What did you say to Colonel Penny?"

"Who is that?" I said.

"Colonel Penny," he shouted at me. "What did you say?"

"Why, I said, 'Colonel Penny, you better not ride out there.' "

Again I walked to the ridge crest. I could see that our corps still was held down by enemy fire, but about a mile to my right General Ewell's Second Corps was approaching to help us, a cloud of dust rising for several miles distant. In the lead were the men of General Rodes, an experienced soldier. He had a big division, with six brigades: the 5th Alabama, the 3rd, the 6th, the 12th, the 26th Alabama, all veteran soldiers, and he had Iverson's North Carolina brigade. Even now as I watched, instead of coming down the center of the road, Rodes led his men out of sight of the enemy into the woods on the far side of the valley.

He was discovered while half a mile from the enemy, but the Yanks, not knowing how large a force he had, sent only two regiments of reserves to meet him. At the moment these reserves reached the foot of the ridge Rodes unleashed his corps of soldiers on them with a charge and a yell which quite well lifted me to my feet. The two Yank regiments were crushed, but when Rodes struck the main force of Yanks, they held. I had not since Sharpsburg seen Yanks fight as desperately as these. Iverson's North Carolinians failed to break the Yank lines and Iverson's leading troops surrendered. I never dreamed I would see the day that Iverson's men would surrender. They had surrendered, but they did not rise from the ground, and gradually the truth came to me that they had not surrendered and would not rise from the ground.

Iverson's failure had left a companion brigade stranded. I believe Daniel's, though the smoke now obscured much of the battlefield. This brigade now attacked, and in the struggle the Yanks fell back. There was Yank cannon fire now, too, hateful in noise, murderous all of it, and I was almost compelled to go to it; one is called, one can scarcely keep himself from running toward such challenging sounds and deeds. I moved along the ridge to be closer, to see it closer, to see it all. I could see splinters flying from the Yank caisson wheels and axles and could see the artillery horses rearing and plunging, mad with wounds and terror, could see boxes of shells explode even as cannons still fired in reply, with artillery men hanging onto the cannons dead and a cloud of dust rising from the advancing infantry, all crash on crash and smoke, splintered steel, wreckage and carnage, the Yanks trying to bring horses forward to pull the gun out, the horses being shot in their harness, the Yanks falling back, while the Rebs fired into their backs and shoulders.

General Rodes was now in command of the battlefield. The Yank corps was in full retreat, falling back to the town. Our own corps came to life and joined in the pursuit. I could see into the railroad cut, and many men of Reid and McRuder's regiments rose from the ground and began to pull their wounded comrades across the field toward a woods. I led my men down into the midst of them and invited the ones who were not wounded to attach themselves to my regiment. The main body of the Rebel army soon was flushing the enemy out of the town and into the hills outside the town.

My men camped in the field, my regiment and the pieces of the other two, and a few of the pieces of General Archer's brigade. As night came, the ambulances arrived; they reminded me of firebugs as they moved slowly back and forth, gathering the wounded of both sides. Hundreds of men were walking about collecting loot, of course. I came upon one of Billy Furr's men sitting beside a dying Yank. "What you doing?" I asked him.

"Waiting for him to die so as I can get his watch," he said dully.

We were all living that night with the dead and wounded but we were not distressed or depressed; we were drugged by a sense of power, for in the midst of battle we had again been saved.

I went over to the railroad cut. I saw one man I recognized and rifled through his pockets to see if a letter was there. None was. His name I had forgotten. I went through his pack and found a bit of cooked bacon, which I thanked him for. His dead face, his eyes now turned in his head, his eyelids halfway closed, his mouth open, the spit still on his lips and thick on his teeth like a foam, all was moonlighted. He was cold and was stiffening. "God forgive you," I said to him.

I left the railroad cut and went stumbling about looking for Colonel Penny's body. Scattered across the field now were the thousand lanterns of the medical aides, those men examining, choosing, lifting, cursing, complaining about their work. I came upon Woofer sitting beside the body of a Rebel soldier. "What's the matter with you?" I asked him.

"I need a pair of pants, but I haven't got the nerve to pull them off of him," he admitted.

247

"Are his legs long enough?" I said.

"I need shoes too," he said, shivering.

"I'll take off his shoes for you," I said. I didn't mind feeling leather, even of a dead man, for leather maintains its own quality. Woofer put on the shoes and said they fit all right. He hobbled, but he said they would do. Then we both sat down and thought about the pants.

"I think I shot a Yank today, but I can't find him anywhere," he said.

"Must not have hit him, Woofer."

"I didn't kill him, I know, for he started crawling toward that railroad cut. Could I have stunned him?"

"Lord, I don't know, boy." We sat there looking about us at the ambulances and the looters. I heard one Reb cry out, "Get your damn hand out of my pocket, buddy." It was weird out there, I tell you, with the moonlight playing down on the field. Some of the men were so drugged that they began dancing, kicking their feet up into the air and pushing and shoving one another.

I took the pants off this dead man finally and threw them to Woofer. "Shake them, will you?" I said.

He shook the death feeling out of them, the chill off them, and slipped them on and began parading around, proud of himself, slapping his behind like slapping a horse's. He went on off across the field.

I found Colonel Reid, quite dead. I came upon Major Crawford, who was looking for Colonel Penny's body. Together we found it underneath two of Colonel Reid's men. We moved the two bodies. Penny's expression was beatific; there was no glimmer of agony. "He died in triumph," I said.

"What a pity he died his first day in battle," Crawford said. He knelt beside him, reached forward and touched Penny's face. His hand came back as if stung. "He's cold," he said.

"He's stiffening, but he's not been robbed yet," I said. I knelt beside him and tried to pull the ring off his finger, but the flesh

248

was swollen around it. I examined his gold repeater watch and chain. "I wonder would he care if I keep them for now," I said. The astonished Crawford gasped, but said nothing. I put them in my pocket. Penny had on fine shoes, and I thought, well, they are better than the ones I'm wearing. I pulled them off and measured them against my feet. I wasn't saying anything and Crawford wasn't either.

Penny had a nice jacket on, of course, with the proper insignia for my rank and brigade and division. I rarely wore a jacket in summer, but this one was tailor-made and of English cloth. It's silly to have premonitions about cloth that don't apply to leather, I decided, so I took the jacket off, Major Crawford watching me. He didn't help me, even though to take a jacket off a stiffening man is something of a wrestling match. I stripped off his pants too, Major Crawford mumbling about how strange it all was. I was as surprised by my actions as he, mind you, I was being driven to rob this man, I wanted to strip him, to take his clothes. Piece by piece I did so too. I put on his silk shirt, which had bloodstains on it, his tailored jacket. I put on his leather belt and leather shoes. I even strapped on his scabbard—I don't know where his sword had landed. I walked about in my new outfit, modeling it for Skip Crawford, who crouched near the naked Penny, his face reflecting his sheer incredulity.

"How do I look?" I asked him.

"Why, I—don't ..." he halted, stammering. "My God, how obscene—"

"Does it fit all right?" I asked.

"Why—it, it is the most brutal—"

"I wish we had a mirror," I said.

"My God," he said, "you are a beast. My God, poor Penny—"

Poor Penny lay there in his smalls, a pitiable, sleeping boy of no charm or character. "He's not a general," I said, "not even a colonel now."

Later, at a time of stark moon shadows on the ground, no

clouds, no promise of rain or any other weeping, I saw Major Crawford walking, his head bent, his shoulders hunched, talking with Sole McKinney. The Major was holding McKinney's arm, and they were walking across the strewn field, stepping over and around the bodies and items of equipment. They saw me and approached me. "McKinney has a gift for you, Colonel," Crawford said.

"I don't want it," I said.

"Yes, you do. You have coveted it for a long while."

"Major, I think I will let it go by the boards," I said.

"No, you have coveted it, so I had Sole fetch it for you," Crawford said.

McKinney held out a closed fist. He was smiling at me in that twisty laconic way of his. I put my open palm under his fist and into my palm he dropped Colonel Penny's ring.

Woofer found the lieutenant he had wounded. At least he was reasonably certain of his choice, and he came to ask for permission to take the man to a hospital. I went with him to see the Yank, a tall, lanky fellow in his early twenties with brown hair and blue eyes, a nice-enough person. He had a stomach wound, so I knew not much could be done for him. "Woofer, the ambulances will be along," I said. "Let them take care of him." The Yank was gasping for breath; he was scarcely able to talk, so much weakness had come over him.

"He won't die, will he, Owen?" Woofer said.

"Oh, no, he won't die," I said. "You come with me."

"He's from Ohio," Woofer said. He had some letters in his hand, the man's letters, I suppose. "I'll go in the ambulance with him. Only for an hour or two," he said.

The Yank did look up gratefully and tried to reach Woofer's arm. He whispered a few words, something or other. I would have said no, would have insisted, but Woofer already thought me so coarse and unfeeling, I let him go. A pity, really. I would have given anything to have saved him the knowledge that the man was dying.

For hours my men and I walked about in a strange, exotic state, not at all mindful of suffering around us. We saw the wounded as from a great, painless distance. We thought not of pain at all, but of our ability to walk about, to throw our arms out, to move our heads, to pick up a dead man's canteen and hurl it, to parade our captured clothes and possessions before others, to preen and polish ourselves, for we had survived, had shown strength beyond our strength, had bathed ourselves in a masculine scent.

But after a while the narcotic effect began to wear off. I began to ask myself what horrors had that day been done by all of us. The death of Penny. My God, had I killed him? The loss of most of the men of two of Penny's regiments. Had I wanted him proved incompetent at this cost? The loss of half the brigade of General Heth—had I contributed to this? Had I wanted to revenge myself on him for his slights and rejections of me? Should I have gone to his rescue? The loss of many of my own men, dead and wounded. Who were they? Why had I not even asked their names? Who was tending to them? What are we doing here? Why aren't we helping with the wounded? Don't we care about our own people?

One after another men would suddenly set about doing chores of all sorts, carrying litters, cleaning up the battlefield, stacking the abandoned goods, cleaning equipment, occupying themselves in any practical chore they could. Other men would set to drinking whiskey, wine, brandy—anything, to keep their minds from settling on the painful thoughts being revealed to them. I came upon several men who were weeping. Many of them didn't know they were weeping. I came upon men who were broken entirely, who were women sobbing, were spent rags of bone and flesh, men who had been celebrating but an hour ago. I came upon men who were feeling pain even though

251

they were not wounded. "I cannot move my arm, Colonel," they might say, or their leg or bend their back or breathe freely. I came upon men fornicating with other men, so drained now of masculinity that they were not men at all. I came upon men shamelessly masturbating. I came upon men who held out their arms to me pleadingly, yet were not able to say what they wanted. I came upon one man cutting with knives on corpses; I don't know why, I can't explain it, but he was mutilating bodies. I came upon men who were moaning in their sleep. I came upon many men who were sitting by a dead fire staring without seeing. I saw Hal sitting near the remains of the trunk of a tree, one blasted apart by shells and bullets, his eyes wide open, his teeth chattering slightly, his lips pulled tightly across his teeth. He is dying a little bit, I thought. They are all dying. They are dying now, so they are desperate to retain life. They are falling now. I am falling now, I thought. I am falling now.

Sleep was a drugged, deep escape, for we were exhausted in body and soul. Sleep.

I was on a rope, dangling from it, holding to it with both hands. General Manger—no, it was my father who stood nearby, watching me, measuring time until I fell. The rope began to unravel.

She was lovely in the dusky light as she kissed my face and neck and chest, and as she and I climbed up the fields past the trees. I thought I saw Woofer seeking me far off, lonely, lonely, and I was lonely seeing him while I watched him kiss her. I could hear the New Orleans girl laughing No, no, no, Owen, let me have something to live with even if you don't love me, love me, love me love me love love love love across the new sky with the herby smell of the plowed field with a child-wife to love and fondle forever. I said, "And where is this road by moonlight and will I go back home with my old thoughts thoughts thoughts?" I stopped even on the field below her distorted house and embraced her to the earth and took her body in my two hands and turned her and kissed her feet, her legs, her thighs.

She was dead now, cold but not still yet, and I didn't know where to put her for it was night and if I laid her outdoors the wild beasts would congregate and if I laid her on the floor I would do a sacrilege to the dead. So I lay beside her all night long. I massaged her body, trying to make it warm again, and I talked to her, and I got excited holding her close to me and made love to her corpse, then lay exhausted beside her, my arm under her shoulders, her dressing gown still up above her hips and open at her breasts, my mouth slobbering where I had tried to awaken a kiss from her hard mouth. I was exhausted completely, horrified at what I had done, ashamed too, and I felt my heart slow down and slow down and slow down and, as I watched it in my chest, it stopped beating and I was dead for a long while, was a prisoner within my body, my heart dead, only my heart for I could think very well and I kept saying wordlessly, desperately, Morla, Morla, Anna Morla, Anna Sory, Sory Anna Morla, where are you, forgive me, forgive me, and I saw a single fluttering of her eyelid in the firelight of the cabin. Then another flutter, another change of expression, a change of her nose, her face dead, I alive, powerless to move.

I was in the river, in the cold water, where a stone had fallen. The stone had fallen into the pool. I smashed my way into the woods. I saw her, she was fleeing from me; I ran after her, shouting for her to wait wait wait. I caught her in the river. Deep in the water I wrestled with her. I held her water-cold limbs and breasts. I love you, I love you, I love love love love, I told her, the sand and rocks touching us as I entered into her body, in the water, in the bed.

CHAPTER TWELVE

General Manger with amusing show of pomp appeared next morning at dawn. I saw him when I first awoke, riding Heth's black mount, at least five couriers around him, he riding about the field where we had fought, peering down at the corpses, looking suspiciously into the railroad cut, riding finally over to where my regiment lay in camp alongside the pieces of other regiments which had come near to us.

"Where is he?" Manger asked Crawford, growling in his throat.

Crawford pointed toward where I was lying, pretending sleep.

"Colonel Wright," Manger called harshly.

I began to snore.

"Colonel Wright, rise up now and listen," Manger said. "I have fallen at least temporarily in command of General Heth's division, for he is wounded, so you will needs be attentive to what I say, though I know this will work hardships on you."

I moved slightly, as if waking. I rolled over on my back and yawned. "How are you feeling, General?" I asked him, lying flat on my back, my head held off the ground by my clasped hands. "Your health all right, is it?"

He rode his mount closer to me. Above him was the overcast, mizzling sky, behind him was the long, open field littered with men and horses and wreckage and beyond all that were the houses of Gettysburg. This conquering lord on a horse was a small, crunchy man, disfigured by persisting irritations and irri-

254

tants, and sourly he was surveying me. "Hey there, Owen," he said, "I need to talk to you."

"I need some coffee first," I said. "Do you have any coffee with you?"

"Take him a handful of grounds," he said grouchily to his aides, and one of them dismounted and came forward with a pouch full of coffee and I poured out what I wanted. Another aide helped Manger dismount, but once Manger felt the ground under him he stood holding to the horse, swaying slightly. I thought he might be drunk, but when he started walking toward me he walked steadily. He sat down on a blanket roll near the fire I was making and scratched his head where he had a bug-bite of some sort, and belched. "Owen, you and me are about the only two left to fight."

"I don't want to fight you, General," I said.

"You bastard. You did me a bad turn, Owen. Now I tell you the truth, I have been angry with you."

"Never in this world would I turn on you—"

"After all I've done for you and all that, yes, and being like a father to you and all such as you could say, damn you. Well, I would have killed you with my hands there for a while."

"Blow on that fire some, will you?" I said.

"But in a war a general needs officers such as you. So I tell myself, anyway, though I still don't know that I would trust you across a shallow creek not to shoot me."

"Hand me that cup, will you?" I said.

He did so, but got confused, for I had interrupted his train of thought. "Owen, get your own cups now, you hear?"

"You don't want any coffee?"

"Yes, I want coffee. Now listen here. I've got to organize Heth's division, such as it is, for Lord knows we have a history of greatness behind us, excusing yesterday. I see your regiment survived very well."

"Oh, yes," I said. "And took eighty-two prisoners."

"Nearer forty, I suspect. The other regiments got busted up, didn't they, Owen? I saw it. I was able to see most of it, though I was denied the use of a horse."

I had a fire going pretty well—I had started it with a knapsack, and the water was in two cups, along with a few grounds of coffee beans.

"Owen, you've always wanted to be a general and I'm going to say this much to you, I am a military man and I can appreciate your achievement yesterday, for look what you did. Think of what able command you had of your own men, in spite of Penny. So I'm going to—" He stopped, apparently awed by his own considerations. "Owen, where did you get that uniform?"

"From here and there," I said. "I wandered around."

"You look the best I've seen you since I met you at—whatever it was—"

"Bull Run," I said.

"These days my mind slips like a mill belt, but it's not illness. Don't go saying it is."

"Oh, no," I said.

"Now then, Owen, you are an able officer, I'll admit, and I'm strapped for leadership, Lord knows, and I'm going to tell you something. I'm going to take hold of Heth's place, and I'm considering putting you in mine."

I was blowing on the fire, idly listening to him, and I stopped still. I looked up at him slowly, cautiously, for I didn't trust him more than I would a pit viper. "That's generous of you, General," I said softly. "What place is that?"

"Yes, I've talked with General Heth and General Hill about it."

"Did they insist on it?" I said. I would even chance rudeness to find out why this turn of events had come about.

"No, they didn't insist on it, damn you. I suggested it. So you are to command the brigade, under me, Owen. Do you hear me?"

I said not a word. I couldn't think of a comment to make to the man.

256

"Do you believe me?"

"I—well, I don't know what to say, for so far as I know—Lord in Heaven, I've never been more surprised."

He took a box out of his pocket and opened it and showed me two brass stars. "Do you see them?"

"I see them," I said, staring at them.

"Stand up."

Many of my men were watching, lying on the ground and sitting around. They watched as Manger snapped off my colonel's insignia, which he kept, and put on the stars, one to a shoulder strap, then he stood back and scrutinized me critically, a little grin working at his thin mouth. "Well, Owen, you got what you wanted, appears to me."

I couldn't speak. I was dumfounded and was confused, of course, and I still felt wary of him; I couldn't understand why I had been chosen this way by him.

"Owen Wright, on order of General Hill dated today in writing, I commission you brigadier general. Congratulations."

I had not a word to say. I saw Hal get up off the ground and come toward me, his mouth open for a cry, but he made no sound. He threw his arms around me and let out a shout, then there came a boiling up of the men as they began to shout and leap about and they started a festivity out there on that field, the bagpipe and drum playing, with General Manger carried aloft on the shoulders of the smith. Somehow or other we had all been recognized and honored, the men decided, and they were glad for me. I prefer ordinarily to have my celebrations in private, I am not overly demonstrative, but there was no closet out here, no room with a door to it, no cove to hide in or gully to lie in. I was carried aloft on the shoulders of my men and there was much singing and music playing—all wild as a jungle dance, with loud noises, guns firing, Manger laughing, coughing, laughing, and everybody trying to get close enough to call my name —"Owen, General Owen," they called to me from everywhere. Everybody except Woofer. I didn't see him at all.

Suddenly a fit of coughing quite overtook Manger. I must say, the attack I had witnessed a few months ago was not as severe as the one which gripped him now as he gasped for breath. The men put him down by his horse, and Manger covered his mouth with a wad of cloth and held to his saddle horn with his arm, tears burning down his face, and all the men grew quiet, their celebrating ripped away from them. There was no sound left out there except the raspy, deep-seated cough, which threatened to disrupt Manger's lungs entirely, and his staff were frantic trying to determine what to do, for they were Heth's old staff, not his, and they had not seen him like this before, in danger of dying, his legs going weak under him and not a one of them daring to touch him. And for some magic reason I went to him, I dared to put my arm around his shoulder and hold him. I had in my hands and arms the emaciated, weak, fibrous body of this fiery man, even while he was weeping, coughing, disgorging blood into a rag.

When he was done I took the cloth out of his hand and wadded it and said I would burn it, and his rheumy eyes looked up at me to question me, to wonder about what I would do and why, and I said, "You can trust me, you can trust me, for God sake," for I was overcome with sympathy for him.

Much of that day was spent in organizing my men into three regiments. I put my old regiment under Lieutenant McGregor, whom I raised in rank to major and promised to raise in rank to colonel as soon as I could. On his recommendation I advanced Sergeant Willis to lieutenant. All this was subject to Manger and Hill's confirmation. I organized the remnants of Reid and McRuder's regiments into a single regiment of 240 men. I organized the remnants of Archer's large division into a regiment of 416 men. All of this Major Crawford wrote out carefully for me, making a copy for Manger and one for each of the regimental commanders. In all I had over a thousand men. They were properly cautious men, too, for they were the survivors of units five times as large.

While all this was going on, Ewell's corps, led by Rodes's division, went on around the town of Gettysburg and took up positions in a valley beyond, and Longstreet's corps, which also numbered more than 15,000 men, approached from Emmitsburg and took positions on the far side of Seminary Ridge. That ridge was smaller than the one the Yanks occupied, which had a cemetery on it; Cemetery Ridge, about two miles long, was in the shape of the letter J. Longstreet's corps lay to the right of the upper part of the shaft. Ewell's corps lay opposite the hook to the left. Gettysburg was below the hook. As for Hill's corps, by midmorning several units of it had left our valley and crept onto Seminary Ridge, taking places to Longstreet's left flank as he faced the enemy, and Peagram's artillery had moved to the top of Seminary Ridge, except for certain rifled cannon which were left on the valley floor itself, near the town, in positions where they could fire onto the Yank hill.

I was much too occupied to pay full attention, to consider the reports of what was taking place up on the hills, and indeed nothing much seemed to be taking place, which was quite surprising, really, for Ewell's corps had but yesterday afternoon put the Yanks on the run, and why Ewell had allowed them to take refuge on the highest ridge in the area, or on any ridge at all, or why he and the others were now letting them build bulwarks at the crest and along the sides of it— I could see them working, even from where I had my headquarters, I could see that the Yanks had got their cannon up there too. Tens of thousands of Yanks were up there by now, more than had been on this field yesterday. Our army had no idea how many, I imagine, for with Stuart's cavalry still off somewhere in Maryland, we had had no way during the night to find out what size force was nearby or what its movements were.

Manger in the middle of the afternoon came down off Seminary Ridge where he had been talking with General Hill. He sat down near me on a cracker box and told my cook to bring him a bowl of hot soup, which he sipped noisily, his lips smacking.

He was perspiring freely. "Owen, they've decided to leave us out of it today," he said. "I'm surprised, for I've assured Hill we're organized by now."

"Leave us out of what?" I said guardedly.

"Whatever battle takes place," he said. "They're up there like two bantam roosters showing their tail feathers to one another, the whole two armies it looks like, and Lee has been trying to get Longstreet to attack the Yanks since early this morning, but he hems and haws and goes and comes and says he would rather find his own hill and let them attack him. Just now he's asleep."

"Asleep? You mean he's unaware?"

"No, he's asleep. He's taking a nap, or so his aides tell Lee's couriers, and he has left word not to be disturbed." Manger laughed, a fretful chuckle which he kept carefully controlled. "I suppose they're going to allow this day to go to waste."

"We might as well move on to Philadelphia anyway," I said. "Let the Yanks attack us, like Longstreet says."

"It's not easy to move an army with an enemy army at your heels, Owen. Lee told us not to get engaged, but Heth did it yesterday."

"How many are up there?" I said.

"Nobody in this world knows, and I'll bet you they don't know, from my experience with the Yanks." He suddenly beat his fists onto his knees. "Ay, God, I do wish they would give us our chance today. We're ready, Owen. I am tired of the war dragging on. A man's life—a man might not live to see his own work finished, but we can charge and win the war most any time. They won't fight."

"They fought Rodes yesterday."

"I wish they would fight me for a while today. I told Hill, 'Let me lead off, let me lead off now, and I will show you,' and he said, 'No, no, Manger, you let General Pettigrew or one of the younger men lead off, give them a chance at it,' and I said, 'General Hill, let your old men have a chance, for we won't all be here all along.'" He was staring off at Cemetery Hill, his hands clenched, his frail body bent forward into the winds of war and challenge. Then he coughed all of a sudden, a single cough, but it changed his countenance in an instant, replaced his ferocity with fear, and he bent over, hiding his face from view, and busied himself writing with a stick on the ground. "Owen, I hope you won't mention that bit of coughing I did this morning to anybody."

"Oh, no," I said softly.

"I fear my aides did mention it to Hill. I think so. I've never had but a few fits like that, and I don't let them handicap me. I feel all right most every morning. Some old men get out of bed slow, they take an hour or two to uncoil and unbend, but I have never had a muscle or bone pain to speak of, and I have most all my powers too. My wife would testify to that, if she dared. I'm good for three times a week." Abruptly he laughed, a big grin breaking through, his eyes twinkling, delighted with his wit. "Ah, Lord, don't count me out."

We heard the sound of shooting over in the far valley, where Ewell's corps was stationed. My couriers got to their feet to see if they could see a battle starting, but soon the shooting ended and they sat back down, crouching at their own fire as was their custom—I found that a general is given a great deal of privacy, which I was glad of in their case, for I didn't know them. Abruptly a single cannon fired, and all of us were on our feet again, and as a little puff of white smoke rose from Longstreet's section beyond Seminary Ridge, a barrage of cannon fire started from his batteries, and from where we sat we could see the Yanks scurrying for cover on Cemetery Hill and could see the shells explode over their heads. A Yank ammunition box exploded and there was a big cheer from my men, camped all around.

Quite a fine show was starting, and Manger was distressed because of it. I suppose because he didn't want anything to happen unless he led it himself.

For perhaps half an hour we listened to the cannons of both

armies, and every time the barrage lifted we could hear a band playing polkas. I think it was Longstreet's band. Directly we heard musket shots, so we knew an infantry attack had begun.

The fighting would rise and fall. Whenever it lulled we could hear the band playing. We learned from several wounded men that Longstreet had captured most of the Yank valley positions and had taken several Yank posts on the lower part of their ridge. At one time his men had even pierced the Yank lines on the ridge crest but were thrown back by Yank reserves. Apparently there were more Yanks up there than had been thought.

When dusk settled, Longstreet forces withdrew to the positions they had captured in the valley; it was about seven o'clock by Penny's watch when the shooting stopped.

Wounded men in greater numbers came past now. They were talking about tomorrow by God they would beat the Yanks more soundly, and they were asking what had put spines in the Yanks at last, such comments as that. Wounded of Joe Kershaw's brigade of South Carolinians came through, of Hunt's Texans, of the 1st Georgia Regulars. Many of Barksdale's Mississippians came through.

That damn band was still playing, so I had my band play us songs. If a military band can play polkas during a battle, I can have a rendition of "Barbara Allen," which I did have, and of "Lily Dale" and "Sweet Evelina" too, from our friends McIlvenna and Clover, the red-faced flower.

In the darkness an engagement broke out far across Cemetery Ridge. Apparently General Ewell's corps was attacking the Yanks now. The sky was lighted over in that direction. When that fighting was over we could hear a Yank band playing "The Goose Hangs High." Longstreet's band soon replied with "When I Saw Nellie Home." The big bands exchanged several songs, then the Rebel band played "Dixie," and the Yank band followed with "The Star-Spangled Banner." When the Rebel band played "Home, Sweet Home," the Yank band joined in, and we all cheered that when it was over and threw hats and canteens into the air.

That evening of the second day at Gettysburg Woofer and Hal and I had a royal feast. From my new, high place I could look back on my life leading to this time, peaking here like a mountain rising. "I admit to being ambitious," I told Hal and Woofer. "I admit it. It has been an obsession with me."

I would get up every once in a while and walk around. I was wonderfully well elated. It was amazing how a sense of well-being had come to me. Even the worry I had about Sory was soothed; I didn't brood on that. I was secure at last, and all the chariots of fathers and kings could not unseat me from my recognition. General Owen Wright. I suppose it's absurd to make so much to-do over a name like that, but it was my name, after all, and the title was all I had to show for thirty-six years of my life. I would walk around my new tent. It was about ten feet square on the ground and a man could almost stand up inside it. It had a cot in it and a little desk; I had two stools and two cracker boxes—a general didn't sit on the ground. A colonel did, but not a general. Nor did his guests, unless he had more than three at a time. I had two smaller tents too, for my four couriers —all of whom could write. I had four wagons under which my cook and drivers slept. I had a commissary officer—I planned to detail him to line duty under McGregor, and I was thinking about asking Hal to take that post, for he would be honest about it. I had more than a dozen horses. I had a banner of my own, one that represented me as a general, and I had a standard for my brigade. I had a great carriage with a star on its door, and with that carriage I could go most anywhere—after the war I thought maybe I would keep that carriage and go riding to the South in it and find me a place. That carriage was a prize of this world. It had four matched horses, black with white feet. It had gold-painted wheel hubs and polished spokes. After dinner I sat

263

in the carriage for the better part of an hour, just being amazed at myself.

I fell asleep promptly that night. I was not worrying now about my guilts and debts and failings, not now. But in the night I was awakened by somebody, a man who was shaking me roughly. "Owen, Owen, you awake yet? I'll take a cup of coffee, damn you, if you'll have your cook make me one. I've got good news."

I called out to the cook and told him to stir the fire. "What time is it?" I said sleepily.

Manger said, "Owen, this matter of attacking the Yanks has come up again—it's about twelve o'clock—and Lee says we have to get them off that ridge, have to defeat them soundly before he'll chance moving his army away from here."

I was thinking chiefly about being awakened and wondering if he was going to be in and out of my life forever.

"Yesterday we didn't have General Pickett's division, Owen, and that made a difference in Longstreet's attack, for they are the best of the Virginians. We wasn't in it either, and I say we're the best of the North Carolinians. Lee's convinced we can unseat them and he's bound and determined to attack where they stand."

"Well, what's he trying to do?" I said, realizing vaguely what Manger meant. "Are they going to attack that damn cemetery?" I still hadn't been on the actual battlefield, but it seemed to be an expensive undertaking for very little gain.

"Lee wants his three corps to advance all at the same time, Owen. Beyond the ridge Ewell is to advance, and on this side Pickett is to lead the charge of Longstreet's corps and Pettigrew is to lead the charge of Hill's." Somber and deep his voice, serious as death, somber and deep his expression, too, as he gripped his veined hands tightly. "What do you say, Owen?"

"I don't know how generals do," I said evasively and roused myself more fully. "I better make the coffee myself."

"It'll be all of us that have it to do," he said.

"All of us?"

"All of us."

"My brigade, too, in a scheme like that? Mountain troops aren't—"

"I've asked to lead off for the left side of the line. I talked to Pettigrew."

I sank back on the cot. I had a sudden remembrance of a last night's dream, papa studying me, trying to evaluate me in that objective, aloof way he had, and I was dangling at the end of a rope that had begun unraveling in my hands. "Are we going to lead good men into cannon?" I asked.

"Lee's going to silence the Yank cannon before we start."

"How can he silence all those cannons?" I said. I got up from bed and felt around for my shoes. "You know, I think Lee is about to end his army, it looks like."

"We want it over, Owen," Manger said. "What's wrong with that? We want to make one charge and prove our invincibility, and to hell with the Longstreets of this world. We with half their number and from inferior positions will attack and destroy them frontally. We want it done with our hands and the butt ends of our guns and done by noon tomorrow, to end this war."

"It wrinkles my mind so much I can't think," I said. I went outdoors and stirred the fire. The cook was dressing, for God sake.

Manger followed me, caught in a great fervor. "Owen, a man's life is a fair price for such a thing."

"I can't make the fire burn," I said.

"It's the challenge of our lives, damn you—"

"General, I can't see walking them out into an open field. How far is it from where we will be starting from? How far do we walk?"

"We'll be on our ridge in the woods, near the top, so it's maybe farther for us than for Longstreet's men."

"How far?"

"A mile."

"A mile?" I said. "A mile?"

"Yes, it's almost a mile. But it'll end the war."

"I've been with you in the army for this is my third campaign, General, and you don't risk your men that way, out in the open for a mile, with cannons and rifles covering them."

"That's what Lee says to do."

"Did Lee tell his officers to sacrifice their men to a whim he has—"

"Lee deserves the loyalty of his generals," Manger said bluntly.

Which stopped me cold and plain, and I huddled down closer to the fire, shivering. It was too clear to be misunderstood, what he meant. "Oh, my Lord, it's coming on us strange, I tell you."

"Owen, is there nothing to be said for deciding here and now the issue of this war, whether this country is to be divided into two countries or reunited into one?"

"It would be a crippled union, I'm afraid."

"Crippled, yes, for years."

"For three generations, the Bible says."

"But I see some point in making it known now, don't you, as to which side wins? Now Longstreet's men yesterday delayed attacking; if they had attacked in the morning, before the Yanks had brought up their valley corps—"

"Do they have their army up there, all of it?"

"I believe they have. Longstreet yesterday delayed, hemmed and hawed, then Ewell didn't attack at the same time Longstreet did, which gave the Yanks a chance to repulse each corps separately."

"Why didn't they attack together?"

"I think Ewell got his orders confused. He's old and sick, Owen—I believe he's sick."

"General, I want to ask you something personal for a minute." I sat down near him, so that the fire would light my face, as it did his. "Do you object if I ask a personal question?"

He did object, I could tell, even before I spoke; he was wary

266

of me, frightened to be asked about himself. "Owen, I am not a subject for your poking about. I have made you a general and you will accept the orders I give you. I told you the other day that I had wanted you as a general. Well, I did not. Heth did, for he had seen Penny shot and had seen Archer captured, and he said from a litter, 'My God, put that battlefield soldier in command, for I have done it wrong.' Even then I refused, for I never have trusted you." He was staring at me, his face close to mine, the smell of his breath, even his spit falling on my face as he talked. "Then it was Hill who told me, said Wright should be given a higher command. 'Look how he survived yesterday, took prisoners while the rest of his brigade and his division were slaughtered and captured and his corps was made to retreat; put Wright in command, as Jackson always said, for Jackson knew.' So I was unable to withstand Hill, and I agreed, though I knew then that Heth and Hill would be inclined to give any credit for any and every success to you. And now by God you'll dictate to me, will you? I have no patience with you, damn you—"

"Or with yourself," I said.

"With delays. I am impatient of delays—"

"You have very little time, I'll guarantee," I said.

"I have very little time. And I have no doubt when I'm gone Hill will say, put Wright in command, give him the command of that old man, and I don't doubt they'll say, decorate Wright for what that old man did with his bravery, and let us all honor Wright, for he survives, his men survive, with even Archer's men saying they want to belong to Wright for he survives, and men all through my division saying Wright is the one who knows battle. Well, I am sick of it, do you know it? I am sick, damn you. I am sick and not so long I have, and I intend to make the most of what rags I've got left to puke in, and of you, damn you, and you'll do as I say, you'll do as I say, for this is the army, this is not a church baptism, we don't use water here, we won't use water up there on that hill, we're all going to be equal tomorrow, the sick and the well will all bleed tomorrow, I don't mean to bleed without you, either, mister, and your men'll bleed because you'll lead them to it, you'll take them out there yourself, and you'll do it because I say it. I volunteered you for it, I order you to and you will, understand me? Now, God damn you, what have you got to say to me that's personal?"

I crawled over to one side and threw up the little bit of Yank crackers and salt bacon on my stomach. I was there on all fours, and I saw him spitting into his rag, then onto the sleeve of his jacket, and I watched as he staggered off into the darkness, and he must have stumbled over somebody sleeping, for there was a cry and then I heard him vomiting.

I crawled to the fire and lay down on my stomach and let its warmth cloak me, my skin comforting itself with it, my mind not in order, not thought by thought; a jungle of thoughts were pressing in, trying to stammer out against each one, to call my mind to itself, so that my mind was confused from its thoughts and the urgency of them, so that I wanted to shout, and I got on my knees on that dark place at Gettysburg, that burial ground, and shouted suddenly into the night with my thousand men around me, ahhhhhhhhhhhhhhhhhhheeeeeeeeeeeeeeee-eeeeee, awakening the dead—let us rise, let us all rise and be about our father's business, let us serve Bob Lee in the wars, let us put on our best West Point suits and get our banners and stand in columns and march into the cannons singing.

Oh, Jesus, damn me, my soul, free me of it. God damn why put me on a rack, why put me in chains on the wheel and turn the wheel down the road, God Jesus, it's too long a road, too long the wars go on, will they stop, will they stop tomorrow on that open field? Jesus, will they, or have the generals found their home now lodged in our bodies, lodged in our houses at our tables, lodged in valley and places and field and woods, we can never get them out of our lives now, for we can never get our lives out of the war now, we are the excrement of the wars, the belly of the war has fed itself with us, it has filled itself and

268

grown bloated with us and our horses and hogs and corn, it has called for more and has taken more men and wealth and iron into itself and gorged itself and now it spews its excrement on us, on the South, and let it be named Confederacy, let the war be named excrement, let the army cover itself again and again with the Confederacy, its own excrement, let it fume across a million acres of plantations with their niggers waiting at the doors and bowing at their waists, Confederacy, let it drown us in our own bile with the final consideration of our pride, Confederacy, for we are proud God knows and tomorrow proudly we will march, our banners flying on the Northern plain even as our pride above our holy heads, for we are God's people going into the field to fight, let it be seen, let Lee see it from his great gray horse, let Jeff Davis see it with his blinding eyes, let us go down one more time into the valley and onto the far hill and let us fight together proudly in God's name, Confederacy.

Oh, Jesus God, where are you, God? Do you see us now? Do you see how we hold to our own hands for support? Do you see how I am nothing left except a general?

I crawled to my carriage and the nigger cook came to me and said what is it general and I said help me up there damn you and I sat in the plush seat and I said put the rug around my legs and he did so as I watched him and he bowed to me and averted his eyes for never could a nigger look at a general, never in his lordly face, for God had laid on generals the powers of heaven and earth to lead even white men to life or death, and I said shut the door damn you and he did so and bowed and backed away not looking at me for I was a god and sat there with my trembling hand resting on the smooth walnut window sill and I could see in the moonlight the Cemetery Hill where the Yanks lay waiting for me and all of us.

Sitting in the carriage, I saw dawn come. I had not moved out of it. I had not slept either. I had called for paper and pen and had written a note to General Hill advising him not to gamble all our fates, our cause, our pride in one charge across a mile-wide field. "There are things infantrymen cannot do," I wrote. In the madness of the night I wrote it out many different ways, and tore up all except one of the letters. "We can perhaps succeed, but only at high cost, to be paid by the lives of our people," I wrote. "Are we to lead our men in a strategy which is clearly to their disadvantage as soldiers? It is not what they expect of us, I suggest. General, I have known these people since my youth."

I could see the streaks of light and my men were awakening now. Dear God, if this day could pass from us, if it could be night suddenly, night now, how welcome night would be. Now generously I would hold out my arms to night and embrace its silky darkness. How feverishly I would perspire affection into it. I would be a nigger before night and avert my eyes, if it could but spare me today, with this mad general dying. God, alter time and I will believe in you devoutly and bow my knees to you. God, let it not be today. Let it be tonight and I will honor you and give you the praise and glory forever. Let me bow now. God, I humbly say let it go from me, let it go today, and I will be your nigger, God, which you want of me, which always you have wanted of me and I have not been willing to bow humbly, my mother even does not bow her head low, but I bow my head low now. See, I touch the other seat of my black carriage. I go down to my knees in my carriage. I bow my body in my carriage, I break my will before you if you will but hear me.

No, you will not. You are a bastard for orderliness. I see you will not. I see dawn coming across the east. You answer me with its colored lights. You make fun of your child General Owen Wright. You make him small and slight in his black hearse before that array of light. You do not hear him pray. You laugh and wait to see the sights of war, for you are one who loves parades as much as General Lee, and battles into cannons' mouths, what a glorious sight, what a harvest for the Lord. The new Red Sea.

Ahhhh, God, if you were merciful and not so full of justice you

270

would on occasions alter time, to serve a greater right than time can serve within its routine boundaries. You would sometimes let a day pass unused, let a night cling to the veil of the dawn. Father, let night rise in the east one time, for Jesus sake I pray, dear Father—

Dear Sory, I am unable to write in a steady hand but I want you to know I am well and I think today is the last day of the great battle in the north which we have longed for. I am a general. I sit in my carriage just now and see the dawn rise, surrounded by my legions, but I have never been so lonely. A general has no freedom in this world over what he commands. He is a tool in another man's hand always. The lowliest sergeant in the army has more mind to use. Sory, I must either lead my men into the hand of death or be a coward in the face of the enemy, both lonely stakes in the field to me. And neither offers me any reward. I have written General Hill asking him to—well, it matters very little what I said. I know that Longstreet is standing firm for the men, and I do hope Hill will bend his way.

Sory, a war turns sour. It starts with a bright vision. We are all clear of conscience. But month by wearying month the life of the creature melts, and now we hold this war's rotting flesh, yet we cannot part with it.

I suspect nothing as large as an army can retain its humanity. Let it be built out of men, it will not be human. Men cannot hold an army to humanity, even a just cause cannot hold an army to humanity.

I feel better now, having written this down, not that I can state any arguments well tonight. I am too hot of mind for that. My dear Sory, why do I write you at all? Why do I worry you with a letter? Only that I gain a wealth of calm by thinking of you. I write you for myself. Do not read it. It is enough that I write you.

I must send my other letter to General Hill, for even now surely his guns are preparing for the day's work. Do not ever judge me for what I do here. I must become myself again, soon as I can. When a man no longer can feel the earth steady under him, must he not cut down his own

271

stalk? I don't know, but I would care to debate it with that dear schoolteacher of mine, Mr. Mabry, who used to discuss the nature of life and growth with me. You never knew him. For some reason he took a liking to me and would give me books to read, and I would go after supper in the summer months, when the light lasts late, and read in the loft of his stable. I was ashamed to let my father and brothers know of his attention. He had soured in his clothes, but he was a kind man to me and would stop me whenever we met, on the road or the bridge or the churchyard, and would grasp my arm and shake it and say, 'Owen, Owen, Owen, what a man you can be.' And when he died I wept at his funeral. I was the only person there who wept for him. I don't know what he meant; did he mean I was someday to be a general?

I think my fate is written by a stern hand and that I have been shackled already; my jail cell is a black carriage with a gold star on its door.

Pity me, dear Sory. Our lives are tender plants, yet they are of value to us dearly. Yours I value, for I think in you is compassion enough even to love me, which is the highest tribute I can pay any of God's creations from here on this battlefield.

Ah, Sory, I ramble on. My men are cooking breakfast and complaining about the chills they feel and their muscle pains. How lucky they are to be alive. How fond tonight they will be of this morning's health. Now they are confident of their army; this evening they will know the truth of it, of those who lead them. Of me. It will be too late by then for many of them. I grow older, Sory. Under the weight of it, I am older now by far than I have ever been before.

I love you. I will always love you, and I will always love you from a distance, for that duty I do accept, and I remain thankful to God even for that privilege. Owen.

CHAPTER THIRTEEN

In the early light, a more somber light than any I had known before, I led my men across the valley floor to the near side of the Seminary Ridge where General Manger waited for his three brigades. I had delayed as long as I could. I was mounted on a great roan. My banner was flying over me. My brigade's standard was flying over my head. My four couriers were riding with me, as was my drummer, my bugler. My men were following in three mighty bodies of themselves, their own regimental standards flying, their commanders mounted.

On my signal my brigade halted. There was a clatter of shouts and orders from many men, horses' hoofs stomping the ground impatiently. Nearby, near Manger's tents, the other two generals waited, each with his brigade occupying a portion of the field. One of them came forward to greet me. "General, can you read signs and omens?" he said.

"No, not clearly," I replied.

"I sense a strangeness in my bones. Lord knows, we were torn to pieces but a day or so ago, and now we are to lead the attack."

"Yes," I said. "God knows what will come of it."

I left my mount with my aides and approached Manger's tent, where his horse waited, the great black horse that had been Heth's before his injury, which today had a gold saddle blanket and a score of brass medallions on it. Fluttering from a pole near the tent was Manger's own banner, that of a general of the Confederate States. About the place hurrying to and fro were couriers and aides and a bugler and runners. I saw a thin, small, white hand appear at the tent flap, pull it aside, and his face appeared, moist, his lips bloodless, his skin pallid.

He studied me.

"General, I have come to ask a kindness of you," I said.

He spat onto the ground. He belched. "What is it? Let me tell you, Owen, I don't want an ill word from you. I will forget last night, for I provoked you, but this morning I want no more discussions with you."

"I have a kindness to request, General," I said firmly. He withdrew his face from the tent opening, but I could see him lurking inside, studying me. "If you would come out where we can talk. I can't talk through a slit in a tent flap, General," I said.

"We have God's work to do this morning, Owen. We have come to the last day, and it is the day of decision as to whether the Union hangs like a plucked chicken from a butcher's hook. We are now on holy ground." He came out of the tent, ignoring me, wandered over to his horse, then came to the fire and stood with his hands clasped behind his back, studying me critically. "What is your request, Owen?" he said.

"To relieve my men of being in the front wall of this attack."

"Why?"

"We are not ready for it. Most of my men were defeated but recently, and their regiments are hastily assembled."

"I refuse the request," he said, staring at me. "Do you think I can go one day to Hill and beg for permission to lead, then the next day explain this—perversity?"

"General Manger, I find it difficult to reckon with—my own feeling is that Lee might be, must be right, but I cannot lead the men into an attack which I believe might be a massacre. I can't trust even Lee beyond my own senses. I know you don't agree, but I am talking about my own judgment. If you cannot spare my men, then at least relieve me from today's command—"

"No, no."

"I will go with them, you understand, but I cannot lead them."

"Oh, yes, you can. Just gather up your courage."

"You don't understand. If I deceive them—"

"You will lead them."

"I could not forgive myself—"

"You lead them anyway. You carry out my orders, Owen."

I sat down on a cracker box and tried to determine what else to say to him. He was looking at me evenly, studiously, all this while. "General, in that case I ask to be relieved of my commission."

He moved slowly closer, staring down at me. "You are a fool."

"I admit anything you please. I wanted it, I admit. I like all the glory I can have, for I need it. I have lusted for such favor as I could find. I have been a general only for a short while—"

"You have been a general for one day only," he said.

"I ask that you do me the personal favor of relieving me of a commission which has become abhorrent to me."

"You will give up your rank, you say?"

"God damn, General Manger, I am—it's a brutal matter for me to ask it over and over."

"To ask any favor of me at all, for a man in your plight—"

"I wrench myself inside each time. I ask that you relieve me of my commission. I ask it, I do plead my own case for it. As a common soldier I will go on the attack."

"Well, you have surprised me, I must say. My Lord help me. Heth is the one who said to give you a brigadier's rank; he was out here on this very field with a head wound, telling me the cardboard band in his hat had saved him from death—some such foolishness, and then he came up with this idea."

"You will be pleased by my resignation, I know—"

"He was out here somewhere near—I don't know just where now. I can't keep track of everything. What is it you want?"

"I ask to be relieved of my commission, General Manger."

"No, no. I won't relieve you. Why, don't you know we are standing here on the edge of history? Never in all history, Owen—"

"I care more for my soul. My men are the best men of many

275

communities. Those men tonight will be racked in pain, broken, dying, scared—I am not talking merely about them as a thousand men, but them as men of communities, a region of my country for which I—many of them I conscripted, and I am to lead them now to be shot down in an open field."

He began pursing his lips, blinking at me reflectively. "I will consider your request at sundown."

"It cost you nothing," I said, astonished at him. "Nothing."

"I owe you nothing," he said.

"General, I am not sure but that you want these men to die with you, and me to die with you, for it all to end with you."

He walked to the edge of his little camp and stood with his back to me, looking at his many regiments. "We are all under sentence," he said, speaking so softly I could scarcely hear him. "We are all under sealed orders. We know not the day or the hour. All those men out there are under orders, and today is God's day, we are going to work for him. Today I hope I—I hope, Owen, I fear I will not see sunset." He turned to me. "A great honor it is for a man to be asked to use his inevitable death for a purpose rather than a waste. We will not whimper because of such a calling. Now get you to your brigade. Ask no quarter of the men, give none to our enemies. The enemies of your country are encamped over that a way; proceed that way, and draw your men into formation facing them."

"I would rather die with some sense of need," I said to him. "I am not under God's sentence of death today, but under yours. You are under God's sentence, not I."

"I confuse myself listening to you—"

"You confuse yourself with us—"

"We will now get about the work at hand. God damn you, you claim to be a soldier. You have presented yourself, passed yourself off as a soldier. You have received an officer's pay and privileges and honors. Now earn your title, earn your keep. No time, no time, no more arguments." He went to his horse. "I have no reason to help you."

"General, do you believe me that it does me no good to see you die so futilely?"

"Yes, I am like a father to you—yes, hell, I know, I know all that." For a moment more he frowned down at me, then he smiled and shrugged. "I suspect you never liked your father." He turned his horse with a heavy pull of the reins and rode slowly to the place where the other two brigade commanders waited for him. Once there, he turned and waved at me. "Come along!" he shouted. I heard him say to another general, "Owen's stomach is weak for the work at hand. You have to have a strong stomach to be a general." Abruptly he stood high in his stirrups and stared out over his many thousands of men. "Remember why we are here," he said to the nearest hundreds of them: "our homes, our children." Again he turned to stare at me—I still watching him. "General Wright will show us the way," he shouted to the men. "Come along, General, show us the way."

I whispered an oath, a prayer. I am not much of a martyr, I tell you. I was not born to lead men to defeat. I once had pride in soldiering. And I had a love for my men, for they were my closest family. "May God forgive me," I said. I had no wish to die, God knows.

The standard of my brigade was sent to me by Manger, that and my mount. I mounted slowly, reluctantly. From horseback I could see out over the heads of my men. A thousand men. Abruptly, viciously, angrily I kicked my spurs into my horse's side, and with a growl, an animal noise, I rode forward to lead the way onto the Seminary Ridge.

I helped my officers form the ranks, all the while trying to dissuade revolt and cynicism.

I encountered much grumbling, but also goodwill and affection among the men, for each other and for me. We were all clutched by the same clawed hand, were close comrades, members of one family. We were pressed close together by the mighty pressure from outside, and by the warm, trembling pressure in our own minds and bellies. "We're going to win the war today," I told them. "Anybody want to go home?"

I walked through my Companies A and B, which had stood with me even when I was a lieutenant and a captain, and I said, "You men know how to bite off a cartridge yet? Aim low, not high."

An elderly man named Curtis said to me, "Owen, don't the Yanks know we're acoming?"

"No, they don't know," I said.

"Won't they see us acoming, Owen?" he said. "There's those of us who've got youngins to home."

"When the smoke settles out there, we'll be ghosts walking out of the smoke, that's all," I said.

"A ghost is what I'm afraid of being," he said grimly. But even so, he showed no sign of deserting us.

I walked through Billy Furr's company. I told McKinney we would measure his courage today, and his sallow frown deepened and he spit into the dirt at my feet. "From a long way off, looks like," he said unconcernedly.

I walked through each company in my regiment, then the other regiments of my brigade, talking quietly, easily, not alarming anybody, not admitting to alarm. "Every man is his own officer today," I told them as I walked among them, knowing even as I said it that never had that been less true than it was today.

Manger kept barking out orders to me and to my regimental commanders. Pettigrew kept giving orders, too, the two of them sometimes giving contrary ones. Further, Heth's division, which was now commanded by Manger and Pettigrew, was supported by other brigades, and these were in formation behind only two thirds of our division, which I mentioned to Pettigrew. "It is your left flank that is likely to be in most need," I told him. "You have no support there." He was young and inexperienced—he was a gallant, well-educated, likable person, but I suspect the excitement of battle had overcome his powers of concentration.

278

In any event, when I pointed out the flaw in his formation—
Heth's division was to lead the left side of the attacking line, as
Pickett's division was to lead the right side—when I mentioned
this serious fault to him he told me he didn't know who was in
charge of forming the lines, whether Hill, who was his commander, or Longstreet, who had been put in charge of the total
attack for this day, or whether he was in charge himself of his
reserves.

"You are at least obligated to report a misalignment," I told
him.

I think he did not report it, or if he did he reported it to Hill,
who did nothing. Finally I even mentioned the matter to Manger. "Our lines will collapse on the left," I told him. But he took
a perverse delight in all the signs of administrative chaos this
morning; he had about as much interest in them as most martyrs
would have in the details of their execution.

There was not much else I could do. My own brigade was
supported adequately. My brigade was on the right flank of
Heth's division, so that we were the link between Heth and
Pickett, almost in the very center of the battle formation's front
line.

I found Woofer and Hal King and sat down between them.
Hal said softly, nervously, "Owen, are they serious about this?"

I said nothing.

"I've been wounded often enough to know they can reach
me, Owen," he said. "I'm not a new man for this war." His voice
was trembling.

I said nothing.

"We been coming a long way to get a decision on this war.
Lord knows how many battles. You want me to lead my men out
there?"

"I suppose Lee has to fight, now that he's here," I said. "It was
a damned expensive error Heth made day before yesterday, to
engage the enemy army like he did."

Woofer was nervous, too, but was not as upset as Hal. He

didn't sense the danger, perhaps, or he had the confidence in his own fortune which young people usually have—it doesn't seem possible to them that they can die.

"How did your wounded lieutenant do, Woofer?" I asked him.

Woofer looked away from me, out over the field. "Not too well," he said.

"I hoped he would recover."

Woofer belched and shook his head angrily. "Damn you, damn it. It's mean, you know it?"

"Yes, I know it," I said.

"He died crying out, Owen."

"Well, they have no morphine, even for our own."

"And talking about his two boys."

"Yes, there are many families out here today, under all these flags," I said. "On both sides," I said. From where I sat, as far as I could see in either direction, to our right or left, men were moving about, getting standards unfurled, giving and receiving commands. "Hal, I'm sorry, I'm only a tool in another man's hand," I said. "You must know how full of despair I feel."

"It's a strange morning, Owen," he said softly.

Heavy fighting broke out on the far side of the Yanks' hill, with artillery and muskets, but I noticed that our own artillery remained silent. I saw Manger send his horse to the rear. I heard him call some question or other to General Pettigrew. Several couriers were racing about on horses, apparently trying to find out what was going on, whether a Yank attack, or if once more Ewell had got his orders wrong, and what we were supposed to do. I could see that hundreds of Yank soldiers were wandering over to the far side of their hilltop to watch what was taking place, but all we saw was a single horse carrying a dead Rebel officer; it came around the bend of Cemetery Hill and passed solemnly in review before us.

When the fighting stopped, the Yanks came wandering back to their stone and log breastworks, which were along the side

280

of the hill facing us. Many of them stacked arms. We could see the glimmer of their rifle barrels and bayonets, and their metal canteens and cups.

"They busted up those peach trees yesterday, didn't they?" Hal said.

"Not much of a crop left," I said.

"Look at that wheat field, Owen," Woofer said, the first time he had called my name in many weeks, just about the first comment he had volunteered to make to me. "It's not got half a crop left," he said.

"That farmer will be cropping haversacks more than wheat, won't he, Woofer?" I said.

"Bodies," Hal said. "I can see bodies in there."

"And on the hill over there," Woofer said. "They didn't pick up everybody last night, Owen."

"I wish there were corpses out front of us," Hal whispered, "to fall behind."

I said, "Yes, if those cannons open fire on us."

"No place to go," Hal said.

"The Yanks are clever with machines," I said. The field was littered with blankets and trousers, caps, muskets and ramrods, bayonets, swords and scabbards, belts, broken haversacks, canteens ... Hundreds of buzzards were in the sky. I suspect they had come from all parts of Pennsylvania. We watched them lazily circling. "Woofer," I said, "don't you try to lead out here today."

He was lying on his belly, and he turned his head forward on his forearm and looked at me. "I'll linger back a ways with you," he said.

"No, I must be with the forward tide," I said.

"Owen, don't get killed," he said.

"I don't mean to," I said. "It's no matter if I die here."

"You have nothing to live for?" Woofer asked quietly.

"Nothing to die for," I said.

Woofer closed his eyes. "Just don't die," he said.

281

"Why do you care? Do you care?' I said.

He lay there for a long while. "I shouldn't care, should I?"

"I never meant you harm."

"But you harmed me. You've never even admitted you harmed me."

"I never meant you harm, Woofer," I said.

"It's not saying the same," he said. And later he said, "I do care, that's the truth of it."

I was moved almost to tears by his comment. "Now listen, I got this thing to do, Woofer," I said suddenly, a sting of affection overwhelming me. I loved the boy, that was the truth of it. I suppose I had never loved any man before in my life. "You are not much of a soldier, Woofer," I said, "and I knew when you first came to my door, back in winter camp, that you wouldn't make much of a soldier, and I told you then to go away."

He watched me carefully, thoughtfully, he and Hal both.

"So I am going to detail you to go see Cutter and let Hal and me carry on this battle."

He looked at me with that utterly incredulous expression he had. "I'll go when you go, Owen," he said.

A wave of relief swept through me, yet of disappointment too. "I conscripted men into this regiment, Woofer. I can't leave them here. What the hell are the smith's men going to do today, will you tell me that?"

"It's going to be chaos out there, Owen," Hal said.

"Maybe the charge won't be made," Woofer said. "Nothing goes the way it's planned in the army, you told me, Owen."

"It might not, it might not," I said hopefully. "God knows, I've been in fifteen battles, and every one was strange as a one-legged dancer. I've had the luck of God Almighty with me, you know it? But I can't base plans on luck. Now then, Woofer, I detail you to sick duty for me, go see Cutter for me."

He looked at me as if I were a stranger.

"God damn you, go and leave me be. Don't you know I'm

tired of looking at you? I don't want you here. You can't even shoot a gun."

"Go to hell, Owen," he said.

"You shut your mouth, talking like that to me. You can take one of my horses and when this battle is over ride south, and nobody will stop you. There will be many a man on the road tonight. And I will be one of them if I have any third-day luck left."

"Owen, d-d-do you think I'd leave you?"

"You damn punk kid, I don't know what you think you can do. I know you can eat meals like a fiend, but we have eaten already. We're not going to be talking big about how you can win women—"

"Owen, I d-d-don't care whether you need me or not."

"Well, I don't want you. Listen here, you came into that log house of mine with that slick, clean face of yours looking around innocent as a sheep, and I said then I wished to God you'd go, for a soldier can't be a family man. Owen do this, Owen do that, and be nice to papa. Papa is nothing but an entrenched old man who can't accept the world changing."

"Owen, if Sory loves you, I can't leave you alone here."

"Hell. All she saw were my colonel's buttons, and all I wanted was a nice farm with a two-story house and a crib. Now get out of here and leave Hal and me alone. I'm your damn colonel or general or whatever it is, and I detail you to go to the rear."

He slowly lowered his face into his folded arm, there on the ground. "Go screw yourself, Owen," he said.

Hal laughed suddenly. "Oh my," he said. He grinned at me. "Well, you said he wasn't much of a soldier."

"He won't listen to an order," I said to Hal, frustrated by him.

"No, he doesn't seem to," Hal said. "I'll go, if you want me to."

"I wish you could," I said.

I put my hand on Woofer's back, rubbed his back gently.

"What if you get wounded, boy? What if you lose part of your body out there? You're too young," I said. "I love you, don't you understand?" I said, and I heard him cry then, a break came in his breathing, and he lay there weeping quietly, trying not to weep. I rubbed his back until he stopped weeping. "Will you go, Woofer?" I said.

He shook his head.

"All right," I said.

A courier came by. He went on, toward where Pettigrew was pacing. This was a time of perfect stillness. Minute by minute, for a long while, we were adrift in a calm on a warm 3rd of July morning. There was no hilarity, no joking by anybody, not even the most lighthearted soldiers. We felt the oppression, just as we did the sun. Some men sat silent, others wrote letters or read the Bible, others were stretched out on their bellies or their backs. "Maybe I loved her because of you, Woofer, maybe in spite of you," I said.

Officers stood together in small groups talking. General Pettigrew beckoned me to come to him. "Your letter troubled Hill, General Wright," he said critically.

"Did it trouble him enough to change his mind?" I said.

Pettigrew blinked at me, considering that. He shrugged. "It's not Hill. It's Lee. He gets so prideful sometimes. He seems to believe that his boys can do anything." He gazed across the open field, at the Yanks' brass Napoleons glimmering on the crest far away. "My God, Wright, it is a long way."

"Is Longstreet still trying to change Lee's mind?"

"Oh, yes. But Lee doesn't budge, once he's set. You know he prays a great deal, and he asks God for advice, and I expect God has told him this is what to do."

A nauseous sense of awe and anger came over me. I felt as if I had lodged myself in a massive mound of fate, that I was a speck on the flesh of this elephantine animal, and was bound to ride it on its mad course.

284

"Who knows but what Lee's right?" Pettigrew said suddenly, hopefully. "After all, he has planned victory after victory before, one after another."

"Where is he now?" I said.

"He won't see you, Wright," he said abruptly. "I'm confident of that."

"But where is he?"

"Over in the far meadow beyond Longstreet's lines, holding a review of Pickett's men."

"A review?" I said. "A review?"

Pettigrew laughed uneasily. "I don't know what to say about it," he said, and he walked along the line of Hill's corps, his own corps to lead today, shaking his head in wonder.

I told Hal where General Lee was just now, while his army waited, and he said, "There has to be a ceremony if there's to be a sacrifice, Owen, doesn't there?"

The lull continued. I told myself I was in papa's field back home, and across the valley Sory had come into her field and was walking in the sun.

Woofer groaned. "Owen, do you still love her?"

"Yes," I said. "But I believe she loves you, Woofer."

"I wrote to ask her," he said. "I wrote the longest letter in the world to ask her. I asked her seventy ways, and I don't know yet."

"You asked her whether she loves you?"

"I asked her whether she loves you."

"And what did she say?"

"She said never to write her another letter like that again."

I laughed softly, more from relief than anything else. "A woman's mind," I said.

"Owen, when you lose someone that's dear as life, what does it do to your insides?"

"It tears them up," I said.

"How long before you forget it?"

"I gave up Anna Morla, don't you know. I never did get over

that, until here lately. And I struck papa and left him, and I try to get over that, but it lingers. I think last time I was home, standing in the yard with him, we were as close as we have ever been in our lives, so it's healing."

"Did you ever lose anything else?"

I said nothing.

"She loves you, I believe," Woofer said, whispering.

"Well, she's just a little girl," I said.

I saw that Plover was asleep. He was snoring. Maybe he was dreaming about one of his daughters. Maybe I ought to dream about one of his daughters, I thought, or dream of Sory in her house when I pulled her close to me and kissed her—I like to kiss her, for she has a full, soft mouth.

Don't, don't think of it, I warned myself, not lying here next to Woofer, in the shadow of our other thoughts.

Life is so much treason, isn't it? We would know all human emotions and excitements, and often we trip over our callings. "My secrets are so beautiful to me," I said quietly. Only I can see my life through the secrets I have, I thought.

"They'll be freeing the slaves now," Hal said, "South as well as North."

"Well, I don't know," I said.

"It will all be changed for us. They will be with us for a long while, the blacks, smiling at us, watching us, until someday . . ."

"Someday what, Hal?" I said.

"They kill us, I suppose," he said. "Or try to enslave us. They are no better than we are, after all."

"Well, I suppose they aren't," I said. General Pickett's Virginians appeared on the field over to our right, in the valley Longstreet had captured yesterday afternoon. They were a proud division, boisterous and confident and beautifully equipped. The men began pelting each other with green peaches they picked up off the ground.

The sun was hot now. The day was clear. "I suppose Lee has decided," I said to Hal.

286

"Those cannon, Owen—"

"He plans to silence them, he says." I pinned my name to my jacket. I unpinned my officer insignia and threw the stars out onto the field. Woofer saw me, and I know he was baffled by it, but he said not a word. "Until last night I didn't think there was an army that could beat this one," I said quietly, "and now I wonder if there's an army that can't."

Officers were taking their places now. Couriers were hurrying back and forth. I saw a group of newspapermen climb into trees at the edge of the woods, field glasses in their hands. They were joking with one another. I saw a group of military observers pass by; they were Germans, I believe.

A single crack of a cannon over to our right, Longstreet's battery; one cannon fired, a distinct, sharp voice which ended the lull, and on that signal over 150 guns of Longstreet and Hill's corps opened fire, almost deafening me. The explosion of the shells enveloped in smoke the top of the Yank hill, stone walls and cemetery and cannons and men in a ball of metal and smoke. As the smoke lifted, a second barrage was fired, and I saw that several Yank artillery horses had pulled free and were plunging riderless across the hillside before us. A Yank mess wagon appeared on the field, being dragged by runaway horses, the driver, a Negro, tugging on the reins desperately; the wagon struck a rock and tore apart, pieces flying all over the place, and the horses went tearing off toward General Pickett's position near the broken peach trees. The earth on which we lay shook with a third Rebel barrage. The South was writhing, crying to be free. Above us were shrieks of metal; rifled shells were hissing. Smoke rolled in torrents above us and darkened over us. Twenty-four-pound shells, twenty-pound, twelve-pound, ten-pound projectiles, as well as solid shot, we were firing everything now and each had its voice and breath, and the Yanks began firing their ten-pound Parrotts, ten-pound rifled ordnance, and twelve-pound Napoleons, using projectiles conical, spherical, spiral. The voice and fire and smoke of over 350 cannons and their shells were all-pervading. Through the smoke we saw men running, couriers falling, now and then an impatient rifleman firing impotently. All other barrages I had heard in the war were but holiday sallies compared with this. Trees were breaking away everywhere, horses were fleeing through the woods from Lord knows where, some of them spraying blood as they galloped past. Many soldiers were wandering about, dazed, completely unaware of what they were doing. They couldn't hear anyone. Sergeants struck them, pushed them back, pulled them by their clothes, threw them to the ground. I saw a ball of flame engulf a Rebel cannon even as I watched, and there in the midst of the flame were the brown muscular arms of a Southerner wielding the rammer and pushing home the cannon's load as he and the load exploded.

General Lee appeared, riding his gray horse. Generals Longstreet and Pickett were with him. Every metal known to artillerists was bounding about now, and here these officers were, conspicuously mounted. My men yelled at them, terrified to see them out here, and Lee took off his hat in acknowledgment of their greeting and waved to them, here in a sulphur cloud lit from within by flashes of fire. "What a proud gentleman he is," Hal said.

The barrage continued until the Federal batteries one by one were humbled. When the Yank cannon had ceased firing entirely, I got to my feet. "Are the Yanks fooling us, Hal?" I said.

"God knows," he said.

Woofer got to his feet. We stood in the wispy, sulphurous cloud beneath an all-concealing darker cloud of smoke. I could not see far to either side. I heard Manger order his division to advance, and at once I ordered my men forward into the field, I leading the men, the smoke screening us from the enemy, the men not yelling, even our drums quiet. The battery and regimental standards were lost in the smoke. We began moving swiftly down the hill. A few minutes later, still in the smoke, we crossed the valley road, a silent army, many rows of men deep. The mist flitted about us. I was walking steadily in the forward row. Woofer was near me, but behind me a few paces. I saw General Manger walking in front of us, walking like my father with his back stiff, his head high, the smoke flailing him.

We were in their valley now. We were moving in solid formation. We moved onto their hillside. Not a shot was fired. Nobody seemed to be alive before us. We heard no sound at all, except the somber, measured thumping of our feet. The men said nothing. There were no yells at all from anywhere. In a moment, in the wind the smoke cleared before us and we saw above us the rocky side of Cemetery Hill, a full view of it, most impressive, and at once Victor Plover rolled the drum he carried—the first drum to sound from Hill's corps. Spread out from us were tremendous lines, 15,000 Southerners in sight, my old regiment in the forefront of the Pettigrew advance, Manger well out front of us all, walking stiffly forward alone. Hundreds of banners were visible. Many drums began rolling now. A cheer went up and I realized the Yanks were cheering us. The moment had come, they knew the moment had come. They were cheering the moment that had come. After three campaigns the battle had come. The Yanks were standing on their breastworks, waving their hats and cheering the sight before them, an army moving toward them in ranks, with colors, with drums and bugles, their brothers advancing.

General Pickett's men were ahead of us, over to our right, they having started in the valley; they were well up on the Yank hillside. A row of about a hundred Yanks appeared before us scrambling away from us up the hill, frightened of so overwhelming a host. We advanced over breastwork, boulder, over every obstacle; we moved over several Yank bodies, even as hundreds of Yanks appeared before us on the hillside and turned and retreated up the hill. McIlvenna's bagpipes were playing. The Yanks were stumbling on the hill, slipping, cursing.

Abruptly before us in a wide line, standing up from behind a breastwork, hundreds of blue-clothed Yanks stood and fired on command, fired in unison into our ranks. My dear friend

Sergeant Silver fell. Four men of the smith's company fell. At once McGregor shouted for his men to charge forward, for the Yanks' muskets were unloaded now, and so he closed with them, rifle butts bashing them. I saw the smith like a wounded bear bashing at a Yank with his musket, a choking cry coming out of him, the yell, the infernal Rebel yell coming out of the smith, the yell coming from many of his bleeding men who had seen their friends shot down. Billy Furr's men were slaughtering as they advanced, wading through fallen Yanks.

A cannon fired. Metal infiladed our line and twenty of my men in a row fell backward, were hurled backward by the iron, and from above us came another roar—all of this was confusing —and I looked higher to see flame leap from four Yank cannons, all of them firing shrapnel at us—hunks of iron straight into us. The cannon tore open wide holes in our forward lines. I saw that the cannon to my right, the one which had first fired, was ready to fire again, but it seemed I could not move fast enough, I could not fall down fast enough, I was stymied by time itself, standing in the line of fire. I shouted at Hal to fall to the ground, and he saw the cannon even as the metal spewed over us, mutilating Sergeant Smith, decapitating Sole McKinney, tearing many men to pieces horribly, striking me—I was thrown to the ground, while Hal stood helplessly watching me, he bleeding even then. The four cannons on the hill fired their second load of iron, this time canister, and I saw the iron strike the bodies of other men as I got to my feet and yelling made a charge forward, irrationally moving toward the enemy. Hundreds of Yanks appeared, some of them only fifty yards away. Red Raper fell. I was hit and fell. I was turned over by two men, one of whom said, "Owen's hit," and they laid me behind the rock wall, even as cannon fired directly into them and their blood splattered over me and another wave of my men went down before me, some of them carried fifty feet down the hill by the iron. I could see all this in a second or two: the field below me where hundreds of men lay, the others of my men retreating

290

now, and I thought, We ought to go as far as General Pickett went. I saw that my little Plover drummer boy was sitting on the ground, bent over, his arms around his drum, his hair covering the surface of the drum; it was as if he had merely gone to sleep.

I could see 15,000 men on the hill and in the field below me, and those who could were fleeing across the valley toward Seminary Ridge now. Manger's division was shattered, was in truth disappearing. All of Hill's corps was falling back. I could see that Pickett's men, their drive having peaked at the top of Cemetery Ridge, were now retreating toward the valley. Bouncing bits of iron skipped across the fields, seeking bodies, and bodies were most everywhere to be found. The field was littered with dead and wounded men, and there were many dazed men who kept walking about in circles, wandering from place to place, until they were shot down.

I sat behind the wall. I sat in the shade of the smoke clouds and watched my men. I watched helplessly as they helplessly retreated, the Yanks killing them like a blight. I was, in fact, near enough to the Yanks to hear them congratulating each other.

I looked to make certain my name was pinned in my jacket.

Quiet now, except for a group of Yanks softly singing "John Brown's Body." A beautiful song. The rain began now. The cold drops of rain. Above me a black sulphur cloud was rolling like the eye of doom. Across the valley Longstreet's band began playing a waltz.

Ambulances appeared at both ends of the valley and began the slow work of sorting the wounded from the dead, lingering at the ends of the valley first, creeping farther into the valley every little while, even as wounded men moved toward them, moved with all manner of disarrangement of torsos and limbs and heads, fiercely trying to limp, crawl, drag their way to the black lightning bugs, men gray and splattered with red, arms dangling, leg bones poked through uniform cloth, a panorama of broken men so immense in scope yet so detailed and specific

291

that I could not cease marveling at it, watching it in spite of its moroseness and my own horror. Men were crawling over men. A man fell sprawling as a leg gave way under him, all of this accompanied by very little noise at all, not much groaning or screaming, for there was not much pain as yet. There was in me no pain at all, except in my mind as I watched my men, and that a somber sorrow. My men lay dead or paining, my regiment was defeated, my brigade was broken, and in the third year of the war our army had lost, we had today lost all our victories.

The earth itched on its skin from the fingers of men who crept across it just now, but the greater loss was earth trembling and had to do with massive forces and with nations.

Lieutenant Willis, so proud to be an officer, dead. I could see his head lolled back from his shoulders. Where was Hal King? Where was Woofer? I tried to call to them but could not locate my voice; I could speak, I was sure, though not on my own command.

In the valley one of the ambulances rolled over a man; I suppose the driver thought he was dead. The man was screaming fiercely now. Well, they should not roll over men, living or dead. See how he is folded in the middle yet tries to rise, his arms outstretched.

I began to weep. I sobbed in despair. I, a soldier.

Dusk, almost full dark. I cut my pants leg on my right leg so I could see the wound, and I held my leg's artery closed as best I could, pressing it with my thumbs, so that the bleeding was only trickling. I sat staring down at my right leg's wound, wondering if in that pool of blood, skin, flesh, metal, bone there were creatures who sometimes congregated for ceremonies, maybe even for battles.

Major Crawford appeared, his hands folded on his lower belly, moving along slowly, studying the faces of the dead, moaning now and then, a womanly sort of tut-tutting on his lips. He saw me and stopped in his tracks. He was not more than thirty feet away. He came toward me, carefully stepping over dead bodies, his gaze on me always.

"Have you got any cloth for a bandage, Skip?" I asked him.

"Skip, is it?" he said. He saw the leg wound I had managed to uncover and his eyes closed for an instant.

"Tear me off a bandage, will you, Skip?" I said.

He did nothing.

"You will watch me suffer, Skip?" I said.

"You have watched me suffer for years," he said.

"I never felt you were suffering," I said, "you were always so lordly."

"Even as a boy I would have given you my horse, my saddle, my slave, to have had you for a friend," he said. "I have told you—"

"Well, I wonder if you have any clean cloth," I said. "I'm sorry about all that other."

"I think you are capable of being sorry, Owen. I have seen you talk to Woofer, and I believe you are capable of affection for him, of love for him."

He was jealous of Woofer, jealous of my affection for him; he was upset because I had never shown affection for him, I supposed. What a strange bundle of emotions he was. I noticed he was white and clammy in his face, even his lips were white, and his eyes were glassy, so that when he turned away I felt it was because he wanted to hide himself from sight. He slumped down against the same wall where I lay.

Slowly I unpeeled my jacket, then my shirt, and tore my shirt into pieces. "I always did admire you, Skip," I said.

His throat gurgled, a groan with phlegm in it, and he said, "Oh, for God sake, shut up, Owen."

I bandaged my leg and poured water from my canteen onto the bandage; water was the best medicine, my mother had always contended. "You waiting for me to die, Skip?" I said.

He stared out at the hillside opposite us, where now the healthy members of our own army were walking about in plain

293

view, unconcerned about the wounded men below them. "You might lose Penny's watch," he said.

"That so?" I said.

"And Penny's boots."

"You think so, Skip? You want them?"

"And his belt and gun and pants and coat, and maybe when you're cold, you'll lose the ring." The frown on his face gave way to a tight, grim smile. It was terrifying, really—his words with that smile, the smile decaying even as I watched, for it was not honest anyway, his mouth becoming as round and hungry as his eyes.

A Yank came down the hill and bent over a dead soldier. He went through his pockets quickly.

"Will you tighten this belt?" I asked him. I was making a tourniquet. He helped me, silently, efficiently. "That white-faced fellow there is waiting for me to die so he can get my things," I said.

He stared at Crawford. "You going to die?" he asked him.

"No, he's waiting for me to die. He thinks I'll die."

"I wouldn't mind having your pistol," the Yank said to me.

"I'll keep it, unless you want to help me to the valley floor."

"Not me," he said, and went on up the hill, stumbling on the rocks.

"Skip, will you help me to the valley?" I said.

He said nothing.

I started crawling toward the valley as best I could, pulling my way along. I saw General Manger's body almost at once. He had come about as far up the hill as I had. He was sprawled out on his back, his chest opened by canister, his limbs thrown out awkwardly, his eyes open but sightless.

Around me were many other bodies, so many I had to crawl over a few of them. Some were alive and asked me to help them, and cursed me for leading them into this battle, even said they would kill me. Mingled in among them were the Yanks we had killed. I took crackers from one of their pockets and ate them.

294

Off across the valley Longstreet's band was playing a waltz.

Crawford followed me, walking slowly, patiently, his hands folded on his belly. He's wounded, I thought. He sat down near me and watched me with his moist, glassy eyes. He'll kill me, too, I thought.

I pulled myself away from him. I came upon McIlvenna, who was sitting up staring at the valley, where fires were being lighted; also there were fires on Seminary Ridge, and when I looked up the hill back of me I saw a line of Yank fires in a row.

"I been wondering about water," McIlvenna said.

"I have none left," I said.

"I recall that my wife wanted me to put a trough to the house from an uphill spring, and ever time she carried a bucket of water to the house she would call out, 'This'n is 2638.' She would shout out so loud I could hear her in the field. Of course, I knew she was one to exaggerate." We listened to the music for a while. "Owen, what in the world is wrong with that band of ours?"

"It's too much brass and not enough music," I said.

"You'd think we could find forty musicians in the South, wouldn't you? I fear the Yanks have us beat on music, Owen."

"You crawling down now?" I asked him.

"No, no. I'm in no hurry, even if I don't get there till morning. We won't try another charge like this tomorrow, will we?"

"I don't know who we would send, do you?"

"How many got hurt out here, Owen? Do you know?"

"More than ninety percent of Heth's division, to begin with," I said.

He sat there fascinated by the fires and the scenes they lighted, no doubt thinking about the marvels he was seeing and the marvels he had that day seen. He was content with that diversion. He was an artist, I suppose.

Lower on the hillside I could hear the rattle of the ambulances. Somebody nearby kept saying his name: Harvey Dale

Long. Nobody wants to die unknown. I was still deep among my men, but it was dark and not many recognized me. Those who did cursed me or asked me to help them. My mind was clear and I did not as yet feel any pain in my body. I was not near death; at least, I didn't sense that I could call death, as papa said he could on occasion.

Sergeant Red Raper was sitting by a boulder. I stopped to rest there. "Where is the rain, Sergeant?" I said.

"It hasn't rained for an hour," he said.

"How did your men do?"

"Oh, they went both directions, once the cannons started," he said. "Plover led the retreat. I think he was the first man to get back to the woods."

"Might have been called by one of his ten-minute bowel movements," I said.

Raper laughed gently. "Will you write a letter for me?" he said.

"No, I have no time to write just now," I said. "I'm wounded, Red."

"I always meant to learn to write," he said.

My leg was bleeding. A throb of pain now. My breath was breathing mist in the air as I pulled myself along.

Hal King. I recognized his gentle hands. "Hal." I pulled myself to him, felt his face with my palm. "Ah, Nell," I said, and laid my head on his chest.

Do you see the stars, Nell? I thought. Nell, see the stars. They make no pattern at all, as Woofer said.

Nell, I will not be a ghost to haunt you, I said, nor will Hal.

Many healthy soldiers were walking through, Yanks and Rebs, asking for friends and robbing the dead. A Pennsylvania farmer and his boy arrived with a wagon half full of hay to carry two wounded men to a hospital. I offered him my ring in payment, but he said he couldn't appraise a ring out here. He wanted a hundred dollars instead, and it had to be in Yank money. I didn't have any. Nobody had that much, so he came down to $80, then to $60, and finally he carried one man for $40 and another for $32.50. "It's not a rich part of the battlefield," I heard him tell his boy.

Litter-bearers were stumbling over bodies, cursing. Martin Luther loomed up before the moon; I recognized his scowling face even in silhouette. "You praying, preacher?" I asked him, glad to see him.

"Who's that?" he said, coming toward me suspiciously. "Who is it?"

"Martin, don't let Crawford get me, you hear? He's a buzzard and wants to eat me."

"We've been looking higher on the hill for you. Woofer said you went high on the hill."

"How is Woofer?"

He cupped his hands to his mouth and shouted out to somebody, "Hey, he's down here!"

"Is that Woofer?" I said.

"It's Betsy. Woofer is somewhere around, looking for a wagon."

"Is he all right?"

"Yes. You know Woofer, how he has the luck of the world about him."

Betsy came down the hill and bent over me, felt of my forehead and took my pulse. "Are you busted in a bone?" he said.

"I feel like I'm not," I said, "but don't let Major Crawford get me, Betsy. He wants to eat me."

"Major Crawford is up there dying on the hill. He was opened up across the belly by a shell," he said.

"Ah, Lord," I said softly. "He's always been—I've always needed him since I was a boy."

"You'll not be pestered with him again, begging your pardon, sir."

"Ah, Skip, dear Skip," I said, tears in my eyes.

Woofer came through the scary place, a Yank in tow, a tall

private. He came forward slowly and touched my face. I was lying on my right side and Betsy was trying to get cloth enough to patch my back. Woofer felt my face and sighed like a little boy. "Owen, are you going to be all right?" he said, his voice trembling like a reed in the wind. "Owen, don't die," he said softly.

"No, no," I said. "I don't feel it nearby, like papa said he did at times. I won't call it, even if it comes to me."

"Can you feel the hurting yet?"

"God, yes," I said. "I think—it's worse than the other times, for they were more slight. Men can't fight cannons, you know it, Woofer?"

"Owen, please don't die, for God sake," he said. "You're the only man left for it, to go home and at least try to set it right." He dug into his pocket and came out with two gold stars and he started to pin one of them on my shoulder strap. "I found them on Manger," he said.

"No, no, Woofer, don't bother me. Go on away with those damn things." He looked so hurt to be set back so roughly that I apologized to him. "I feel cold, Betsy," I said, a chill sweeping through me, as if an icy hand had been laid on my back. "My God, Betsy."

"Get Owen some blankets," Betsy said. "Anybody have a blanket for Owen?"

Two men began to curse me from somewhere off in the dark. "Where is he?" one of them kept asking aloud.

"What Yank you got in tow, Woofer?" I said.

"This man's from Ohio and knows that lieutenant I shot at Chancellorsville."

"Does he?" I felt Woofer's face. He scarcely needed to shave, he was still such a tender boy. "You worried still about that man?"

"His family I worry about. I been asking about Cousin Bee, as well."

"He's not out here, is he, in this battle?"

298

"No, I don't think so," Woofer said.

The Yank private came close and knelt beside me and felt my forehead. He frowned at me. "We can carry him," he said.

I could barely see Woofer now. His hand was hot on my skin. I saw him dig into his pocket and come out with those stars, and he gave them to Martin. "Go tell them it's a general sent for a wagon," he said.

"With straw in it, plenty of straw," Betsy said.

Way off in my mind I heard the sound of guns firing, the swish and tearing noise of metal slashing through the air, plopping hard into bodies and the earth, sounding like the beating of the hoofs of a horse on the wooden planks of a stall; the rattle of muskets followed, and I heard a cry like a boy makes.

Blotches of darkness and moonlight. The sound of hoofs on the wooden wall beating, my heart beating; the sound of muskets around me firing, our men firing, the horse's leg in pain, its back in pain, my father watching, calculating, measuring, estimating, but never touching, loving, Betsy saying where is the straw, the straw on my back, my leg beating the wooden slats in pain, my hand squeezing the gun firing the Yank falling the man saying over and over his name. I with my hand on his shoulder. The shells breaking, he rising on the litter ...

A line of tents, stacks of arms and legs outside the tents, hogs eating them. "Ahhhhh, Owen, ahhhhh, Owen," Woofer saying. "Ahhhhh, Owen," he leaning close to my face, staring into it.

"What you want, boy?" I said.

"They didn't cut it off," he said, "we wouldn't allow it, but I had to put your stars on you or they would have cut it off."

"What they say? No lies to me, Woofer."

"You don't feel it close, do you, Owen?"

"No, not yet."

"Your back is strapped. It took them longer on the back then the leg. You were hit six times, Owen."

"Uh-huh. It doesn't pain me now."

"They use morphine, they have morphine for the generals."

"Did I see hogs," I said, "last night—or did I dream it?"

"Yes, there are hogs here," he said.

It was raining. The cold rain sobered me and my mind was clear. From my litter I could see a big house and barn, and the open barnyard was crowded with moaning and wailing men, and the road was full of ambulances and wagons coming toward us, most of them passing on by us, and with wounded men walking toward us, legions of men in the rain. From where I lay I saw long rows of men lying under the eaves of buildings, water pouring down on their bodies in streams. Most of the operating tables were in the open where the light was bright. The surgeons stood in the rain or under tarpaulins or blankets, their shirt sleeves rolled up to the elbows, their bare arms as well as their linen aprons soaked with blood. Around them were pools of blood and amputated arms or legs in heaps. I saw a man, I heard him shriek with pain as he was lifted onto the table; the surgeon examined his wound and in that same instant took his knife from between his teeth, wiped it across his apron, and began to cut. He cut off the man's arm at the elbow. He looked around with a deep sigh of weariness and said, "Next."

As far as I could see men were on the road moving south, wounded and well, men helping each other, sludging through the mud of the road, going into the fields sometimes to rest, men with glassy, staring eyes, open, gasping mouths, an army going south, many of the men going home. The soldiers seemed to pay no attention to the guards who tried to stop them. They knew the Confederacy's back was broken, the long chain of victories was ended. We were the slaves now.

A wagon stopping. "It'll cost you your ring, Owen," Betsy said. I was lifted into it. I remember the road being rough, and there were no springs in the wagon. I lost consciousness. I awoke at a train which was packed with men, and other men were holding to the sides of the cars. Betsy and Martin gave a sergeant my watch, bought with it room to stretch me out on the

300

floor of a car near the stove, and Woofer came to me again. I saw him as in a glass darkly and he took my hand as if saying good-by to me, why, I don't know, and pressed my hand firmly, tears in his eyes, why, I don't know. I was too vague of mind to ask him much of anything. "Do you love her?" he said. I remember him saying that over and over, and I must have told him again that I did, for tears took form and rolled down his cheeks, but he was such a strong boy, such a staunch man inside, that he didn't even turn away.

The train moving. The tree limbs passing by the broken side of the boxcar. The stars beyond the limbs. The smell of anthracite coal, the smoke of battle filtering across the great field where my men lay; the train jolting, men hanging to the sides of the train, men shouting; a pain as thick as stone in my body; somebody singing, somebody not Woofer sitting by the wall, not Manger either; the room in the inn, the little nigger girl nearby who looked like him, my father's face cold as dawn in the dawnlight standing by the wall, my mind wandering, my bed creaking, sitting on my bed my father's body close by while he watched. Ahhhhhh, Owen, ahhhhh, Owen, the words filled with concern I had never known him to express. The smell of mint. Nell at the doorway watching me. Papa near the wall now, waiting, his scowling face watching me. Above me the pine slats of the inn room. A rain began splattering on the glass panes. The black girl standing nearby with his face.

"Where is Crawford?" I said. "Where is Skip?"

"He spoke, did you hear it?" my father said. "Thank God, please God."

"Skip, where is Woofer?" I said.

Mint. Vaguely I see her.

"Sory?" I said.

Her cool hand on my forehead. "It's only Nell," she said.

"Only Nell," I said, "only Nell," tears coming into my eyes. "Only my baby," I said, and took her into my arms.

"How is he?" she whispered.

301

"Oh, hush, baby, hush," I said, and held her close to me, and rocked her.

Let all generals come down to this. Let us hold our sister when we can, once we have killed her lover. Let our father watch us one by one in pain. Let God forgive us for what we do with what we have, for what we do to the straggly woods and the wide fields.

CHAPTER FOURTEEN

"So I said to the nigras, well, if you want to go away, I will find somebody to take you up on the ridge where the trail to the North is, and they all got their clothes packed in bags and took as many hams as they could, not that we had many left after those six soldiers came through and said they was buying for the army and took most everything that could walk or hang from a string. I asked at church one morning of your brother Phillip if he knew the way to the North, and he said he did, and he said also Jesse came back from time to time and could show them, so when the night came they sang all the sad songs they knew and I led them over the bridge, and Jesse took them from there." She was sitting on the front porch of papa's house with her belly poked out from her pregnancy, rocking back and forth, her rough, work-worn hands folded and resting on her lap, her pretty face wan and solemn, as was her mood.

"So Jesse took them up there for you, did he?"

"Yes. They said good-by to Eli and me at the bridge and went singing in a column up through your papa's pasture, and I realized then that a night about three years ago when Mr. Crawford and I was sitting up late, I saw a strange procession in that very field. I remember saying to him, 'See the ghosts go,' and he couldn't see so well, poor dear. It was Jesse leading another company of nigras to the trail, I suppose."

"Did all of yours leave, Sory?"

"They all come back," she said.

I laughed out of surprise. "Oh, Lord, Sory."

"The male workers have sneaked off since, taking what wasn't nailed down. I believe the women and children got up there and saw so many spirits and spooks, with the limbs shifting and the vines drooping and the wind moaning, that they scared the men, so they all come back down, weighted with packs of clothes and food, and my Mattie with four jugs of brandied peaches."

She was pretty in the late-afternoon light. She always came to see me in the afternoon and sat with me, fanning herself with a feather fan; later I would walk to the bridge with her, she helping me, and papa would come to help me home, he or Phillip, for I was still mending.

"I hope I never carry another full baby in the heat of summertime," she said.

"You look like you're carrying two or three."

"I was big as this with Eli. My family pokes out more than the Ellises or anybody who lived near us. When I was no more than three months gone with Eli, my papa saw that I was in more than a cupful of trouble and wrote to Mr. Crawford. I was showing, even in church with a wool shawl on. My breasts got full too. Most women wait till toward the end of the nine months, but I begin to bloom out at the start, and this time when I was only a month gone I knew I was in danger."

I laughed, she was such a dear person, talking along in that staccato, sad voice with a smile on her face, her black eyes glancing at me, seeking ways to entertain me.

"It'll be born this month, won't it? When did Woofer come to your army?" she asked.

"December, about the middle of the month."

"I had just noticed my condition and I told Woofer my fears about him and that riverbank, and he turned white as snow and next I knew was running off to find you, for he never could talk with his father about anything personal."

"Let's see now, that would be the middle of November or

304

later—sometime the last half of November that—that is, you and Woofer must have—"

"Right over there on the far bank of the river on a warm morning," she said.

I rocked for a minute or two, considering that. "This is near the middle of July, I believe, about the twenty-first, isn't it?"

"And you got home the night of the ninth, all wrapped up, and I said to myself, no, no, Sory, don't go over there, don't go see, for they brought your husband Pinky home with soldiers milling about him like that. But I—I took Eli's hand to guide me and we came across that bridge, the longest journey I ever made save the one with Mr. Crawford, and we passed his grave and came up that little rise to the house, and I saw the wagon and thought the worst, for there were scores of people milling about, talking about what you had done and Plover telling it in a sorry song, and you saw me and raised your hand to me and the sweetest smile, Owen, why, it was the gentlest smile, as if you had seen the worst men do and had come home and now cared about me over that distance that separated us."

"I do care about you," I said. "Lord, yes." I took her hand and pressed it to my lips, held it for a moment.

"So how many months does that make it? Is it nine?"

"I would say this month you should bear, the latter half of this month. This must be the twenty-eighth or -ninth, itself."

"When I was walking over here I wondered if I ought to cross the bridge, for fear the baby would call time about halfway over." She clutched her little hands together and sighed. "And it not named."

"You do have a woman or two over there to help you when you bear, do you?"

"There's three of them left and one of them will sometimes come when she's called. The other two I caught wearing my dresses, and I got so fiery at them that they won't speak to me, or listen either. They were on the staircase, Owen, flouncing

305

about, going up and down modeling my dresses and talking with my accent, with those broad vowel sounds—I can't help the way I talk any more than they can, and acting like the hall was full of Yankee soldiers come to take them away and free them and Lord knows what all."

"How do you feed all those women, Sory?"

"We have a garden we planted for ourselves and have worked ever since. And even when the six military men came to take most everything, they didn't get it all, for Mr. Crawford had part of my herds and flocks and I claimed them later, and I had hid enough pigs for the hams and bacon we needed, and chickens too, and even a steer. And we have two milch cows."

"And the oxen."

"Yes, the government men said they didn't want to buy the oxen."

"And they paid you with scrip?"

"And it worth less than the paper they wrote it on, as I decided, so I kept back all I could, and Mr. Crawford was surly with them and told them he had given all he would to the war. Mr. Crawford's patriotism stops where financial sacrifice begins."

"We'll all need to start over here anyway. Saturday Phillip helped me as far as the mill and I listened, and I judge most everybody will have to start over. It takes two or three years of being lean, then we'll be gaining again, provided we can get the road to market repaired. And provided there is a market."

Her fingers were clutched tightly. "Is it nine months even, Owen, that a baby is born?"

"It's ten moon months, 280 days, papa says. He has it all determined for stock and people both."

"The best time to conceive would be summer, then I would bear in the spring. This next month or two would be the best time to conceive."

"Does it kick?"

"Law, yes, since it was four months old. It's like Woofer,

306

always on the move," she said, her voice soft and sad, as it was whenever she mentioned him. "It kicked my napkin off my lap at supper last night."

"Did Woofer write you again?"

"Never but the one letter I showed you, saying how pretty Ohio was and how this woman had let him come to eat dinner with her and her two boys. He only wrote me that to make me angry as a peacock that sees its reflection. Have you ever seen a peacock fight itself, Owen?"

"No, not that I recall."

"They will almost drown themselves trying to kill their reflection in water, and once a tinker told me a peacock saw himself in one of his pots and tore the pot to pieces."

"Oh, hush."

"It's the truth."

I laughed with her and reached over and took her hand and held it. "You're a funny little girl," I said. We sat there for a while, content with one another. "Martin Luther said he would come to see me today, but he hasn't yet. He worries much of the time, Sory, and he asked me the other week if I had seen God at Gettysburg."

"Did you?"

"I told him I was busy watching the ground that day. Martin said to me, 'Owen, do you ever have any doubts?' I told him no, except sometimes about General Lee. He said he did have doubts from time to time and that it worried him, for if Jesus revealed God, why isn't God more like Jesus, he said."

"I wouldn't speak about such matters, Owen, or you'll get struck by lightning for your trouble, for I don't think the wisest man on earth is safe to argue with the Bible or with God. You'd best hush."

"I told Martin it was a fine question and he ought to preach on it. I said Jesus was always asking questions of people. Martin said, 'But I don't have the answer.' "

"He probably doesn't have the answer, for Mr. Crawford

307

always told me nobody in Andrews had answers to much of anything."

"I told him to use parables then."

"Is he a preacher, Owen?"

"Why, he preaches some. He was visited by an angel, Sory."

"Was he now?" she said, her mouth round with wonder. "Was he?"

"Same one that visited Mary, I believe he said. A pretty one, anyway."

"Owen, I've never heard of anybody—"

"There in winter camp. I suppose the angel was getting his roll in order for the campaign."

"Did Martin talk to him?"

"Oh, yes. It was all reported to me officially, Sory."

"I'll bet he's a Virgo. Is he quiet and patient and dutiful?"

"Yes, I suppose I could say—you mean the angel or Martin?"

"I wish my new son would be a Virgo, but I don't suppose I'll last till August. They don't talk much, but they are given to noticing kindly all manner of details. I could bear a Virgo, if I would start later of a year."

"Martin's a preacher, the best I know, the same way the smith's brother is. That is, he was called by God. They tell me the smith's brother makes more money preaching than black-smithing now."

"And him still living in the house with his dead brother's wife."

"They say when he holds out those hands and they see the scars on them, and him standing there with pain on his face—"

"Can Martin marry people, Owen?" she said, fidgeting nervously with her blouse tie. She was tense as a string drawn tight, and was concentrating on the road out front, her rocking chair still.

"You wondering about marrying in the next day or two, Sory?" I said.

308

"I've been wondering about marrying for eight or nine months now," she said.

There was a shallow wind coming in from the east and it nestled among the trees there in the yard. "I went into church Sunday, Sory, and saw that empty section where the men always sit, and I almost collapsed and would have if Phillip hadn't been holding me."

"No, there's not many men left to go to church here."

"And those that are, half of them are crippled. And the women ask how their men died, and Mr. Crawford came up to me after the service white as a ghost, and asked me again how Skip died. He said he understood that he was heroic and was leading the charge and might be medaled, and I said, 'Oh, yes, he was a brave man.' And Hal's mother was the worst for crying Sunday. Nell's been staying over at their house for two weeks now, though I guess she'll come home soon. She's mourning."

"He was such a quiet, pleasant person. Was he prepared for dying?"

"He was. Hal knew it was stalking him. His older brother said Sunday how sorry he was, and I told him Hal told me to ask him to take his place in personal matters. Which I guess is a lie, though Hal might have asked it if I had found him earlier on that hill."

"What did the brother say?"

"He said, 'Well, all right.' "

She fidgeted with her hands. "What does that mean?"

"I don't know, all those King boys talk so calm, but I take hope from it for he has had two weeks to acquaint himself with her at home. No doubt she has been cooking for them."

Sory looked slowly over at me. "Did you send her over there yourself?"

"Yes, I told her she might easier mourn over there for Hal."

"Did you have all this in mind from the start, about the other brother eating her cooking while she mourned?"

"What you staring at me so hard for, Sory? You angry with

309

me?" She was so serious and perturbed about something that I didn't know what to make of her.

"I never in my life have known a man to send his sister to mourn with intent to find a husband among the brothers."

"Oh my, I've done something wrong, I know. Let's not talk any more about it."

"Worrying more about Nell than about me, seems like, with your own brother off in Ohio, where they probably will kill him for a spy."

"No, they don't do like that out there."

"Me so worried, for I do have honor enough to ask what name my baby will have? And I've—Owen, I get so confused and hurt to think Woofer would do like that, knowing I've had one husband die and another man who wouldn't marry me. And now Woofer, he won't come home even when his baby is ready to be born."

"Sory, could he be telling you something about you and me? I wonder most every night about it. I lie awake wondering."

"Wondering about what?" she said, turning those black eyes on me again. "Owen, what?"

"Now, you take Woofer, I think he held me close in his heart too. I remember him saying to me—I was halfway lost at the time, as he knew, but his face was close, and he said to me, 'Do you love her, Owen?'"

"You told me several times that he said that to you."

"He was wanting that assurance, and I had a notion when I heard about him going on to Ohio that he might not come back for a while, that he might give us time to decide."

Her little hands were tightly clutched and she was still as death, staring at me. "What are we to decide?" she said.

"Whether we ought to marry each other or not."

A long while she sat there, before slowly she said, "Owen, please tell me what you mean, please don't linger with it."

"I mean he grew up enough in the battles to know he ought to give you up, and I lost enough to know a man can lose it all, if he doesn't mind, so he must guard some things, he must take them. And I want you to marry me, Sory," I said.

She bent her head and pressed her face against the palm of my hand. "Owen, will it hurt him deeply?"

"Yes, it will. Though I believe that's what he's expecting us to do. God knows, I hope so."

"I love you, I do," she said, "but it's his baby."

"Yes, and it's my life," I said. "It's all complicated and no simple answers will unravel it." I touched her hair, tucked a few strands of it behind her ear. "I have the same last name he has," I said.

She looked up, her round black eyes moist with tears. I put her hand against my lips. "I told him I loved you," I said.

"I believe maybe you do," she said, "for you don't seem to mind my talking myself to death every afternoon. I've been accused of talking too much."

"I believe Woofer would understand that you have to name his baby most any day and Wright ought to be the baby's name," I said. We sat there for a while quietly. "There's that little tan dog again," I said. "I wonder who owns that dog, Sory? It comes around here every now and then and gets papa's two hounds to baying. Maybe we ought to take that dog home to Eli."

"Owen, can you—when should we get married, since it's nine months almost to the day?"

"Why, when Martin gets here we'll ask him to go get a license for us. I don't mind his performing the ceremony, do you? I mean, his doubts don't bother me, for nothing is set and clear in this life, much less the next one."

"I don't mind," she said, whispering.

"And he did see an angel. It was warming by his fire, Sory."

"Why, I never knew that an angel got cold."

"Oh, yes, they often do, he told me."

"Owen, I don't ever want—I don't—oh, law, when I can't talk I feel sick."

"You sit there and rock. Don't worry. We're going to make our

311

move, you and me. I feel it's right that we do. It's right to wrong Woofer this way. We'll go over to your house directly."

"I don't even want to say—to hear—Owen, I do think I'm happier than I was ever meant to be. I do want to be with you."

"We'll wait for a little while yet, an hour or two," I said. "By then the sky ought to be twilighted."

CHAPTER FIFTEEN

Once I had time to do so—recovering from an illness gives one time—I began writing down notes about the war and began working on a list, a roster of the names of the men from this one community, not by any means the entire region, who had as of 1863 fought in this war, on either side, including the one Negro man who was hanged and another Negro man who was beaten a month ago for singing "The Star-Spangled Banner." I think it is well to add him to the list. I cannot in good conscience say that he was wounded in the war, and indeed if I include him I ought also to include white men who have been beaten—I should include the smith's brother in any event. I will do so. Their children and grandchildren have a right to know what part they played, and certainly the Negro descendants will owe a debt to the white and black men who fought to liberate them. Whether all the Yanks fought for that purpose or not I can't say. I suspect as many fought to enslave the Rebel whites as fought to free the Negro, there being nothing clear as a bell in the purposes of any mass of people, any big nation. I do believe many Yanks fought for the Negro, however, and recall even now as I sit at papa's desk and write these notes the song sung by a group of Yanks after the final charge we made, that beautiful song they sang about John Brown.

The notes about the war and my life in it I am writing for my children once they are grown should they seek an explanation for the reputation I have, for I am sometimes called a traitor and sometimes a hero by my own people. Also, they will know that

313

one of their brothers is the son of Eli Crawford, though in fact
he is not his son, and that the second son is Woofer's, who has
recently denounced me angrily for stealing the boy from him,
he doing this before he left for California, it being his intent to
go to California even before he arrived here, it never having
been his intent to stay here and feed or care for the boy. He
claimed even as he arrived and announced his intentions to go
west that he was astonished to find Sory married, none of which
is true, but all of which was needed to be claimed by him as
balm, comfort, for his hurt soul. He must blame someone; in
truth he must blame me, must hurt me at least as much as he is
hurt, and must hurt Sory. Well, let the record show the truth of
it, as near to truth as I can come with pen and ink and paper.
Let it show I took her from him and that he gave her to me, the
truth lying somewhere between.

My father maintains staunchly that truth is not my purpose,
that facts are my purpose—what are the battles, the size of the
armies, the names and dates: what was the confusion of General
Manger's authority on the final day—a most interesting detail,
indeed, for it seems that General Hill appointed Pettigrew to
command Heth's division in the charge and asked General
Manger to remain with the reserves, which the old man did not
do. He would not relinquish anything before the battle, not so
much as a standard, for he must insist on dying in the charge
rather than die later without any authority or cause to comfort
himself with. Which is why in the reports of the battle some
writers say Heth led the advance of his division, which is not
so, and others say Manger, and others say Pettigrew. Now,
details of this sort my father considers to be of much importance. I find them irrelevant, now that Manger's dead. What is
the credit worth, after all? Also, my father wants me to set down
a scene I witnessed on the third day of Chancellorsville, in the
Wilderness. It is too gruesome for me to like it very well. We
were on the afternoon of the third day at a field, an open field
of grass and weeds. I had called for my regiment to halt there,

314

but Manger, who was in a rage at me, came himself to the front and ordered me to advance. I told him I would do so when he supplied us with cartridges, for we had few. He said to advance my men anyway, at which point Billy Furr had a dozen of his men let out a yell and advanced into the field, and then two of the smith's men and five or six of Raper's—there were no more than twenty in all. I ordered my other men to stay where they were and I shouted for these nineteen or twenty to come back, but they would not. When they were halfway across, the cannon opened up on them and held them to the ground for the rest of that day, and in the evening of that day, so many fires having started in the woods that the air was thick with smoke, I knew I must take my men away from there, and I ordered all except the remaining men of the middle section, Crawford's section, to withdraw. I stayed with them in hopes we could save the twenty men somehow, but there was no chance of it. Manger, coughing on the smoke, found his way to where I was and himself ordered us to go out and save them. I think he feared I would report him for bringing about their loss. He ordered my men forward, but of course they would not, could not go, for fire had begun to sweep across the field and the heat was unbearable, even where we were. As it burned across the field, cartridges on dead men would explode, and now and then a wounded man would rise and try to flee the fire. And then, most awful sight, men on fire would rise and try to flee the fire and like burning torches would fall and set other fires and would explode, so that we in the heat watched as our men rose and fell and burned and exploded out there, Manger watching, his teeth chattering, his skin wet with drops of sweat thick as glycerine. I left him standing beside the burning field and led my men up out of the Wilderness.

Men who have come home from the war do what they can for shelter; they have no time to notch cabins properly, and Zill Cole, who was the best for dovetailing anywhere around, is dead in the Shenandoah, and his son Howard, who was also a fine craftsman, was wounded at Gettysburg on the first day. He was one of the Company B men who took the first load from the cannon and he and the other wounded men were gone in ambulances before I saw him. I didn't see Howard again until we met on the road recently. I was taking corn to the mill, for Sory and I had no meal at home; I wheeled a hand cart across the bridge and Howard came along, going the same way, he with a shoulder harness full of corn, for I saw that some of it was dropping out the back and a little pig was following him and eating the grains one by one, and I saw he had lost an arm. "Howard, can you make a cottage for Phillip, for he is marrying most any day he can get the preacher?" I asked him, and Howard said no he couldn't do that work any more.

"Because of the arm?" I said.

"No, no," he said. "Because of other things."

"What are they?" I said.

"Well, what else is being done right around here?" he said.

We are every day aware through just such attitudes that the loss of a war is not merely the loss of men in battle, or money or cattle or horses or railroads or industry. It is also the loss of what we can call our civilization, which has been built up here for three generations; its seeds were brought from Scotland, North Ireland, Wales, England, Germany, Holland, France. And from the war we have inherited the warped shingles on the roofs of the houses, the crooked barn wall that never will be fixed, the orchards overgrown, the fields overcome with joe-pye weeds and erosion, the fences down, the walls fallen, the roads impassable much of the way for a wagon, the bridges sagging, the schools closed, and nobody left to do but half of what must be done, and nobody to care much now.

And then, too, whenever I visit the mill I notice that even the men who are left, many of them begin to hear the drums way off, the roll of drums. The young men hear it, as well as men who have been with me in the Shenandoah and before Richmond, who have been with me at Fredericksburg and Chancellorsville and Gettysburg. They hear the call coming in from the outlands, where once again an army is being assembled to defend our land from the invaders from the North. For we have not yet done with the war, neither side has done with it. Though we have lost, the North will not allow us to quit without unconditional surrender; President Lincoln will not negotiate peace on any other terms, and we cannot surrender until somehow we take from our generals at last their stars and entourage and power and send them to their busted houses and ruined families. There is no one to send them now, for they control everything, and they will not send themselves.

So each season for a while we will have recruiters come up here, and conscripters will try to conscript men for our faltering legions. I will receive other letters from Hill or some such officer, asking if I can be persuaded to come back to lead a regiment or a brigade "for I remember how Jackson always said of you that you could be counted on to fight on the front lines from the first through the final day of a battle, knowing always how much could be expected of your men and what could not." And each spring for a while we will sense in ourselves the awakening of the old calling, and in the nights several men will leave—the boys will sneak away to have their adventure, and some of the veterans will sneak away again, ashamed, I suppose, to admit they are going, and those of us left at home will try to bind the community together and make-do for a while. How difficult it is to get stock enough to breed, to get seeds enough to plant, to get salt enough to cure, to get sugar enough to preserve, to get food enough for us all to eat, and cloth enough to clothe ourselves. Or to get the will to do anything.

Yesterday I recall, out in the field, I was plowing, the earth moldy under my feet, Eli following in the row as best he could, birds pecking at the rows we had opened, Sory waiting in the eastern end of a row, a letter in her hand, she reading, a letter from Woofer she told me as I turned the oxen, and she read me a part of it:

317

For never having given up anything that was dear to me, I was not able to know how it was done, but I have gained more age and growth from it than from most anything in my life, more than from years, themselves, and I know Owen realized that I must lose part of my life in order to grow into another one . . .

"Ah, Lord," I said, heavy with the weight of the thought. Way off I saw the farm I had once farmed, which I had not returned to and which I had not even thought about for months, nor had I thought about my first wife, so we do lose our old lives one by one, we can lose them and take on new ones. And Woofer surely can find new ones, for he was born for the wide road. "When's he coming home and help papa and me?" I said.

"He writes so scrawly that I can't read all of it," she said. "I think he wants us to come out there. He says the war's not poisoned the springs out that way. Can you read it?" she said.

"Tonight I can, when we have time," I said. "I want to finish this, Sory, lest it rain."

"Why, there's no sign of rain, Owen."

"I know, but there might be." I kicked a clod of earth open. "It's all right," I said. "It's a good time to plow it now. It's moist and ready. It's the same," I said, "though everything else has changed," and I clicked my tongue and set my weight against the plow, the oxen moved, and the earth opened to me as it had in many other times.

That night I read Woofer's letter. It rambled about from one marvel to another. The world of the West was new and untrampled and it astonished him, I judged. In some ways I saw even in his infant son the same sense of enchantment with perfectly ordinary matters and people. And in my own child, should one be born to me, in him or her I would perhaps find also the wonder of it, the marvel of it all—not perfect, not kind, not even sane, not controlled and not controllable—life scattered on the sky like seeds sown into the wind long ago.

318

Southern Army Soldiers from Harristown Alone

ADAMS, HOWARD. About 28. Killed in the Shenandoah. A farmer. He made good cider.

ADDISON, MARSHALL. 19. Killed at Gettysburg the third day. Company B. I don't know where his body or the bodies of others killed there finally were laid. He had one daughter, I believe, Cindy.

ANDERSON, CHARLIE. 17. Wounded at Gettysburg the third day. Company B. He died later, his mother tells me.

ATKINS, FORDIE. 54. Returned to his home well. Fought in Company A in the campaigns of 1862 and 1863. He is father and grandfather of many people in this place. He left Saturday, presumably for a new campaign.

BRANT, JASPER. 35. Wounded at Fredericksburg, but he stayed on to fight the third campaign, returning home after Gettysburg. He was with Company B.

BROWN, HANSON. About 24. Deserted during the third campaign. One of the smith's raiders. I hear he is fighting in the North for the Yank army. Father of two, husband of Rachel Collis Brown.

CARTER, ELEASE. About 35. Dead at Chancellorsville. Son of Cary Carter, who received this final message from his son: "Tell papa I died facing the enemy."

CHEEK, VAUGHN. He must be 60. Wounded at Gettysburg on the third day but now at home. Father of eleven children, all except one of them sons.

COLE, ZILL. 52. Killed in the Shenandoah. The best for corner work on Houses.

CRAWFORD, ELI. 70. Killed in Tennessee. Husband of Sory. One son.

CRAWFORD, SKIP. 35. A major. Died at Gettysburg on the third day. A friend from boyhood.

DENNY, FRED. Company G. A planter's son, one year of college. Wounded in the chest the third day of Gettysburg. At home but sick. About 18.

ESSER, CHARLES W. About 40. Company C. He and his son Brown fought in the second and third campaigns and both fell wounded at Gettysburg on the third day, the son dying finally in a hospital near Richmond.

FORTNER, BRANT. 22. Company C. Dead at Gettysburg the third day.

FORTNER, CALEB. 25. Company H. Sergeant. Wounded at Chancellorsville; killed at Gettysburg the third day.

FORD, BUDDY. 35. Company I. Given to drink, but the best wood carver I ever saw when he was sober. Dead at Gettysburg the third day.

GADDY, DAN. Company H. 20's. Father of six. Wounded at Gettysburg, third day, in his left hand. A shell took off three fingers. Also wounded in his thigh. He makes good brandy.

GOTT, LOUIS. Company B. 45. He made the best wine. Killed at Gettysburg the first day.

GREEN, GORDON L. 31. Company F. Captured or deserted at Gettysburg.

GRIFFEN, LEE. 27. Company F. Wounded in the hip and back at Gettysburg the third day. Died in the hospital near Richmond. His father, Hariston, brought his body home in a wagon. Father of four. He was a good hand to break and train horses.

HANES, COMUS. 23. Company C. Disappeared at Chancellorsville, the second day. I believe he was killed. Later his father went to the battlefield to find out if he was there, and nobody had buried any of the men; this was months after the battle, and the stench of men and horses was so great he could not enter the woods. When he told me I said to say the boy wasn't there so far as he could determine, which was the truth and has helped comfort his wife.

HASTINGS, HERBERT. 23. Company A. Father of two. He once drove 80 swine to Old Fort by himself. A big man, about 6' 3", 200 pounds. Left leg lost at Gettysburg the third day, but he is home now. He has made a crutch out of his musket.

IDOL, LANE. About 20. Company I. A fat boy. He fought in the second and third compaigns and returned home mildly wounded. Recently married Faulkner Brown's daughter Lucy.

JORDAN, TERRY. 25. Company B. Killed at Gettysburg the third day.

KIGER, EDGAR. 21. Company G. Planter's youngest son. Killed at Gettysburg the third day.

KING, HAL. About 25. Lieutenant. Seven brothers and sisters. Wounded six times during 1861 and '62, twice in his arms and four times in his torso. Twice hospitalized. Yet he fought at Chancellorsville and later was killed at Gettysburg the third day.

MCBRIDE, WINFRED. 21. Company F. Killed at Chancellorsville the second or third day. Made sleds and wagons, like his father.

MCDANIEL, WILL. 40. Company B. Wounded at Fair Oaks. Lost the sight of his right eye and hearing in his left ear. Is a fine bear hunter but doesn't do much else.

MCILVENNA, BRUCE. 60. Bagpipe player at Chancellorsville and Gettysburg. Wounded but now at home.

MCLENDON, ERIC. 34. Company H. Father of seven. Wounded at Fredericksburg; killed at Gettysburg the third day.

MCRAE, ANGUS. 31. Company H. Oldest son of a planter who lives between here and Hobbs. They have at least thirty slaves. Killed at Gettysburg the third day.

MORGAN, MOCK. 16. Company G. Killed at Chancellorsville the second or third day, never buried as far as I know.

MOORE, BOBBY. 18. Company E. Captured at Chancellorsville; at least, he was one of Billy Furr's men and advanced with him that first day and never came back, and Herbert Hastings tells me he thinks the boy was captured.

O'BRIEN, ALEX. Company F. Bearded. I don't know his age. Unmarried. Died of wounds received at Gettysburg the third day.

OULD, EUGENE. 37. A planter from downriver a ways. Wounded at Richmond, wounded at Fredericksburg, wounded at Chancellorsville, wounded at Gettysburg the first and again the third day. Now at work again, mean as ever. Company G.

Perry, Reid. About 17. Company D. Killed at Gettysburg the third day.

Powell, Orville N. About 30. Company E. Father of seven. Excellent tanner. Killed outright at Gettysburg the third day.

Plover, Elvir. 40. Company F. Fought in the third campaign. A musician and fisherman.

Plover, Victor. 15. Company F. Drummer boy. Killed at Gettysburg the third day.

Queen, Patsy James. Company A. 35 years old, father of three girls. Excellent breeder of horses, best wheelwright, taught two sons to be coopers. Killed or captured in the Shenandoah. General Jackson ordered me to leave twenty men with horses or oxen to drag boughs of trees on the roads to fool the enemy, to make them think by the dust that our army was going west when in fact we were moving south to attack the Yanks at Richmond. I left Queen and never saw him again. A close friend. God spare him.

Rawls, Eben. Company D. The best singer I ever did hear. Shot down at Richmond, recovered, shot down at Gettysburg the third day and I suppose he died.

Reynolds, Hardin. Company G. About 20. Wounded at Gettysburg the third day, now farming, as I am. No complaints except in cold weather, he says.

Rollins, Park. Company I. About 20. Father of four, two sets of twins. Killed at Gettysburg the third day.

Russell, Patrick. Company B. About 20, though he's bearded. Wounded at Gettysburg the first day. He came home but went off again yesterday.

SAYERS, PAUL. 45. Many children and a few grandchildren. Wounded at Gettysburg the third day, now farming. Company D.

SEVIER, NORMAN. Company F. 18 or 19. Wounded at Sharpsburg. Killed at Gettysburg the third day.

SHUBERT or SCHUBERT, J. C. Company D. About 35. Father of two girls. Wounded at Richmond and again at Gettysburg the third day. Now hunting again, and farming. He killed a 450-pound bear February last, biggest for spring I ever did see. He's talking about going back to the army.

SILVER, ERNEST. 45. Sergeant, aide to his regimental commander. Killed at Gettysburg the third day.

SIMMONS, SPURGEON. 24. From downriver. Killed in the Shenandoah. Company H or I.

SMITH, HORACE (Actual name, Horace Roberts). 45. Blacksmith. Killed at Gettysburg, third day. Of Company D.

STALLINGS, LESTER. 17 or 18. Company H or I. Lost his left leg at Sharpsburg.

STONE, PHONSO. 21. Company B. Married, two children. Killed at Gettysburg the first day.

THOMAS, A. Ray. 33. Company C. Married with four children. A friend of mine from school days. Captured in the Shenandoah or killed there.

VADEN, ARTHUR. 24. Company G. Father of two. Killed before Richmond, 1862.

WALKER, MARION. 18. Company I. Wounded before Richmond and I have heard nothing more about him since, nor has his father.

WILLIAMS, RONALD. About 20. Company D. Killed at Bull Run, the first day of fighting.

WINGATE, EDELL. 34. Company B. A friend of mine. Father of four, son of Thomas and Lillie. Wounded at Sharpsburg, saw limited service at Fredericksburg, wounded at Gettysburg the third day, now in the army hospital near Richmond and there has been no report since September.

WOLFE, DOCKERY. 19. Company H. Wounded at Sharpsburg, wounded at Fair Oaks, wounded at Fredericksburg, fought all three days at Chancellorsville, wounded at Gettysburg the first and again the third day, now at home with his parents, who are planters. He is to be married this spring to Thelma Starnes, daughter of Worth. He hates Yanks worse than anybody I ever did see.

WRIGHT, JAMES PINKNEY, called Woofer. 18. Company B. Saw service at Chancellorsville and Gettysburg. Brother of Owen. Now in California.

WRIGHT, OWEN. 35. Service spring 1861 to July 4, 1863. Wounded at Richmond and Gettysburg. Now farming.

Yank Soldiers from Harristown

ADAMS, FLOYD. About 40. Father of six. Killed in Tennessee.

BARLOW, RICHARD. 20. Left home spring of 1862.

CASEY, GORDON. 18. Left home spring of 1862. Wounded at Antietam, as his people call Sharpsburg.

CHILDRESS, GAITHER. 19. Left home in February, 1863, and was killed at Chancellorsville.

DETTLE, CHARLIE. 51. Father of about twenty children by three wives. Four of his sons attended college. He took two sons to the North with him in 1861 when the war started. He was killed at New Bern.

DETTLE, MIKE. 19. Killed at Sharpsburg.

DETTLE, TOMAS C. 29. Killed at Chancellorsville.

FRIDAY, ROBERT. About 35. I went to school with him. No report since 1861.

GREGORY, JERRY. About 20. Reportedly captured at Richmond and put on Belle Isle. Pity him, God, I hope not.

ILLMAN, EVERETT. About 25. Left home spring of 1861, reported seen by Sergeant Willis at Fredericksburg.

JORDAN, WALTER. About 20. Missing in the Yank navy.

JOYNER, RONNIE. About 20. Missing since Fredericksburg.

LaFEVERS, JAMES. About 40. A planter's son who turned against his father and brothers. Wounded at Bull Run, wounded at Fair Oaks, reportedly killed at Fredericksburg on the first day.

LINCOLN, PRESTON. About 20. No report since he left home to join the army in April, 1862. Married with one son, but his wife has since married Will McDaniel.

LOVE, ARTHUR. About 30. A mail carrier for the Yank army.

McDANIEL, LONNIE. About 30. He won the caber toss summer of 1861, then left for the North walking.

McMILLAN, ROBERT. About 25. Killed at Gettysburg.

MOSS, LESTER, JR. About 25. Wounded at Chancellorsville. He came home four weeks later, said he had walked all the way. He's a fine chair maker.

PETREE, JULIUS. About 25. Wounded at Fredericksburg, or so

he wrote his parents in December, 1862. No report since.

RUPARD, ARLIS. 58. A lieutenant or even a captain by now. A man most deeply opposed to slavery. Fought at Bull Run, Chancellorsville, Gettysburg.

SHAVER, NEIL. About 35. A father several times over. Fought with a Pennsylvania regiment at Chancellorsville and reportedly was captured by an Alabama brigade. God help him in that case.

SMITH, SELDON. About 25. Killed at Chancellorsville or Gettysburg. Brother of Spurgeon.

RANDAL, JEWELL. About 25. Reportedly seen at Fredericksburg in the uniform of a sergeant.

TUTTLE, HOY. About 35. Seen in the Shenandoah and again at Fredericksburg when the Yanks charged across the open field and up the hill and we slaughtered them—but we learned nothing from it, as we proved at Gettysburg.

VENABLE, DARRELL. Another planter's son. About 20. Angry about slavery. Was seen in the front lines at Gettysburg the first day by his uncle, who shot at him and shouted obscenities at him.

WALKER, MONROE. About 40. An excellent bear hunter, son of a bear hunter who killed more than 200 bears in his lifetime. Monroe killed more than 100 before leaving for the North in the spring of 1861. He has not been heard from, but his wife says he is fighting with the Northern army, probably in the West.

WIGGINS, NORMAN. 15. A drummer boy with the Yank army in a New York regiment when last heard from in October, 1862.

LaFEVERS, TIM. About 30. Hanged in January of 1863 for trying to escape to the North, a slave. His body was thrown into the river between here and Hobbs.

PATRICK. A slave who was beat almost to death for singing "The Star-Spangled Banner." Actually this was in Burnsville, not Harristown, though his masters, the O'Sullivans, lived near here.

ROBERTS, ROGER. Nailed to his brother's barn, January, 1863. Now preaching.

WRIGHT, JESSE. 38. Repeatedly endangered his life 1850 to 1863 helping slaves escape to the North. Now farming with his father. A man of much courage and stamina, whom I have come as I grow older more and more to appreciate.

70 71 72 73 10 9 8 7 6 5 4 3 2 1